BASEBALL ON TRIAL

BASEBALL ON TRIAL

The Origin of Baseball's Antitrust Exemption

NATHANIEL GROW

UNIVERSITY OF ILLINOIS PRESS
Urbana, Chicago, and Springfield

Manufactured in the United States of America
1 2 3 4 5 C P 5 4 3 2 1

♾ This book is printed on acid-free paper.

Library of Congress Cataloging-in-Publication Data
Grow, Nathaniel.
Baseball on trial : the origin of baseball's antitrust exemption / Nathaniel Grow
pages cm
Includes bibliographical references and index.
ISBN 978-0-252-03819-8 (hardcover : alk. paper) —
ISBN 978-0-252-07975-7 (pbk. : alk. paper) —
ISBN 978-0-252-09599-3 (e-book)
1. Baseball—Law and legislation—United States—History. 2. Antitrust law—United States—History. 3. Professional sports contracts—United States—History. 4. United States. Sherman Act. 5. National League of Professional Baseball Clubs—Trials, litigation, etc. I. Title.
KF3989.G76 2014
343.7307'21—dc23 2013023552

To Lara

CONTENTS

ACKNOWLEDGMENTS

I would not have been able to write this book without the assistance of a number of individuals. First and foremost, my wife, Lara Grow, and father, Michael Grow, dutifully reviewed drafts of each chapter as they were being written, providing invaluable substantive and editorial guidance. The book also benefited greatly from the feedback provided by Professors Ed Edmonds and Mitchell Nathanson, who both reviewed an initial manuscript for the University of Illinois Press. Daniel Levitt, author of the terrific history of the Federal League, *The Battle That Forged Modern Baseball: The Federal League Challenge and Its Legacy*, courteously shared an advanced copy of his book with me to facilitate my own research. My research assistant, Holt Coltharp, assisted me with the collection of articles from relevant baseball periodicals. Freddy Berowski and his colleagues at the National Baseball Hall of Fame Library aided my navigation of the library's pertinent holdings, while the staffs of the National Archives facilities in Chicago, Kansas City, Philadelphia, and Washington, D.C., as well as the Cook County Circuit Court Archive in Chicago, helped me locate the original court documents from many of the lawsuits discussed in the book. Last but certainly not least, this project would not have been possible without the extremely generous financial support provided by my home institution, the University of Georgia. In particular, a Junior Faculty Research Grant from the Willson Center for Humanities and Arts facilitated my travel to all of the necessary research archives, while a Terry-Sanford Research Award from the Terry College of Business supported my writing efforts. To all of the above: thank you.

BASEBALL ON TRIAL

INTRODUCTION

The United States Supreme Court's 1922 decision in *Federal Baseball Club of Baltimore, Inc. v. National League of Professional Baseball Clubs* ranks among the most frequently criticized opinions in Supreme Court history. In a unanimous ruling authored by Justice Oliver Wendell Holmes Jr., the Court held that the "business of base ball" was not subject to the Sherman Antitrust Act because it did not constitute interstate commerce. Although the Supreme Court has subsequently acknowledged the anomalous nature of this ruling, it has nevertheless affirmed *Federal Baseball* on two separate occasions, first in 1953 and then again in 1972. As a result, Major League Baseball is not only the sole professional sports league to enjoy antitrust immunity, but is in fact the only industry in the country operating under a judicially created exemption from antitrust law.

When considering baseball's unique antitrust status, the obvious question to ask is: how could this be? Today, Major League Baseball is a multibillion-dollar venture, with its commercial operations—ranging from its television and Internet broadcasts of games to its extensive merchandising efforts—increasingly conducted on not just a national but an international scale. How then could anyone, let alone a legendary Supreme Court Justice the caliber of Oliver Wendell Holmes, conclude that baseball was not interstate commerce and thus not subject to federal antitrust law?

To date, legal scholars have been unable to provide a fully satisfactory answer to this fundamental question due to the lack of a comprehensive account of the *Federal Baseball* litigation. Although baseball's unique antitrust status has been considered in several books and a number of law review articles, none of these works have thoroughly explored the exemption's origin, but instead have typically provided only a cursory account of the *Federal Baseball* case.[1] Because relatively little was known about the lawsuit itself, commentators have been forced to appraise Holmes's decision without the benefit of a complete understanding of the proceedings that helped shape its outcome. As a result, although a few authors have defended *Federal Baseball* by arguing that it was consistent with then-prevailing judicial standards,[2] most scholars have criticized the opinion as being wrongly decided and reflective of a fundamental misunderstanding of professional baseball. These critical analyses tend to judge the decision in light of the sport's present-day commercial operations, however, rather than the state of the business in 1922, and frequently fail to fully consider the contours of the applicable law at the time. Moreover, because no thorough account of the litigation existed, these scholars were largely unaware of the many strategic—and in some cases questionable—decisions by counsel that framed the legal issues on appeal and help explain the Supreme Court's ultimate ruling in the case.

The lack of a comprehensive history of the *Federal Baseball* case is particularly surprising given the colorful path the suit took to the Supreme Court. The origins of the litigation date back to the formation of the Federal League of Professional Base Ball Clubs in 1913. The Federal League sought to establish itself as a third major league by challenging the supremacy of the American and National Leagues. Following a lackluster first season, the Federals attempted to elevate their league's profile by raiding the rosters of "organized baseball" during the 1913–1914 offseason, successfully convincing approximately fifty major league players to join the new circuit. The Federal League believed it could sign these players based on advice from its legal counsel, who asserted that the standard major league playing contract was legally unenforceable. Not surprisingly, the major leagues disagreed, and as a result thirteen different lawsuits were filed in 1914, with both organized baseball and the Federals seeking injunctions to prevent their players from jumping back and forth between the leagues. After an ill-fated attempt to negotiate a resolution to the dispute in November 1914, the Federal League turned to another legal strategy, filing an antitrust lawsuit against the American and National Leagues in federal district court in Chicago in January 1915. The litigants staged a four-day hearing before Judge Kenesaw Mountain Landis—who would later become the first commissioner of baseball—in the process offering a preview of the legal arguments that would eventually be asserted before the Supreme Court. Following the hearing, Landis proceeded to withhold judgment in the case for a year in the hope that the two sides would amicably resolve their differences. With its financial losses mounting, the Federal League ultimately agreed to a settlement with organized baseball in December 1915, thereby dissolving its operations.

This detailed backdrop set the stage for the *Federal Baseball* case. Although seven of the eight Federal League clubs were satisfied with the peace agreement, the league's Baltimore Terrapins refused to accept the settlement terms. The team instead opted to file its own antitrust lawsuit against organized baseball in 1916, alleging that the American and National Leagues had conspired to destroy the Federal League. After being presented with unfavorable evidence during an abbreviated trial in Philadelphia, however, Baltimore voluntarily withdrew its case in 1917, only to refile a broader antitrust lawsuit a few months later in Washington, D.C. This latter suit proceeded to trial in 1919, ultimately culminating in the Supreme Court's infamous 1922 decision.

The lack of a definitive account of the *Federal Baseball* litigation has had significant practical implications. Not only have a number of important details regarding the case been widely overlooked—most existing analyses completely omit any mention of Baltimore's 1917 trial in Philadelphia, for instance—but the absence of an authoritative record of the proceedings has also led to inconsistent subsequent judicial decisions. Specifically, lower courts have disagreed in recent years regarding the extent to which baseball's commercial activities are protected by its antitrust exemption, with some courts holding that the exemption only shields those facets of the business that were at issue in the *Federal Baseball* case. Because no complete account of the 1922 litigation existed, however, these subsequent lower courts were forced to try to discern its scope from the terse appellate and Supreme Court decisions in the case, resulting in a series of divergent—and in some cases incorrectly decided—opinions.

Drawing upon contemporaneous newspaper accounts, original court records, and a recently released collection of attorney correspondence from the case (available at the National Baseball Hall of Fame Research Library in Cooperstown, New York), this book attempts to fill this gap in the literature by providing the first full-length history of the *Federal Baseball* litigation. It begins by providing a complete account of the Federal League–related lawsuits of 1914 and 1915, establishing the necessary background for its subsequent discussion of the Baltimore Terrapins' antitrust attack on the major leagues. Ultimately, the book concludes that many of the common criticisms of Justice Holmes's opinion in *Federal Baseball* are unjust, as the decision was consistent with the prevailing judicial precedents of the day, and reflected several critical tactical mistakes Baltimore's counsel committed throughout the litigation. In the process, the book offers an explanation of how Major League Baseball first came to be exempt from antitrust law.

1

The Rivalry Begins

1913

"It will be war to the hilt with organized baseball from this time forth," exclaimed J. Edward Krause. "We have the money, and the money will tempt the players we want."[1] The "we" that Krause was referring to was the Federal League of Professional Base Ball Clubs, a new league that began play in 1913. Following the successful completion of the organization's inaugural season, Krause—president of the league's Indianapolis franchise—was serving notice that the Federals had their sights set on challenging the supremacy of the two established major leagues, the American and National, in 1914.

The Federal League had formed from the remnants of two failed 1912 ventures, the Columbian League and the United States League. The Columbian League was the creation of John Powers, the former head of the Wisconsin League, a lower-level minor league. Powers hoped to compete with the two major leagues by forming an eight-team circuit based in the Midwest, with franchises in Kansas City, Milwaukee, Cleveland, Detroit, Indianapolis, St. Louis, Louisville, and Chicago. Powers was forced to abort his plans prior to the scheduled start of the 1912 season, however, when one of his primary financial backers—St. Louis brewer Otto Stifel—backed out of the venture. Meanwhile, the United States League ambitiously established a national circuit of teams located in New York, Washington, D.C., Reading, Richmond, Chicago, Cincinnati, Pittsburgh, and Cleveland. The league got off to a more promising start than the Columbian, successfully holding its opening day on May 1, 1912. The United States League ultimately shared the Columbian's fate, however, collapsing in late June due to bad weather and low attendance.[2]

Despite the failures of the Columbian and United States Leagues in 1912, Columbian founder Powers did not abandon his dream of organizing a third major league. After reaching out to some of the former owners from the two failed circuits to gauge their interest in establishing a new league for 1913,

Powers was eventually able to enlist the support of William McCullough, owner of the United States League's defunct Pittsburgh franchise, and Otto Stifel, the St. Louis businessman whose change of heart had doomed the Columbian League, among others. The founding owners officially organized their new venture—the Federal League—on March 8, 1913. The league established a six-team circuit for its inaugural season, placing franchises in Chicago, Cleveland, Pittsburgh, Indianapolis, St. Louis, and Covington, Kentucky (across the Ohio River from Cincinnati). The owners hoped that by locating all of their franchises within relatively close proximity of one another they could reduce travel costs and boost profitability.[3]

Rather than initially compete head-to-head with the American and National Leagues for playing talent, the Federal League primarily recruited minor league journeymen and local semipro players to fill out its rosters. To attract and maintain fan interest, the new league hired aging, former major league stars to serve as team managers. The Pittsburgh Federals signed former Pittsburgh Pirates star pitcher Charles "Deacon" Phillippe to manage their club, for example, while Cleveland's team hired the legendary Denton "Cy" Young as its manager. Despite providing what was generally considered to be lower-quality baseball than the two established major leagues, the Federal League nevertheless managed to survive its initial season. While many of its teams struggled financially, only one proved to be completely nonviable, as the league was forced to transfer the Covington franchise to Kansas City forty games into the season.[4]

By August, the Federal League magnates had grown optimistic enough about their long-term prospects that they began to plan a more aggressive campaign for the 1914 season. During a secret meeting held on August 2, 1913, the owners removed Powers from the league's presidency. They had become dissatisfied with several aspects of Powers's administration—including his management of umpires and inability to generate more press coverage for the league—and believed that new, more vigorous leadership was necessary to elevate the Federal League's stature. In his place, they appointed James A. Gilmore as the league's new president.[5]

The thirty-seven-year-old Gilmore had joined the Federal League earlier that summer when a friend persuaded the longtime sports enthusiast to invest in the organization's Chicago franchise. Gilmore was a consummate salesman. After serving in the Spanish-American War, he honed his craft selling coal before eventually becoming president of a ventilator manufacturing company in 1911. So impressive were his sales skills that an acquaintance once proclaimed, "Gilmore could not only convince you the moon is made of green cheese, but he could sell you a slice of it."[6] Extremely talkative and outgoing, Gilmore was dubbed "Glib Jim" and "Gabby Jim" by the sporting press.[7]

James Gilmore was the Federal League's president throughout its battle with the major leagues (Library of Congress, Prints & Photographs Division, LC-DIG-ggbain-15080)

As Edward Krause's declaration of war suggested, Gilmore and the other Federal League owners decided to elevate the stature of their fledgling circuit by signing prominent stars from the American and National Leagues for the 1914 season. The Federals were confident they could convince established major leaguers to jump to the new organization for two reasons. First, they believed their strong financial backing would allow them to outbid the two major leagues for talent. Second, and perhaps more significantly, they believed organized baseball was vulnerable to legal attack on several grounds. In particular, the Federals concluded that two provisions in the standard player contract used by both major leagues and most of the minor leagues rendered the agreements legally unenforceable: the so-called "reserve clause" and the ten-day release option.

The reserve clause gave teams the unilateral right to renew their players' services for the following season. First proposed by Boston owner Arthur Soden in 1879, the clause was intended to reduce roster turnover and help keep labor costs in check by restricting the market for each player's services to a single team, thereby eliminating any bidding competition between clubs.[8] Specifically, clause ten of the standard player contract provided that the player "agrees and obligates himself to contract with and continue in the service of [the team] for the succeeding season at a salary to be determined by the parties."[9] In other words, if the player and his team were unable to agree upon the terms for a new agreement at season's end, the club could automatically renew the player's contract for the following year, with the player then forced to choose to either accept the team's final salary offer or else find a new profession.

Not only did the reserve clause thus bind a player to his team for the following season, but it effectively allowed teams to control their players in perpetuity. Under then-existing major league rules, teams were required to include the reserve clause in every player contract, meaning that each time a player's contract was renewed, his new agreement would also include a reserve clause. As a result, a team could continue to renew the player's contract year after year, effectively binding the player to the club for the entirety of his career.

Although a player was potentially bound to his team for life under the reserve clause, the accompanying ten-day release provision permitted the team to terminate the player's contract for any reason simply by providing ten days' written notice. In particular, clause eight of the standard player contract stated, "[t]he club may, at any time . . . give [the player] . . . ten days' written notice to end and determine all its liabilities and obligations" under the agreement.[10] The contract did not grant players a corresponding right to terminate the agreement themselves. Major league owners asserted that the ten-day release provision was critical to maintaining discipline and loyalty by deterring players from slacking off or disregarding their manager's orders.

Taken together, Federal League officials believed that these two provisions rendered the existing major league player contracts legally unenforceable. To enforce a player's contract, a major league team would typically seek an injunction by filing what was known at the time as a suit "in equity" (that is, a lawsuit seeking a remedy other than money). Under prevailing legal doctrine, a court would not order the player to actually perform as agreed for the team under his original contract, but would instead issue an injunction preventing the player from playing for anyone other than his original club. In other words, even though the player would not be forced to abide by his initial contract, he would be unable to earn a living by playing for anyone else during the term of his agreement. Although such an injunction would not fully alleviate the harm inflicted on the player's original team, it would at least prevent the player from directly competing against his former club by working for a rival.

To obtain such an injunction, major league teams needed to satisfy several legal requirements. First, the court would typically want to see that the player had agreed not to work for anyone other than his original team during the term of his contract by signing what was known as a "negative covenant." The standard player contract utilized by the major league teams satisfied this requirement, with clause two providing that "[the player] agrees to perform for [his team] and for no other party during the period of this contract (unless with the written consent of [the club])."[11] Second, the court would require that the player possess such unique skills or abilities that he could not easily be replaced by another player, with his loss thereby inflicting an "irreparable injury" on his original team (that is, one that monetary damages alone could not fully remedy). Major league teams typically also satisfied this element, as courts had generally concluded that most professional baseball players were highly and uniquely skilled employees whose services were not easily replaced.[12]

Although a major league team could meet the first two requirements for injunctive relief, the Federals nevertheless believed courts would refuse to enjoin players from playing in their league because of a third requirement: mutuality. Mutuality is a legal principle specifying that in order for a contract to be enforceable, it must impose roughly equivalent obligations on both parties. When a contract so disproportionately favored one side as to render it unfairly prejudicial, the court would declare the agreement "unconscionable" and refuse to enforce it via an injunction because of its lack of mutuality.[13]

The Federals believed that the combination of the reserve clause and ten-day release provision rendered the standard major league player contract far too one-sided to warrant injunctive relief, as the agreement potentially bound a player to his team for life while only obligating the team to employ him for ten days. Indeed, as one subsequent legal scholar concluded, "the coupling of the reserve clause with the 'ten-day clause' . . . most acutely raised the specters of unconscionability and lack of mutuality."[14] Therefore, the Federals were confident that a court would not enjoin major league players from performing in the new league.

The Federal League's legal position was not merely theoretical; a number of prior baseball legal precedents supported the circuit's contention. The enforceability of the reserve clause and ten-day release provisions had been litigated during two earlier baseball wars: the Players' League challenge of 1890 and the American-National League war of 1901–1902. In both cases, the new leagues disregarded the reserve clause and employed players previously under contract with the established league. Not surprisingly, in each case the established league went to court to seek injunctions preventing the players from performing for the rival organization.[15]

In a series of decisions, courts refused to grant the established leagues injunctive relief. These decisions typically focused on the issue of mutuality, emphasizing the unbalanced nature of the player's contract. For example, in the seminal case of *Metropolitan Exhibition Company v. Ward,* a New York state court refused to enjoin Hall of Fame shortstop and pitcher John Montgomery Ward from playing for the rival Players' League in 1890, holding that Ward's prior contract with the National League's New York franchise was unenforceable due to a lack of mutuality.[16] The *Ward* decision emphasized the disproportional rights afforded to the two parties under the contract, noting, "we have the spectacle presented of a contract which binds one party for a series of years and the other party for ten days, and of the party who is itself bound for ten days coming into a court of equity to enforce its claims against the party bound for years."[17] The court also concluded that Ward's reserve clause could not be enforced because of its indefiniteness, noting that the provision only stated that the parties would enter into a contract for the following season, without specifying the relevant terms of that subsequent contract (such as Ward's salary). Given these infirmities, the court refused to enjoin Ward from playing in the Players' League.

Most subsequent courts considering the enforceability of the standard player contract followed the *Ward* precedent.[18] The only significant exception to this consensus was the Pennsylvania Supreme Court's 1902 decision in *Philadelphia Ball Club v. Lajoie,* a suit in which the National League's Philadelphia franchise sought to prevent future Hall of Fame second baseman Napoleon Lajoie from playing for the crosstown Athletics of the rival American League.[19] The court concluded that Lajoie's contract did not lack mutuality because it specifically provided that a portion of his salary was being paid as compensation for Lajoie's agreement to be bound by the reserve clause. However, the strength of this precedent was limited in at least two respects. First, the Pennsylvania Supreme Court's opinion noted that Lajoie's contract was only renewable for three years, arguably rendering it distinguishable from the perpetual reserve clause contained in the standard player contract in 1913. Perhaps more significantly, though, the American League was easily able to circumvent the Pennsylvania court's decision by orchestrating a trade that sent Lajoie from Philadelphia to the circuit's Cleveland franchise. The Ohio courts refused to enforce the Pennsylvania injunction, permitting Lajoie to play for Cleveland. Thus, Lajoie was generally able to fulfill his American League contract with the exception of those games his squad was scheduled to play in Philadelphia; for those series, Lajoie avoided enforcement of the injunction "by going to Atlantic City, New Jersey, for vacation."[20]

Therefore, given that most prior courts had refused to prevent players from jumping to a rival league, and with the only significant outlier appearing distinguishable and easily usurped, the Federal League was confident that the existing American and National League player contracts would prove legally unenforceable. Indeed, during the 1913–1914 off-season, the Federals sent recruitment letters specifically arguing that major league players need not respect their prior contract's reserve clause because "it is not mutual."[21]

In addition to the potential contractual arguments at their disposal, Federal League officials also believed that organized baseball was susceptible to another line of legal attack. Specifically, they thought that a strong argument could be made that the American and National Leagues had formed an illegal monopoly in violation of the Sherman Antitrust Act. The Sherman Act was enacted in 1890 in response to growing public outcry over the domination of critical sectors of the national economy—including the railroad and oil industries—by a single firm or small handful of companies colluding in the form of a trust or cartel. The act attempted to eliminate these restraints on competition in two ways. First, Section One of the Sherman Act attacked collusion between two or more companies by prohibiting "[e]very contract, combination . . . or conspiracy, in restraint of trade or commerce among the several States."[22] Meanwhile, Section Two outlawed the monopolization, or attempted monopolization, of "any part of the trade or commerce among the several States."[23]

The Federals believed that professional baseball was dominated by a trust vulnerable to challenge under the Sherman Act. At the time, the baseball industry was governed by what was known as the "National Agreement," a pact signed not only by the two major leagues, but also by the majority of the nation's minor leagues. The agreement was formed in January 1903 at the conclusion of baseball's last major war, pitting the upstart American League against the dominant National League.[24] The American League challenge to the National League's supremacy was orchestrated by Byron "Ban" Johnson, a former sports editor for the *Cincinnati Commercial-Gazette* newspaper. Bold and brash but quite shrewd, Johnson had entered the baseball business in 1893

Byron Bancroft "Ban" Johnson, the autocratic president of the American League (Library of Congress, Prints & Photographs Division, LC-DIG-hec-18042, photograph by Harris & Ewing)

when his friend, Charles Comiskey, recommended him for the presidency of the Western League, a midwestern minor league. Johnson spent the rest of the 1890s building the Western into one of the nation's top minor leagues, all the while harboring greater aspirations.[25] In 1900, the National League gave Johnson the opening he had been waiting for when it eliminated four teams for the forthcoming season. Johnson quickly moved to elevate his circuit to major league status, renaming the Western League the American League, and declaring his intentions to challenge the National League's supremacy in 1901. He placed American League franchises in three of the four cities abandoned by the National League, building a major league organization by signing away many of the senior circuit's established stars (including the aforementioned Napoleon Lajoie). In the process, Johnson utterly disregarded the National League's reserve clause.[26]

The American League and National League waged a costly battle for two years before finally agreeing to a truce following the 1902 season, culminating in the signing of the National Agreement in January 1903. The agreement re-established a rigid hierarchy for organized baseball, with the two major leagues on top, followed by various classifications of minor leagues. The National Agreement specified that all of its signatories must honor the reserve clause and refuse to employ players under contract with other member-teams; any club or league not respecting the reservation practice was considered an "outlaw." The agreement was enforced by the so-called "National Commission," a three-member tribunal consisting of the presidents of the American and National Leagues and August "Garry" Herrmann, president of the Cincinnati Reds.[27]

The Federal League believed that the centrally organized monopoly created by the National Agreement violated the Sherman Act. Specifically, by standardizing and enforcing the reserve clause, the agreement enabled organized baseball to control practically the entire supply of highly skilled professional baseball players. Moreover, the agreement also allowed the major leagues to restrict where professional teams could be located and who they could play against. Through these provisions, the American and National Leagues were able to all but ensure that their supremacy would not be challenged, making it nearly impossible for a rival organization to acquire the talent and cities necessary to legitimately establish itself as a "major" league.

The Federals believed they could use antitrust law as a weapon against the American and National Leagues in several ways. First, organized baseball's monopoly potentially provided courts with an additional reason to refuse to enjoin major league players from jumping to the new circuit. Specifically, in addition to the mutuality requirement discussed above, courts also demanded that a party seeking an injunction come to the proceedings with "clean hands." Put differently, courts refused to enforce a contract via injunctive relief if the plaintiff had itself acted unethically with respect to the agreement. As the Federal League's chief legal counsel, Edward Gates, explained in December 1913: "Any baseball club that attempts to secure an injunction to restrain a player from playing in the Federal League must come into court with clean hands. Otherwise, no matter what contract it may seek to enforce, and no matter how binding on the face thereof such contract may be, the court will decline to enter into the merits of the case and dismiss the bill in equity at once."[28]

Gates argued that organized baseball's hands were unclean because it had used the reserve clause to prevent new leagues from forming to challenge its monopoly:

> The National Commission if it goes into the court will immediately be confronted [with a] very serious proposition[:] . . . is the commission a trust within the meaning of the Sherman Anti-Trust act? . . .
>
> There is no doubt in the mind of any one, we take it that organized baseball as organized under the so-called national agreement, has in the past monopolized the baseball business not only by attempting to crush competition, but by tieing [*sic*] up by contract the professional baseball clubs and players of the United States from the largest down to the smallest minor league club, and that the ball player cannot play ball with any competitor whatsoever.[29]

Not only did Gates assert that organized baseball had used the reserve clause to unfairly prevent rivals from acquiring talented players, but he also alleged that the National Agreement unjustly punished players who dared to violate the provision by banishing them from the sport: "Do the clubs operating under the national agreement maintain a blacklist? This proposition must be presented to and determined by a court before it will enter into a consideration of the reserve clause, which complainant will attempt to enforce in a court of equity."[30] Taken together, Gates was confident that organized baseball's blacklisting practices and use of the reserve clause to maintain its monopoly would cause a court to conclude that the major leagues' hands were sufficiently dirtied to preclude the granting of injunctive relief.

In addition to the unclean hands arguments, the Federals were also hopeful they could use the Sherman Act to attack the American and National Leagues in another way: by convincing the federal government to launch an antitrust probe of organized baseball. This hope was not as unrealistic as it might first seem. In 1912, Representative Thomas Gallagher of Illinois had introduced a resolution calling for a federal investigation of the "baseball trust" under the Sherman Act.[31] Although Gallagher's resolution failed to gain traction in 1912, it was revived early the next year by two Georgia congressmen upset over the recent suspension of baseball great—and Georgia native—Ty Cobb. Cobb had been suspended when he insisted upon a $15,000 salary for the 1913 season—a raise of $6,000 from the previous year—and refused to report to the Detroit Tigers' spring training facility in Mississippi after the club balked at his demands. Any potential momentum for a congressional investigation waned, however, when Cobb ended his holdout by agreeing to a $12,000 salary with the Tigers for 1913.[32]

Nevertheless, reports emerged throughout the first half of 1913 that Federal League officials intended to press the government to launch an antitrust investigation of organized baseball. William McCullough, head of the Pittsburgh Federals, stated in March 1913 that the new league would soon be asking Congress to investigate the National Commission under the Sherman Act. Then in June, reports surfaced that a delegation of Federal League officials had traveled to Washington, D.C., to meet with various government officials, including Attorney General—and future U.S. Supreme Court Justice—James McReynolds and Congressman Gallagher.[33]

Both publicly and privately, however, organized baseball appeared unconcerned. The National Commission sent out a confidential memorandum to major league and minor league owners stating that baseball had "nothing to fear . . . from a Federal or other investigation of any kind."[34] So long as organized baseball was "given the opportunity to fairly and fully explain the principles and practical operation of the National Agreement," the commission was confident that nothing "but good results can come to the game from an impartial and thorough investigation by Congress or searching inquiry by the Attorney General into the system under which National Agreement Base Ball has grown in popularity and gained in prestige."[35] Just to be safe, though, the commission encouraged owners to contact their local congressional representative to secure his aid on behalf of the sport, spurring a significant lobbying effort by organized baseball. Not only were dozens of letters sent to Congress on baseball's behalf, but the American League's Washington franchise went so far as to give the U.S. Speaker of the House, James "Champ" Clark, a pass entitling him to free admission to any American League game.[36]

In addition to these back-channel lobbying efforts, officials for organized baseball also launched a public media campaign. The chairman of the National Commission, August Herrmann, issued a statement inviting a congressional inquiry, stating his belief "that if this is done nothing but good can result to the game."[37] The fifty-four-year-old Herrmann was a particularly effective spokesman for organized baseball. After first making a name for himself in Cincinnati as part of the local Republican political machine in the late 1800s, Herrmann entered baseball in 1902 as part of a group purchasing the Cincinnati Reds. The notoriously gregarious executive used his political skills to quickly rise through the leadership ranks of organized baseball, becoming famous for holding court during both the World Series and annual meetings of the National League when he would take over a local bar and pick up the tab for all of the owners and reporters in attendance. He used the relationships he had cultivated with his generosity to successfully disseminate his message through the media.[38]

August "Garry" Herrmann, the affable president of the Cincinnati Reds and chairman of the National Commission (Library of Congress, Prints & Photographs Division, LC-DIG-ggbain-17539)

Others within organized baseball followed Herrmann's lead and stated their case to the press. For instance, Detroit Tigers owner Frank Navin went one step further than Herrmann, admitting that "[b]aseball in this country is controlled by a trust," but stating that it was nevertheless a "beneficial" trust "necessary for [the] preservation" of the national pastime.[39] This argument played into an ongoing narrative at the time distinguishing between "good" and "bad" trusts. For example, despite his reputation as a "trust buster," President Theodore Roosevelt had in fact advocated that the Sherman Act only be applied to those monopolies that harmed the public interest, a view that was widely shared in the 1910s.[40] Thus, by characterizing its activities as beneficial for the public, organized baseball hoped to avoid antitrust scrutiny.

As a result of these lobbying and public relations efforts, by mid-1913 the National Commission appeared confident it had weathered the congressional storm. The irascible Ban Johnson—never one to mince words—declared in June, "[i]f Congress is going to do any investigating why don't they get busy and probe or else shut up."[41] The press largely agreed that federal action was unlikely given "the friendliness of the Wilson Administration to base ball, and the pressure of vastly more important business" for the "overworked" Department of Justice.[42] Ultimately, no formal federal investigation was commenced.

Despite the Federal League's inability to drum up support for a governmental investigation, several owners within organized baseball encouraged the National Commission to treat the emergence of the Federals as a legitimate threat. In May 1913, Bob Quinn, owner of a minor league franchise in Columbus, Ohio, warned Ban Johnson that the Federal League could "cause considerable trouble" in the future, and suggested that "[a] little attention to the matter now might save a lot of trouble later on."[43] A few days later, St. Louis Browns owner Robert Hedges informed Johnson that although the Federals were "not at all dangerous now . . . I cannot tell how soon they will get a foot hold."[44] Despite these prophetic warnings, the National Commission paid little heed to the Federal League for much of the 1913 season. Indeed, as late as May 31, Ban Johnson was still expressing his doubts that the rival organization would "last until the first of July."[45]

By August, however, the National Commission was forced to begin taking the Federal League more seriously as speculation started spreading that the organization intended to launch a more formidable challenge to the major leagues in 1914. Ernest Barnard, president of the American League's Cleveland franchise, warned Ban Johnson on August 4th that "[t]here seems to be so much activity on the part of the Federal League officials lately that it is possible that some of the promoters . . . may have courage enough to gamble on a larger scale next season."[46] Even the skeptical Johnson was forced to concede that the Federals would survive the year, a feat he acknowledged would "be regarded as a marked achievement," giving the organization "much prestige."[47] In a letter to August Herrmann, Johnson cautioned that the Federal League organizers "will not be easily 'turned back'," and predicted that "[w]ith new parks and better locations, [the Federals] will be a menace to some, and a positive blight to many of the Leagues of the National Association" in 1914.[48]

Anticipating war on the horizon, organized baseball began to prepare its legal defenses. August Herrmann hired his friend John Galvin—along with Galvin's Cincinnati law partner Ellis Kinkead—to undertake an analysis of both the enforceability of the standard player contract as well as the legality of the National Agreement under antitrust law. Although the attorneys believed there was "no reason to question the validity of" the ten-day release provision in the player contract, they concluded that the enforceability of the reserve clause was in "serious doubt." In particular, they cautioned, a court could strike down the existing form contract as indefinite due to its failure to specify "any of the terms of the contract for that succeeding [reserve] year." The attorneys thus characterized the reserve clause as "merely a contract to make a contract if the parties can agree." Accordingly, Galvin and Kinkead recommended that the standard agreement be revised to state that the player would receive the same salary for his reserve season unless he and his team otherwise agreed.[49]

With respect to the antitrust issue, the lawyers counseled that organized baseball was technically restraining trade given the restrictions that the National Agreement imposed on the independence of its member teams and leagues, such as those specifying when and where games could be played.[50]

Attorney John Galvin provided legal counsel to organized baseball throughout the Federal League war of 1914–1915 (Chicago History Museum, DN-0071967, photo by the Chicago Daily News)

Nevertheless, Galvin and Kinkead believed that federal antitrust law did not apply to professional baseball because it did not constitute "commerce." Consistent with the U.S. Constitution's Commerce Clause, the Sherman Act expressly governs only the monopolization or restraint of "trade or commerce among the several States."[51] In other words, for baseball to be subject to federal antitrust law, a court would first have to conclude that the major leagues were engaged in "interstate commerce," a phrase traditionally construed to mean the production, transportation, or sale of physical goods or commodities across state lines. Because organized baseball did not produce any tangible products at the time—but instead merely sold tickets to ephemeral exhibitions of baseball—its attorneys believed that it was not involved in trade, consistent with an analogous series of judicial rulings holding that theatrical performances were not commerce. However, they cautioned that should a court determine that the major leagues were engaged in commerce, then their business would likely be characterized as interstate in nature—and thus subject to federal antitrust law—given that their teams were located and played games in a number of different states.[52]

As a result of Galvin and Kinkead's analysis, organized baseball revised the standard player contract following the 1913 season. Specifically, the contract was modified to state that the player was receiving a specific sum of money—typically one-fourth of his annual salary—as compensation for consenting to the reserve clause. The reserve clause was also amended to specifically provide that the player's contract would be renewed for the same total compensation he received the previous year unless the player and club agreed otherwise, thereby addressing Galvin and Kinkead's concerns over the definiteness of the provision. Moreover, all references in the contract to either the National Agreement or National Commission were removed in hopes of preventing a player from challenging organized baseball under antitrust law when contesting his contract in court. The major leagues implemented these changes to mimic the contractual language that was ratified by the Pennsylvania Supreme Court in the *Lajoie* case, believing the modifications would be sufficient to persuade future courts to follow the *Lajoie* precedent and uphold the enforceability of the contract. Indeed, the revised agreement reportedly received the blessing of several outside legal experts, including former U.S. President—and future U.S. Supreme Court Chief Justice—William Howard Taft.[53]

The National Commission publicly declared its confidence that the modified player contract was fully enforceable, with August Herrmann stating at organized baseball's annual meeting in November 1913: "In former years there existed a doubt with reference to the reservation clause in the player's contract, it being contended and probably correctly so, that it was not an equitable arrangement. This condition has now been changed.

A player signing a contract containing a reservation clause, is [now] compensated for his action, whether he is reserved or not."[54] Recently appointed National League president John Tener expressed similar confidence in early 1914, declaring, "it is well known that the legality of the present form of contract between the league and players was attacked, but its validity in law and equity was sustained by the Supreme Court of Pennsylvania in the *Lajoie* case."[55]

Tener was joining organized baseball's leadership at a particularly tenuous time given the brewing baseball war. To compound matters, he was unable to devote his full attention to governing his league during the 1914 season because he was simultaneously finishing his term as the governor of Pennsylvania. Nevertheless, it is easy to understand why organized baseball wanted Tener to join the National Commission; not only was he politically connected, but he was also intimately familiar with professional baseball. A former major league pitcher, Tener had helped organize the rival Players' League in 1890. The physically imposing, six-foot four-inch, 240-pound Irish immigrant would be the first former big leaguer to serve as president of either major league.[56]

Despite the National Commission's public declarations of confidence in the enforceability of the reserve clause, some believed that organized baseball had erred by revising the standard player contract. A January 1914 article in the *Sporting News,* the nation's leading baseball publication at the time, speculated that the decision to modify the contract would only embolden the Federal League's recruitment of major league players. The paper warned that by revising the form agreement, the National Commission indicated that the prior contracts were "too weak from a legal standpoint to be dragged into court."[57] As a result, the article predicted that the Federal League would point to the modifications as evidence that players were free to disregard the reserve clause in their prior contracts.

Meanwhile, some within the baseball establishment did not believe that the changes went far enough. Ban Johnson proposed eliminating the ten-day release provision entirely in December 1913, believing that the "the ill feeling and possible legal ramifications it created" dwarfed any benefits provided by the clause.[58] Indeed, including the provision in contracts during a period when the major leagues were fending off a rival challenger made little sense, as the Federals would likely sign any player released by an American or National League team under the clause.

As the 1913–1914 off-season progressed, organized baseball continued its war preparations, with the American and National League owners settling on a legal strategy to deter players from jumping to the Federal League. In December, August Herrmann announced that major league teams would seek to "enjoin any of the players who jump contracts or reservations.

John Tener served as both the governor of Pennsylvania and the president of the National League in 1914 (Library of Congress, Prints & Photographs Division, LC-USZ62-54075)

This will take their cases into the courts and force the players to remain idle until decisions are handed down."[59] Meanwhile, although Herrmann insisted that there would "be no blacklist," he warned that "any players who ignore organized baseball to the extent of jumping either contracts or reservations will always remain outside" the game in the future.[60] Despite these dire warnings, however, the two major leagues would soon learn that some of their players were nevertheless all too willing to take their chances and jump to the Federal League.

2

The Opening Salvos

December 1913 to June 1914

The news of December 27, 1913, sent a shockwave throughout professional baseball: star shortstop Joe Tinker had signed a three-year contract with the Chicago Federals, or "ChiFeds," for $12,000 per season. The future Hall of Famer—immortalized in Franklin P. Adams's poem "Baseball's Sad Lexicon" regaling the Chicago Cubs' famed double play combination of "Tinker to Evers to Chance"—jumped to the Federal League after his contract was sold earlier that off-season from the Cincinnati Reds to Brooklyn for $25,000. Following the sale, Brooklyn rejected Tinker's demand for a $7,500 salary, offering him no more than $5,000 per season. Tinker balked at the offer and instead agreed to terms with the ChiFeds on one of the richest contracts in baseball history, in the process giving the Federals instant credibility with other major league players.[1]

A driving force behind Tinker's signing was Charles Weeghman, a recent investor in the ChiFeds. Weeghman was a self-made millionaire, having earned his fortune by opening a chain of twenty-four-hour, quick-service diners throughout Chicago. His involvement with the Federals would cause some of the more dismissive media outlets to dub the organization the "Lunch Room League" or the "Flap Jack Circuit." Having long sought to enter professional baseball, Weeghman agreed to join the new organization after hearing a recruiting pitch by Federal League president Jim Gilmore. The *Sporting News* described the forty-year-old Weeghman as "a clean-cut man, as lively as a cricket," and noted that "[w]hen he talks his voice is well modulated and good to hear."[2] Weeghman used his youthful energy to build his team and league.

Upon learning of Tinker's defection, Brooklyn announced that it would seek to enjoin him from playing in the Federal League prior to the start of

Charles Weeghman, the energetic head of the Chicago Federal League team (Library of Congress, Prints & Photographs Division, LC-DIG-ggbain-17663)

the 1914 season. In response, the Federals issued a statement denouncing the legality of the reserve clause and proclaiming that they would stand behind any player joining the league by furnishing his defense in court. Fearing that Tinker's contract did not provide the strongest test case for determining the validity of the reserve clause—no doubt instead preferring to rely on the newly revised 1914 player contract in any litigation—the National Commission ultimately convinced Brooklyn owner Charles Ebbets not to pursue legal action. Instead, Brooklyn was left to fight it out with Cincinnati over the return of the $25,000 it had paid for the rights to Tinker.[3]

Tinker's defection forced organized baseball to begin taking the Federal League challenge more seriously. The baseball press speculated that major league teams would be more amenable to compromising with players in salary disputes that off-season to prevent a mass exodus to the rival circuit. Recognizing that it had a fight on its hands, the National Commission sought to prevent other players from jumping to the new organization. American League president Ban Johnson attempted to deter players by publicly discrediting the benefits of joining the Federals, noting that the rival league's standard player contract itself included both a reserve clause and ten-day release provision. Indeed, the Federal League contract did include both provisions. However, its reserve clause was more favorable to players, guaranteeing them at least a 5 percent raise each year and permitting them to become free agents after ten years. Moreover, the Federals often omitted the ten-day release provision in order to entice players to sign.[4]

Meanwhile, National Commission chairman August Herrmann reiterated his earlier threat that organized baseball intended to forcefully defend its contracts in court against both defecting players and the Federal League itself: "Rivalry will not be resented so long as league and club rights are not ignored, but illegal and unsportsmanlike interference with an utter disregard of established privileges of national agreement clubs will justify the adoption of vigorous-defense methods."[5] The Federals bristled at the charge of "unsportsmanlike" behavior, arguing that they were only signing players subject to the invalid 1913 reserve clause, and not those already under contract for the 1914 season.

Despite organized baseball's retention efforts, other players soon followed Tinker's lead and jumped to the Federal League. On January 5, 1914, the Baltimore Federals (or "BaltFeds") announced they had signed Otto Knabe, the longtime second baseman of the Philadelphia Phillies, to serve at their player-manager. Around the same time, the Federal League announced that Mordecai "Three Finger" Brown—so nicknamed following a farming accident to his throwing hand—would be pitching for the St. Louis Federals.

Then on January 9, 1914, Weeghman's ChiFeds announced the signing of four more major league players: pitchers Ad Brennan, Gene Packard, and Leonard "King" Cole, along with catcher William "Reindeer Bill" Killefer.[6]

Notwithstanding these signings, the Federal League was disappointed by both the relatively small number of players it was able to sign as well as the cost it took to sign them. In total, the Federals would secure only fifty big league players for the start of the 1914 season, fewer than seven players each for the circuit's eight teams that year. Meanwhile, only sixteen of these men had played a significant role for a major league club in 1913, meaning that many of the rest were fringe big leaguers.[7]

Of the players signed by the Federal League that off-season, catcher Bill Killefer would prove the most significant legally. Just a .207 career hitter in 296 major league games, Killefer was nevertheless regarded as one of the National League's premier defensive catchers. He was particularly valuable to his former team, the Philadelphia Phillies, because he was the backstop of choice for the club's pitching ace Grover Cleveland Alexander.[8]

Upon learning of Killefer's defection, Philadelphia quickly sought to persuade him to return to its team. The club wrote to Killefer's father, a Michigan probate judge, explaining its legal claim to his son under the reserve clause and urging him to persuade Killefer to reconsider. The team included Killefer's 1913 contract and a copy of the Pennsylvania Supreme Court's 1902 decision in the *Lajoie* suit to help bolster its case.[9] The letter convinced the father of the validity of the reserve clause, and he implored his son to return to Philadelphia.

At his father's urging, Killefer agreed to travel to Philadelphia to meet with the team's officials. The club sent its secretary, William Shettsline, to accompany Killefer on the trip from Chicago to Pennsylvania. While waiting at the station for the train to Philadelphia, Killefer noticed Jim Gilmore—who by happenstance was himself traveling to Philadelphia aboard the same train—walking down the platform toward them. Shettsline quickly moved in front of Killefer to block him from Gilmore's view, and the Federal League executive passed by unwittingly. Killefer eventually made it to Philadelphia without incident, and upon arriving quickly agreed to re-sign with his former team for three years at $6,500 per season, a significant raise over his 1913 salary of $3,200, and nearly $700 more per year than the Federals had offered.[10]

The news that Killefer had re-signed with Philadelphia both shocked and angered the Federals. ChiFeds owner Charles Weeghman declared, "I can't understand the report. I have the signed contract of Killefer in my possession."[11] He then threatened retribution, stating, "If Organized Baseball

William "Reindeer Bill" Killefer spurned the Federal League to return to the Philadelphia Phillies in 1914 (Library of Congress, Prints & Photographs Division, LC-DIG-ggbain-12268)

starts taking players we have signed, I will start the same thing, and I'll have Christy Mathewson and Ty Cobb and some more of them playing for me on the north side, because I'll give them more money than anybody else."[12] Meanwhile, Weeghman's player-manager Joe Tinker was more circumspect: "Organized ball knows it has no legal right to sign our ballplayers. It merely wants to tie them up so they can't play with us."[13] Killefer's disloyalty also resonated with the public, inspiring the following anonymous jingle:

Weeghman Weeghman Federal man
Make me a contract as fast as you can,
Pad it and sign it and mark it O.K.
And I'll go to the majors and ask for more pay.[14]

The Federal League did not take the loss of Killefer lightly. Shortly after his re-defection, the league announced it planned to file a lawsuit blocking his return to organized baseball.[15] To help lay the foundation for the case, Gilmore sent Philadelphia a telegram stating: "We hereby officially notify you that Ad Brennan and William Killifer [*sic*] have signed contracts with Chicago Federals and have received advance money. Both our players and our contracts will be protected."[16] Meanwhile, the Federals' general counsel, Edward Gates, hoped to extract some benefit from the potential loss of Killefer by arguing to the press that Philadelphia's decision to re-sign the player showed that organized baseball knew its contracts would not hold up in court.[17] Otherwise, the team would have simply sought an injunction based on Killefer's 1913 reserve clause.

At the same time Killefer was repudiating his ChiFeds contract, the Federal League learned that organized baseball was actively recruiting other defectors back into its fold. The Federals had underestimated the ferocity with which the major leagues would seek to win back their players. In February 1914, the National Commission circulated a bulletin to all major league teams, encouraging owners to "make special efforts to have their deserting players sign contracts at once and report by the first day of the major league pennant races without regards to their having signed Federal League contracts."[18] The bulletin also suggested owners should come to terms with any unsigned players as quickly as possible, preferably on two-year contracts, and inform their players that any jumpers would face at least a three-year ban from organized baseball. Cognizant of the risk of an antitrust investigation, however, the bulletin urged teams "to make it plain to newspaper interviewers that Organized Baseball is not a trust or monopoly."[19]

Following Killefer's desertion, several other lesser-known players—such as Gus Williams, George Baumgardner, and Samuel Agnew—announced they were repudiating their Federal League contracts and returning to organized baseball. The Federal League hoped to stem the tide of player losses by announcing it would sue any player breaking his contract with the organization. Ultimately, however, these threats largely failed to materialize into litigation.[20]

In addition to battling for players, officials from organized baseball and the Federal League also continued to fight a public relations battle in the press. In late January, organized baseball publicized a meeting held with Attorney General John Bell of Pennsylvania, during which Bell reportedly expressed his opinion that the reserve clause was legal. The next week, word was leaked that major league owners had held a secret conference in Pittsburgh where they agreed to tie up any defecting players in court for one to two years to prevent them from playing in the Federal League. Meanwhile, Jim Gilmore announced that he had received additional legal advice in support of the Federal League's position regarding the invalidity of the reserve clause. Although it recognized that the legal maneuverings were of critical importance to the baseball magnates, by February the *Sporting News* nevertheless bemoaned the posturing as being "decidedly tiresome to the fans."[21]

With the 1914 season approaching and spring training camps beginning to open, any hopes the Federal League may have held that Bill Killefer would honor his contract with the ChiFeds faded when newspaper reports emerged that the player had reported to Philadelphia's spring camp in Wilmington, North Carolina. As a result, Gilmore instructed the Federals' general counsel, Edward Gates, to file a lawsuit to enjoin Killefer from playing for his former team. Gates announced that he would soon be filing a complaint against the player in federal district court in Grand Rapids, Michigan (the closest federal court to Killefer's home in Paw Paw, Michigan).[22]

Moreover, Gilmore declared, the Federal League would be going on the offensive, signing any big league players it wanted without respect to the contracts they may have signed with a major league team. "The policy of respecting the contracts of organized leagues in the search for players is a thing of the past," Gilmore announced.[23] This marked a significant shift in the Federals' strategy; whereas the league had previously targeted only unsigned players bound by just the reserve clause, Gilmore was now sanctioning the signing of players under contract for the upcoming season. The approach was premised on the invalidity of the ten-day release clause, with the Federals believing that a court would refuse to enforce any contract containing the provision as being so unfairly one-sided that it was rendered unconscionable. Justifying his league's new position, Gilmore proclaimed: "It's war to the end. We will show the public that the Federal League is not a piker and that Ban Johnson of the American League is a four-flusher. . . . We have been clean and above board in our efforts to secure the services of players who are not under contract. We have not made any overtures to players under contract, but as long as one of our players who is under contract to one of our clubs has been 'lifted,' we are perfectly justified in going after players who are under contract to the clubs of Organized Baseball."[24]

Following Gilmore's declaration, the Federals began to send agents to organized baseball's spring training camps in the hopes of signing additional players. These recruiting efforts came to a head in early March when Kansas City Federals manager George Stovall showed up to the Boston Braves' spring training site in Georgia to sign some of the team's players. Angered by the Federals' audacity, Boston owner James Gaffney filed suit in Georgia state court seeking to enjoin Stovall from stealing his players. The Bibb County Superior Court issued an injunction on March 10, 1914, barring Stovall or any other agents of the Federal League from inducing Boston's players to break their contracts, or from otherwise loitering around the team hotel. In particular, the court identified thirty-one players under contract with Boston and found that the loss of any one of them would inflict an irreparable injury on the team because there was not enough time left before the start of the season to find suitable replacements.[25]

Meanwhile, on March 20, 1914, the Federal League filed its long-awaited suit against Bill Killefer in federal district court in Grand Rapids, Michigan. Formally captioned Charles Weeghman and W. M. Walker (Weeghman's co-owner) versus William J. Killefer Jr., the case was assigned to Judge Clarence W. Sessions, a former Michigan state court judge in Muskegon who had been appointed to the federal bench by President William Howard Taft in 1911.[26] In the complaint, Weeghman asserted that Killefer had signed a three-year contract with the ChiFeds on January 8, in which he had agreed not to perform for any other team. In what would become fairly typical language in these types of cases, the ChiFeds' owner alleged that Killefer possessed such "unique and extraordinary skill" that he was impossible to replace with another player. In particular, he argued that the loss of Killefer was especially damaging because he played a position—catcher—that was one of the most important and difficult to fill. Not only would the ChiFeds thus be harmed on the field by Killefer's defection, but the complaint further alleged that the team had also incurred significant expense advertising his participation to fans. As a result, Weeghman asserted that his business would be irreparably harmed by the loss of "a most attractive drawing card for the public," and urged the court to issue an injunction preventing Killefer from playing for anyone but the ChiFeds.[27]

Because Judge Sessions was out of town at the time the suit was filed, the ChiFeds were unable to obtain immediate, temporary injunctive relief. Instead, the case was scheduled for an initial hearing on Saturday, April 4. Reached for comment, Killefer expressed doubt that he would be served with the court papers, adding that he would retire before ever playing in the Federal League.[28]

At the same time they were suing Killefer in Michigan, the Federals continued their recruitment of players under contract with organized baseball by sending Samuel "Howie" Camnitz of the Pittsburgh Federals to Hot Springs, Arkansas, where the Pittsburgh Pirates were training. Camnitz, himself a former pitcher on the squad, offered two Pirates—George McQuillan and Jim Viox—$5,000 each to defect to the Federal League. Upon learning of the inducement, and undoubtedly buoyed by Boston having successfully obtained an injunction in Georgia, Pittsburgh owner Barney Dreyfuss ordered his attorneys to file suit in Arkansas state court to enjoin Camnitz from recruiting his players.[29]

Samuel "Howie" Camnitz was sued in Arkansas after attempting to recruit players from the Pittsburgh Pirates to the Federal League (Library of Congress, Prints & Photographs Division, LC-DIG-ggbain-09321)

In a complaint filed on March 23, 1914, in Garland County Chancery Court, Pittsburgh alleged that Camnitz and another unknown person—later identified only as "Happy"—were attempting to induce the team's players to break their contracts and jump to the Federal League. As in Boston's earlier suit, Pittsburgh asserted that the loss of any player at this juncture would inflict an irreparable injury on the club because all talented players were already under contract with other teams. Therefore, the team requested that the Arkansas court enjoin Camnitz and any other Federal League agent from "talking to or writing to or in any way approaching" its players.[30]

The news of Dreyfuss's suit angered Ban Johnson, who feared that the Federals might use the case as an opportunity to obtain copies of Pittsburgh's player contracts to ascertain the players' salaries. Johnson expressed his frustration in a letter to August Herrmann: "I regret exceedingly that an issue of this sort should have been raised in a distant city and possibly under unfavorable conditions. The restraining order issued against Federal League agents could have no substantial value and I am surprised that some of the National leagues Clubs should have resorted to such a course. . . . I certainly am not in favor of combating the suit in the courts of Arkansas."[31] Herrmann agreed that the "Pittsburgh Club should have kept in touch with the Commission before filing suit." Nevertheless, he defended the team by reporting that "Mr. Dreyfuss told me that everyone was so rattled they did not know what to do; that Camnitz had $5,000 in cash and was running around with some of the players of the Pittsburgh club."[32]

Three days after the suit was launched, Camnitz filed an answer presenting a multifaceted defense. First, although Camnitz admitted that he had tried to sign several Pittsburgh players, he denied that he had acted wrongfully. Instead, he argued that the players' contracts were invalid for a lack of mutuality due to the inclusion of the ten-day release provision, and therefore that he had done nothing wrong because the contracts were unenforceable in court. Meanwhile, Camnitz further contended that Pittsburgh should not be granted injunctive relief because it had unclean hands after illegally conspiring with the other American and National League clubs to fix ticket prices and player salaries in violation of both federal and state antitrust law. Then, as Ban Johnson had feared, Camnitz asked that Pittsburgh be forced to produce its player contracts in court to prove that the alleged contractual relationships existed. Finally, Camnitz requested $1,000 in damages to cover the expense and inconvenience caused by the suit.[33]

August Herrmann took Camnitz's answer in stride, arguing to Ban Johnson that there might be a silver lining to the case. In particular, Herrmann noted that the National Commission's outside legal counsel, Ellis Kinkead, "seems to be positive that this case can be won if it is presented to the Court in the proper way." Given Camnitz's attack on the validity of the major leagues' standard player contract, Herrmann hoped that a favorable ruling could provide a valuable precedent for future cases: "If we can get the proper kind of decree in the present case, I am sure it will do us a world of good for the future."[34]

The Arkansas court scheduled a hearing in the *Camnitz* case for April 2, during which it heard testimony from various Pittsburgh players and team officials. In response, Camnitz's counsel emphasized the antitrust argument to the court, arguing that Pittsburgh's unclean hands made it improper to grant injunctive relief. Meanwhile, although Pittsburgh objected to presenting all of its players' contracts in court, the team grudgingly agreed to provide the contracts for the two players in question (Viox and McQuillan).[35] The court promised to issue its decision shortly.

Chancellor Jethro P. Henderson released his opinion two days later, enjoining Camnitz from recruiting Pittsburgh's players. Specifically, the court reasoned that Camnitz's actions were wrongful because he knew the players were under contract with Pittsburgh and that their loss would cripple the club. Despite granting the injunction, however, Chancellor Henderson shared the Federals' belief that the ten-day release provision rendered Pittsburgh's player contracts unenforceable because of a lack of mutuality. The court nevertheless concluded that this finding did not excuse Camnitz's conduct, because only a player could rightfully challenge the validity of his contract on this basis. Thus, it was up to the player to decide whether to contest his contract on the grounds that it was unconscionable; until he did, Chancellor Henderson concluded, third parties had no right to interfere with the contract. In other words, legally speaking, the contracts were not automatically void, but merely "voidable" by the player.[36]

After reviewing the *Camnitz* decision, organized baseball's attorney, Ellis Kinkead, tried to spin the opinion as a positive one. He emphasized the fact that the court had issued the injunction as requested, and trivialized the opinion's language regarding the unenforceability of the player contracts as mere "dictum" (that is, an unnecessary, nonbinding statement in a judicial decision). Although the attorney was forced to concede that the Federals' argument that the ten-day release provision rendered the standard player contract unconscionable "apparently commends itself at first blush to most lawyers," he remained confident "that when the question is fully considered, and particularly in view of evidence which in the Arkansas case the Chancellor refused to admit, showing the purpose and reasonableness of the clause, its validity will be sustained." To mitigate the harm of the *Camnitz* opinion, though, Kinkead recommended that organized baseball quickly pursue a case to a "court of last resort of standing and dignity to determine the validity" of the standard player contract.[37]

Nevertheless, the *Camnitz* decision upset Ban Johnson. He believed that Chancellor Henderson had "departed from the real issue" in the case by discussing the ten-day release clause, and in the process "uncovered a vital flaw" that would only lead to "embarrassment" for the major leagues. As a result, Johnson expressed his frustration to August Herrmann by once again arguing that the case never should have been filed in the first place.[38]

The same day that the Arkansas court handed down its opinion in the *Camnitz* suit, the federal district court in Grand Rapids heard argument in the *Killefer* case. Following the initiation of the ChiFeds' suit, both Killefer and his Philadelphia club—which was granted permission to intervene in the case to present its own defense in support of its player—filed answers alleging that the Federals had known Killefer was under a contractual obligation to his former team but had nevertheless induced him to breach his contract.

As a result, both the player and club argued that the ChiFeds' hands were unclean, and thus that injunctive relief against Killefer was unwarranted.[39]

The Federal League's general counsel, Edward Gates, represented Weeghman at the hearing. Gates had been involved with the Federal League since its founding in March 1913, owning an interest in the organization's Indianapolis franchise. The respected attorney had gone to college at Yale University, and then attended law school at both Indiana University and New York University, before returning to Indianapolis to begin his legal career. Gates rose to prominence in the Indianapolis bar when he represented the local Chamber of Commerce in a high-profile railroad dispute before the Interstate Commerce Commission in 1907.[40] Upon joining the Federal League a few years later, he would quickly take a lead role in formulating its legal strategy.

Opposing Gates in the argument was renowned Philadelphia attorney George Wharton Pepper, a University of Pennsylvania Law School graduate widely regarded at the time as one of the nation's premier corporate attorneys. Pepper was so well respected that he had once been offered a judgeship on the United States Court of Appeals for the Third Circuit by President William Howard Taft, but declined to remain in private practice. Later, in 1922, he would be appointed to the United States Senate.[41] Perhaps Philadelphia's most esteemed lawyer at the time, Pepper was a natural selection to represent the Phillies in the first major legal battle of the Federal League war.

Edward E. Gates, the Federal League's general counsel (Library of Congress, Prints & Photographs Division, LC-DIG-ggbain-17672)

Noted Philadelphia attorney George Wharton Pepper would represent the major leagues in a number of Federal League–related lawsuits (University of Pennsylvania Archives, UARC20020621003)

At the hearing, presiding Judge Sessions focused his attention on two primary issues. First, Sessions questioned whether the Federals were entitled to injunctive relief against Killefer when they had knowingly convinced the player to break the reserve clause in his contract with Philadelphia. Second, the judge explored whether the ChiFeds could properly challenge the reserve clause in Killefer's contract when it appeared both the player and team were now satisfied with the agreement.[42]

Pepper emphasized the first point during his argument, asserting that the Federals did not deserve an injunction because of their own unclean hands: "Should the seducer of an employe [*sic*] be entitled to equity in court?" Gates attempted to rebut this contention by arguing that the reserve clause was legally unenforceable, and thus that the Federals had done nothing wrong by recruiting Killefer once he had fully performed all of the valid obligations in his 1913 contract.[43] Judge Sessions frequently interrupted Gates, hinting that he favored Philadelphia's side of the argument: "He who seeks equity must himself come into court with clean hands. You, having been a party to the breach of obligation, claim you are entitled to an enforcement of the contract not withstanding your actions in that regard."[44] After the hearing concluded, Judge Sessions announced that although he was ready to rule, he would hold off on issuing his decision for a week so that the parties would have time to cite additional legal authority.[45]

Judge Session's focus—not to mention that of the *Camnitz* court as well—on whether the Federal League had itself acted unethically when recruiting players bound by the reserve clause appeared to take the organization by surprise. Indeed, the Federals believed they had done nothing wrong by negotiating with players bound only by what they thought was a blatantly invalid provision. As Charles Weeghman would later state, "I can't understand how [a] judge could hold the reserve clause illegal and at the same time rule that we went into court with unclean hands."[46] In hindsight, the Federals may have been too personally invested in their dispute with organized baseball to objectively evaluate the optics of their position.

Notwithstanding the unpromising tenor of the hearing, the Federal League believed it was well positioned in the *Killefer* case and would emerge victorious no matter the outcome. As Edward Gates explained to the media, if the court granted the ChiFeds an injunction, then other players who had signed with the Federal League would also have to honor their contracts, meaning the league could reclaim the services of any player that organized baseball had recruited back into its fold. On the other hand, if Judge Sessions denied the injunction, then Gates believed the court would effectively be holding that all baseball contracts were worthless, allowing the Federals to raid organized baseball's rosters without regard to the contractual status of its players.[47] Indeed, the major leagues anticipated that the Federals would attempt to use an unfavorable decision in the case to recruit players to their organization. Along these lines, National League President John Tener wrote to August Herrmann shortly after the hearing in Michigan, recommending that the National Commission advise players that courts would view the repudiation of an existing contract in midseason much differently than Killefer's case, which only involved the enforceability of an outdated version of the reserve clause.[48]

Judge Sessions announced his ruling in the *Killefer* case on April 10, 1914, issuing what the *Sporting News* described as a decision "strewn with jawbreaking phraseology and technical legal terms which probably stump the average fan."[49] In the opinion, the court refused to enjoin Killefer from playing for Philadelphia but nevertheless held that his 1913 contract was legally unenforceable. Specifically, Judge Sessions found that the prior contract with the club was invalid due to a lack of definiteness and mutuality. The court concluded that because the reserve clause did not state what Killefer's salary would be for the subsequent season, it was indefinite and nonbinding. In other words, Sessions characterized the player's agreement as "[n]othing more than a contract to enter a contract." In addition, he agreed with the Federals that Killefer's 1913 contract was unenforceable for a lack of mutuality, owing to the inherent unfairness of the ten-day release provision.[50]

Although the court agreed that Killefer's prior contract was unenforceable, it nevertheless refused to grant the ChiFeds an injunction. Like the *Camnitz* court, Judge Sessions determined that even if Philadelphia could not enforce the reserve clause against Killefer, it did not automatically render his contract legally void. Instead, the court characterized the contract as being valid until the player himself repudiated it. In other words, unless Killefer himself contested the validity of the contract, the agreement was binding, and thus no third party could rightfully interfere with it. As a result, Judge Sessions concluded that the Federal League lacked the clean hands necessary to obtain injunctive relief: "Knowing that the defendant, Killefer, was under a moral, if not a legal, obligation to furnish his services to the Philadelphia Club for the season of 1914, [the Federal League] sent for him, and by offering him a longer term of employment and a much larger compensation induced him to repudiate his obligation to his employer. In so doing, a willful wrong was done to the Philadelphia Club, which was none the less grievous and harmful because the injured party could not obtain legal redress [against Killefer] in and through the courts of the land."[51]

Both sides declared victory after the opinion was released. Edward Gates stated that he regarded the decision "as a victory for the Federal League in that it sustains our contention in regard to the reserve clause and that the 1913 contract of organized baseball is not enforcible [*sic*] because of lack of mutuality on account of the ten-day release clause." Gates minimized the court's finding that the Federal League's hands were unclean by suggesting that future courts may rule differently: "it may be said to be a close question, upon which even courts might differ."[52]

Similarly, Jim Gilmore declared the decision to be "our greatest victory," and predicted that by striking down the reserve clause, it would "give our organization an opportunity for a bigger raid next year." Gilmore stated that the Federals would appeal the unclean hands finding to the highest possible court, while the ChiFeds' local Grand Rapids counsel suggested that the team would likely file an additional lawsuit seeking damages from *Killefer* for his breach of contract (a claim that would not hinge on the righteousness of the Federal League's own activities). Despite the Federals' public declarations of victory, in private league officials recognized that the Killefer decision undermined their plans to pursue injunctions against other players that had repudiated their Federal League contracts to jump back to organized baseball, forcing the circuit to shelve its planned legal action against Gus Williams and George Baumgardner, among others.[53]

Meanwhile, officials for organized baseball also announced that they were pleased with the outcome in the case. John Tener praised the opinion, stating that "Judge Sessions' decision in the *Killifer* [*sic*] case is timely, and its effect will be far-reaching and beneficial to baseball."[54] August Herrmann minimized the effect of the court's holding regarding the invalidity of the reserve clause, arguing that the "ruling is not in the nature of a surprise to my associates and myself for the reason that the defects pointed out by Judge Sessions have been remedied in our 1914 contract."[55]

Philadelphia's lead attorney, George Pepper, also issued a statement, declaring, "We naturally feel much gratified at the decision, because the contention of the Philadelphia club is sustained in every particular . . . we insisted that until the club and the player had agreed to disagree, our friends of the Federal league must keep hands off." Pepper then hinted that the decision might spur additional litigation by organized baseball, concluding "[i]t will be perceived that the same conduct that disentitles the Federal league to [injunctive] relief also gives the Philadelphia club the right to sue for damages for past injury and to seek protection by the injunction from any future interference with its business."[56]

In private, however, organized baseball's attorneys took issue with Judge Sessions's holding regarding the enforceability of the reserve clause. In a letter to August Herrmann, Ellis Kinkead noted that the *Killefer* court had relied on a Supreme Court decision (*Rutland Marble Co. v. Ripley*) that the Court had itself not followed in three subsequent cases. He also criticized Judge Sessions's conclusion that the one-sided nature of the ten-day release provision rendered the player contracts unenforceable, quoting from a leading legal treatise that suggested contracts do not have to grant both parties the same rights in order to be mutual.[57]

As Pepper's comments following the *Killefer* decision had foreshadowed, two major league teams quickly sought to capitalize on the opinion. Three days later, on April 13, 1914, two clubs filed lawsuits against the Federals, each alleging that Federal League officials had conspired to persuade major league players to break their contracts and jump to the rival circuit. The first case was filed in federal district court in Baltimore by the Boston Braves against the Federal League, Jim Gilmore, the BaltFeds, Edward Hanlon and Otto Knabe (two officials from the team), and pitcher John Quinn. In the suit, Boston alleged that Quinn had agreed to pitch for the Braves in 1914 for $3,600, but then was persuaded to sign a three-year contract with Baltimore for $4,800 per season. Boston argued that Federal League officials had convinced Quinn to repudiate his contract by telling him that the reserve clause was invalid, and offering to indemnify him for any legal costs.[58]

However, rather than request an injunction to prevent Quinn from playing in the Federal League, Boston merely sought $25,000 in damages. As a result, L. Edwin Goldman, Baltimore's attorney, dismissed the suit as "an obvious bluff, and a confession that [Quinn's] contract" was not enforceable via injunctive relief.[59] Meanwhile, Boston president James Gaffney described his motivation for filing suit: "I don't want Quinn as a pitcher on my team under any circumstances, but I do propose to show the baseball world the actions of Gilmore, Hanlon, and others in carrying out their conspiracy to get this player to jump his contract."[60]

On the same day that Boston sued the Federals in Baltimore, the Philadelphia Phillies filed two lawsuits in federal district court in Chicago against Charles Weeghman, his partner William Walker, Jim Gilmore, Joseph Tinker, and Brooklyn Federals owners Robert and Walter Ward, the first seeking $25,000 in damages and the other an injunction restraining the Federal League from further interference with the club's players. In particular, Philadelphia alleged that the Federals had induced four of its players—Tom Seaton, Otto Knabe, Michael Doolan, and Ad Brennan—to repudiate their contracts even though two of the players (Seaton and Doolan) had already agreed to terms for the 1914 season. The franchise also asserted that the Federals had approached other players from the team, and had threatened to raid the club if the *Killefer* case had been decided differently. As a result, Philadelphia contended that it would be irreparably harmed if the Federal League induced any more of its players, and asked the court to enjoin the Federals from interfering with its employees.[61]

In response, the defendants denied that they had conspired to harm Philadelphia, arguing that the reserve clause—the entire basis for the plaintiff's claim to the players' services—was legally unenforceable.[62] Although Philadelphia's counsel, Horace Tenney, told reporters that the suits would be "vigorously pushed," they ultimately languished in court for the better part of the next two years. Nevertheless, Tenney characterized the suits as "part of the war all along the line that will be waged against the Federals."[63]

Indeed, shortly after the Boston and Philadelphia cases were filed, rumors spread that additional lawsuits would soon be initiated by teams in the International League, similarly alleging that the Federals had conspired to steal players from the upper-level minor league.[64] Fearing that it was losing centralized control over the legal battle, the National Commission issued a confidential bulletin on April 23, 1914, stating that it had "unanimously agreed that a major league club should not under any circumstances or conditions, begin court proceedings against a Federal League Club or player who has deserted to that League . . . without first applying for and securing the Commission's consent and cooperation." The commission justified its pronouncement by arguing that "uniformity in the method and efficient conduct of suits [would] minimiz[e] the chances of defeat in the courts, through inadequate presentation, and the establishment of adverse precedents."[65]

Meanwhile, although the Federals had initially ruled out the possibility of pursuing injunctive relief themselves following the *Killefer* opinion, one team in the league nevertheless opted to sue two players who had defected back to organized baseball for damages. Within a week of the release of Judge Sessions's opinion, the Kansas City Federals filed two lawsuits in Missouri state court—one in St. Louis and the other in Kansas City—against pitchers Fred Blanding and Earl Hamilton, respectively. Both men had signed contracts with the team for the 1914 season, but nevertheless repudiated those agreements shortly after they were signed to return to the major leagues. The Kansas City Feds asked the St. Louis court to order Blanding to pay $10,000 in damages for the breach of his contract, and sought $25,500 from Hamilton. As with Philadelphia's suits against Weeghman and company, however, Kansas City did not seriously pursue either case once it was filed.[66]

As Kansas City was filing its lawsuits in Missouri, the Federal League also sought to take advantage of the *Killefer* decision on the playing field. In light of Judge Sessions's declaration that the standard player contracts would be unenforceable if challenged by a player, Gilmore and Gates gave Federal League owners their blessing to go on the offensive and sign players currently under contract with organized baseball. Charles Weeghman instructed Joe Tinker to wire players throughout the country, inviting them "to come to the Federal League quarters in Chicago and discuss terms. Even if you decide not to sign a contract, all your expenses will be paid by the Federal League."[67]

As part of the recruitment effort, Kansas City Federals' president C. C. Madison traveled to Cincinnati on April 20, 1914, to meet with Native American pitcher George "Chief" Johnson of the Cincinnati Reds. Johnson had become disgruntled with the Reds after he believed he was unjustly fined for being out of shape. Madison offered Johnson a three-year contract for $5,000 per season, an $1,800 raise over his current salary with the Reds. Madison then enticed the pitcher by placing an advance of twenty-five $100 bills on the table before pausing, and then laying down five more. Johnson accepted, and the two men boarded a train for Kansas City that evening.[68]

Johnson was scheduled to make his Federal League debut in Chicago on April 23, 1914. By coincidence, Johnson's former team, Cincinnati, was also in town for a series against the Cubs. Cincinnati president August Herrmann and his attorneys went to the Cook County Superior Court in Chicago and persuaded Judge Charles Foell to temporarily restrain Johnson from playing for the Federals, just minutes before he was scheduled to pitch. They then rushed to the ChiFeds' stadium—Weeghman Park, better known today as Wrigley Field—with deputies to serve the injunction papers on Johnson and Madison. Upon arriving at the park, the deputies found Jim Gilmore in the stands and asked him where Madison was. Not realizing who the men were, Gilmore unwittingly led them to their target: "Boys, Mr. Madison isn't up here, but I think I can find him for you." After locating Madison, the deputies then served the injunction papers on Johnson while he was walking off the field at the end of the second inning. In retaliation, the Federals marched over to the Reds' hotel that evening to recruit some of the team's other players.[69]

In total, the Reds initiated four lawsuits that day, two each against Johnson and Madison, one seeking to enjoin the respective defendant, and the other requesting an award of damages. In its injunction suit against Johnson, Cincinnati stated that the player "was generally regarded as one of the foremost base ball pitchers on the American base ball field," and asserted that his defection would inflict an irreparable injury on the team.[70] The club further alleged it would sustain additional financial harm from the loss of Johnson insofar as it had paid his travel and accommodation expenses while he prepared for the season in spring training, and had mounted a significant advertising campaign around the pitcher. As a result, Cincinnati requested

George "Chief" Johnson warming up in Chicago moments before the inaugural game at Weeghman Park (better known today as Wrigley Field), in 1914—he would be served with injunction papers during the second inning of the game (Chicago History Museum, SDN059371, photo by the Chicago Daily News)

that he be enjoined from playing for the Federals, and that he be ordered to pay the team $10,000 in damages for his breach of contract.[71]

Meanwhile, the suits against Madison alleged that the Kansas City Feds' president had attempted to induce not only Johnson but also Cincinnati players Armando Marsans and John Benton to disregard their contracts in order to sign with the Federals. The Reds asked the court to enjoin Madison from continuing to interfere with the team's players and order him to pay $20,000 in damages for the harm he had already inflicted.[72] Although Cincinnati would vigorously press its injunction suit against Johnson, the others cases would ultimately languish for the next year and a half with little activity.

Indeed, organized baseball had high hopes for its injunction suit against Johnson, with Herrmann predicting that if the court entered a permanent injunction in the case "we will have no more trouble insofar as players jumping their contracts is concerned in the future."[73] The National Commission's co-counsel, John Galvin, estimated that if Judge Foell agreed to grant the permanent injunction, it would take the Federal League at least six to eight months to get a hearing before an appellate court.[74] However, Galvin cautioned Herrmann that the Federals appeared to be winning the public relations battle in the press regarding the lawsuits, which he feared "might create a better impression on the minds of the public." Although the attorney acknowledged that winning the lawsuits was ultimately more important, Galvin nevertheless encouraged the National Commission's chairman to try to get more favorable press coverage for their side of the legal dispute. Herrmann agreed, assuring Galvin that "[e]very effort will be made in the future to correct this condition."[75]

Johnson and the Federals responded to the lawsuit on April 26, 1914, by filing a multipart answer. First, Johnson argued that his contract with the Reds was unenforceable because the team had fraudulently induced him to enter the agreement. Specifically, the pitcher alleged that he been negotiating with the Federal League that prior off-season when August Herrmann told him that the Federals had no parks, were not financially responsible, and would not survive until the start of the 1914 season. Herrmann also allegedly threatened that any players jumping to the new league would be blacklisted by organized baseball. Johnson asserted that he had relied on these misrepresentations when entering his contract with the Reds, and therefore argued that because Herrmann had lied to him about the financial condition of the Federal League, his Cincinnati contract should not be enforced.[76]

Second, hoping to draw upon the favorable language in the *Camnitz* and *Killefer* decisions, Johnson argued that the ten-day release clause in his Cincinnati contract rendered the agreement void and unenforceable. Third, he further alleged that he had good cause to terminate his contract, asserting that the Reds had improperly fined him when he was unable to play due to a case of tonsillitis and "La Grippe" (the flu) that he had acquired after being forced to practice in the rain.[77] The Reds would later contest this claim, alleging that Johnson had in fact been fined for his excessive drinking and cavorting with "lewd women."[78]

Finally, Johnson contended that injunctive relief was not warranted because his departure would not inflict an irreparable injury on Cincinnati. In particular, he argued that there were numerous replacements available to the Reds throughout the minor league system. Moreover, the pitcher asserted, any injury to Cincinnati could not be "irreparable" by definition because the team had simultaneously sued him for $10,000 in damages (thereby placing a dollar value on any injury it had sustained).[79]

Despite Johnson's defenses, organized baseball remained confident it would prevail in the case. Following a hearing before Judge Foell on May 14, 1914, Cincinnati's attorneys Galvin and Kinkead wrote to August Herrmann summarizing the proceedings and predicting a victory in the case.[80] Several days later, one of the major leagues' other attorneys reported that Judge Foell had requested copies of Herrmann's testimony along with a few other documents referenced in the hearing, a sign the lawyer interpreted as indicating that a favorable decision would be forthcoming.[81]

As organized baseball's attorneys had anticipated, Judge Foell ultimately granted Cincinnati a permanent injunction on June 3, 1914, restraining Johnson from playing in the Federal League. In the opinion, the court rejected the defense's assertion that the ten-day release provision in Johnson's Cincinnati contract rendered it invalid due to a lack of mutuality. Specifically, the decision cited several cases standing for the proposition that a contract was not invalid simply because it only gave one party the right to terminate the agreement. Moreover, Judge Foell noted, substantially similar contracts had been used throughout baseball for years, making it hard for the jurist to believe that so many players would have agreed to such terms if they were as unfair as Johnson alleged: "It seems improbable that the many members constituting the great fraternity of base ball players should have, for a score or more years, voluntarily in contemplation of law signed such contracts if the practical effect of [the ten-day release] clause . . . resulted in the infliction of an unconscionable hardship upon the players."[82]

Judge Foell's observation was at odds with the practical reality of the players' predicament. Under the National Agreement, teams within organized baseball were specifically forbidden from issuing contracts without a reserve clause or ten-day release provision. As a result, players did not have any choice in the matter; they could either accept the terms that were offered or else forgo a professional baseball career entirely.

Judge Foell's decision went on to reject each of Johnson's other defenses. First, the court determined that the pitcher had been properly fined under his contract, before next concluding that Johnson had not been fraudulently induced because the allegedly false statements made by Herrmann were all "merely expressions of opinion." Finally, Judge Foell held that Johnson's departure would inflict an irreparable injury on Cincinnati, as the team had subsequently been unable to find a replacement with similar abilities.[83]

After issuing the permanent injunction, Judge Foell granted the Federal League's request for an immediate appeal to the Illinois Court of Appeals. Edward Gates believed the decision would be reversed by the appellate court, telling the press that "[t]he opinion of Judge Foell is contrary to what we understand to be the law, therefore we have appealed with the hope of getting justice."[84] In the interim, though, Jim Gilmore announced that the Federals would honor the injunction, even though Gates had suggested that the court's order would be ineffective outside Chicago (raising the possibility that the Federals could mimic the strategy of the American League in the *Lajoie* case twelve years earlier by letting Johnson play everywhere but in Illinois). Just to be safe, August Herrmann quickly sought to rule out Gates's suggestion by declaring that the Reds would file a similar suit in every Federal League city to prevent Johnson from playing in the league.[85] For his part, Johnson shrugged off the talk of continued litigation by reaffirming his commitment to the Federal League: "All the decisions or injunctions in the world can't make me go back to Cincinnati," he insisted.[86]

Meanwhile, Herrmann went on to praise the *Johnson* decision as "a decisive one. It is clear and distinct and a great victory for organized baseball."[87] The press similarly viewed the outcome as a significant triumph for the major leagues, with the *Chicago Tribune* declaring it to be a "crushing blow" for the Federals.[88] Indeed, not only did the decision negate the defection of Johnson, but it may have also prevented an even larger exodus of players from organized baseball to the Federal League. Anticipating a victory in the *Johnson* case, the Federals had reportedly persuaded as many as thirty-seven major leaguers to jump to the league if it received a favorable judicial decision in Chicago. When Judge Foell sided with Cincinnati, however, the planned raid collapsed, with the majority of the players deciding to stick with organized baseball rather than risk being enjoined from playing in the Federal League.[89] The *Johnson* decision was thus a significant setback for the Federals, derailing what might have been a decisive shift of momentum in the war between the leagues.

The *Johnson* case capped a disappointing few months for the Federal League. First, the Federals had been unable to sign as many players as they had hoped over the off-season, only to see many of those that they did sign quickly defect back to the ranks of organized ball. Then, even though two judges—in the *Camnitz* and *Killefer* cases—were amenable to the argument that the reserve clause and ten-day release provision were invalid and legally unenforceable, the Federals had nevertheless lost all four lawsuits decided to date, largely owing to their own perceived malfeasance. Despite these setbacks, however, the league would continue to fight on. And its persistence would soon be rewarded, as the Federals' courtroom luck was about to change.

3

The Federal League Strikes Back

June 1914 to December 1914

Although the Federal League's large-scale raid of organized baseball collapsed following the Illinois court's June 1914 decision in the *Chief Johnson* case, the circuit was nevertheless able to convince several players to defect from organized baseball shortly after the opinion was issued. The same day that the *Johnson* decision was released, outfielder Armando Marsans announced that he was leaving the Cincinnati Reds to join the Federal League. The twenty-eight-year-old native of Matanzas, Cuba, first came to the United States to play professionally in 1908. Marsans had developed into a strong everyday player for the Reds by 1913, his third season in Cincinnati, hitting .297 with thirty-seven stolen bases that year. The club rewarded him the following off-season with a three-year contract for $4,400 per year. Upon reporting to duty for the 1914 season, however, Marsans was upset to discover he was being underpaid in comparison to other big leaguers, who had more effectively used offers from the Federal League as negotiating leverage with their major league teams. Marsans was further aggravated when Cincinnati refused to renegotiate his contract.[1] In his mind, it was simply a matter of respect: "Several players on the club . . . have been given new contracts that call for more money than they signed for at the beginning of the season and that do not contain the 10-day notice of release clause. I claim I am as good a ballplayer as they are, so why can't I get a raise in salary and a contract with the 10-day clause marked out?"[2]

Marsans's frustration soon spilled over into the clubhouse, where he began to clash openly with Cincinnati manager Buck Herzog. Following a dispute with his manager at the end of May—in which Marsans alleged that Herzog did not support him in a dispute with an umpire—Marsans elected to jump to the Federal League, which had been recruiting him since the start of the season.[3] On June 3, 1914, Marsans sent the following handwritten letter—obviously ghostwritten by a Federal League attorney—to Cincinnati's team president:

> Mr. August Herrmann,
>
> Dear Sir—As my alleged contract with you lacks mutuality and is voidable for various reasons, including the ten-day reserve clause, I herby [*sic*] notify you that I now elect to cancel and void said contract, hereby offering, however, to render my services to you for the same salary proportionally for said ten days, including payment of expenses as in said alleged contract provided, but without in any manner or respect ratifying or adopting said alleged contract. Furthermore, if you desire expiration of said ten days, you must within two days after receipt of this notice offer the items satisfactory to me or I will after two days consider myself free of contract to render my services elsewhere after expiration of said ten days.
>
> —Armando Marsans[4]

In effect, Marsans and the Federals were seeking to turn the ten-day release provision on its ear, contending that if the team has the right to terminate a player's contract upon ten days' notice, then the player must possess the same right under the contract. Otherwise, the argument went, the agreement would be unenforceable because of a lack of mutuality. Upon receiving Marsans's letter, Cincinnati suspended the player indefinitely.

Privately, organized baseball's attorneys derided the Federal League's legal theory. As John Galvin, the National Commission's outside counsel, put it: "Some lawyer for the Federals has worked out the theory that if the Club has the right to give a 10 days' notice of the termination of the contract, the player also has the right. . . . I think this proposition is absurd, but it seems to be effective with some of the players. Either our contract is void because of the 10 days' clause by lacking in mutuality and therefore can be broken without any 10 days' notice from the player, or it is good and the player has no option or right to break the contract in the same way or at all."[5] Nevertheless, baseball's attorneys counseled Cincinnati that its indefinite suspension of Marsans was legally unsound, given that the National Agreement required teams to provide players with written notice stating the duration of any suspension.[6]

Anticipating that organized baseball would try to persuade Marsans to return, the Federals holed him up in a St. Louis hotel room and placed a guard outside his door to prevent any major league representatives from contacting him. Although Marsans had already agreed on the terms of a contract with the St. Louis Federals, the team elected to wait a full ten days before formally executing the agreement. During that time, Cincinnati resorted to threatening Marsans by enlisting one of his friends to write the

Armando Marsans, the Cuban outfielder who defected from Cincinnati to the St. Louis Federals (Library of Congress, Prints & Photographs Division, LC-DIG-ggbain-13619)

player, warning that organized baseball would boycott his homeland of Cuba—by no longer sending major league teams to play exhibitions on the island—if he did not come back to the Reds. Marsans remained resolute, however, and signed a three-year, $21,000 contract with the Federals just after midnight on June 14, 1914. He made his Federal League debut later that Sunday afternoon, and with the courts closed, Cincinnati was unable to obtain an injunction to stop him before the game.[7]

At the same time the Federals were coordinating Marsans's defection, the league also sought to take advantage of the *Johnson* decision by pursuing injunctive relief of its own against pitcher Fred Blanding in Chicago. The Kansas City Feds had previously sued Blanding for damages in Missouri state court in April after he repudiated his Federal League contract to return to organized baseball. The team now sought to prevent the pitcher from continuing to play for the Cleveland Indians by filing for an injunction in the same court that had enjoined Chief Johnson a few days earlier. This time, however, Judge Foell refused to issue an immediate, preliminary injunction in the case, instead opting to first hold a formal hearing on the matter. Blanding ultimately defended himself by explaining that when he signed with the Federals he "did not have in mind" his obligation to return to Cleveland pursuant to the reserve clause in his prior contract with the Indians. He further asserted that because the Federals had recruited him despite knowing that he was obligated to re-sign with Cleveland, his agreement with Kansas City was legally unenforceable. For unknown reasons, however, Judge Foell does not appear to have ever issued a decision in the case, and as a result Kansas City's suit languished over the ensuing months.[8]

Meanwhile, shortly after Armando Marsans played his first game for the St. Louis Federals, news reports emerged that the Buffalo Federals (or "BuffFeds") had signed two additional major leaguers: New York Yankees pitcher Al Schulz and Chicago White Sox first baseman Hal Chase.[9] While Schulz was a relatively undistinguished pitcher, Chase arguably represented the Federals' most significant signing to date. Indeed, "Prince Hal" was widely regarded as one of the best first basemen of his era, considering his .291 career batting average and stellar defensive abilities. However, he also had an unsavory reputation for associating with gamblers and allegedly throwing games. Hall of Famer Edd Roush later described Chase as "the best first baseman I ever saw. He was also the worst if he wanted to lose a game. . . . You could tell after an inning or two whether he was in there to win or in there to lose."[10]

Chase had become disgruntled with the Chicago White Sox after the club's notoriously frugal owner, Charles Comiskey, allegedly cut his salary from $8,000 to $6,000 for the 1914 season. With rumors swirling that Chase was considering defecting, Comiskey tried to repair the relationship by asking the player to sign a revised contract. In particular, Comiskey reportedly offered to omit the ten-day release provision from Chase's contract, in the hope that that would prevent him from exercising the option himself (as Marsans had done). Chase refused. As he would later recollect: "At the time Comiskey called me into his office, and asked me to have the ten-day clause stricken from my contract. I demurred at this. A contract, it seemed to me, ought to bind both parties to the agreement. If that agreement allowed him to dispose of my services with ten days notice, I didn't see why I shouldn't enjoy the same privilege."[11]

When press reports surfaced that Chase had agreed to terms with the Federals, American League president Ban Johnson immediately ridiculed the story, declaring, "I don't believe it. . . . The Federal League can't get sensible players to climb aboard a sinking ship. Hal Chase above all others. The Federals are running to cover. They're through."[12] When reached for comment, Chase at first denied the reports before ultimately conceding that they were accurate: "Yes, it is true the Feds have been after me and I have decided to serve the ten day notice on the Chicago American League owner."[13] Suddenly realizing that his initial response may have been a bit too flippant, Ban Johnson now predicted that "if Hal Chase jumps his contract he will never . . . be permitted to play with a Federal League team—you can set that down as a certainty." Johnson also threatened that "any player in the American League who jumps his contract to play in the Federal League will never be permitted to appear on the rolls of an American League team again."[14]

Despite these threats, or perhaps because of them, Chase abruptly cleaned out his locker at the White Sox's stadium on June 21 and traveled across town to join the BuffFeds at Weeghman Park for a game that afternoon against the ChiFeds. As was the case with Armando Marsans the week before, because Chase's Federal League debut fell on a Sunday the White Sox were unable to obtain an injunction before the game. Nevertheless, Ban Johnson announced that litigation was forthcoming: "I notice Chase played with the Federals on Sunday. . . . As it was a Sunday, that could not be helped, but action will be taken to keep him from playing with the Buffalo team, which is equally culpable with Chase."[15]

Indeed, organized baseball did not take the latest defections lightly. The Cincinnati club quickly sought an injunction blocking Marsans from playing in any further games for the Federals, filing suit against the player in federal district court in St. Louis on June 18, 1914. As had become standard by this point, Cincinnati alleged that Marsans's defection inflicted an irreparable injury on the team because no suitable replacements were available to be signed so late in the season, let alone one that could make up for someone like Marsans, who was "generally regarded as one of the foremost players in the baseball fraternity" and "a most valuable drawing card."[16] Federal marshals served Marsans with notice of the suit later that day at the Federal League park in St. Louis.[17]

Cincinnati's attorneys believed they had had a stroke of luck regarding the timing of their lawsuit against Marsans. At the time the suit was filed, the only federal district court judge in St. Louis, Judge David Dyer, was out of town and not scheduled to return for nearly three weeks. As a result, under local judicial procedure, Cincinnati was able to take its request for injunctive relief straight to Judge W. H. Sanborn of the U.S. Court of Appeals. Cincinnati's attorney, Ellis Kinkead, viewed Sanborn as "one of the strongest of the U.S. Circuit Judges, and I think much superior to the regular District Judge of this District."[18] Kinkead hoped that Sanborn would hear the case within a few days.

Following a preliminary hearing, Judge Sanborn enjoined Marsans from playing in the Federal League on June 22, 1914, pending an eventual trial in the case. In a brief, one-page decision, Sanborn reasoned that Marsans had accepted the terms of his contract with Cincinnati—including the ten-day release provision—and had been well compensated in return. As a result, he declared that Marsans's agreement with the Reds was valid and binding. From there, Sanborn asserted that injunctive relief was appropriate because Marsans possessed unique and extraordinary skills and had promised not to perform for anyone else during the term of his contract. His defection would therefore inflict an ongoing, irreparable injury on Cincinnati.[19]

August Herrmann praised the opinion and hoped it would mark the end of player defections to the Federal League: "This decision is the most important of all of our legal victories. Organized baseball has won every case against the Federal League. The independents must now feel convinced that the contracts of organized baseball are above reproach of any kind. I think that this latest decision in the *Marsans* case will bring the players to their senses."[20]

With Marsans indefinitely tied up in court, organized baseball turned its attention to stopping Al Schulz and Hal Chase from continuing to play for the BuffFeds. Specifically, the New York Yankees filed a lawsuit against Schulz with Judge Foell—the same jurist presiding over the *Chief Johnson* case and second *Fred Blanding* suit—while the BuffFeds were in Chicago, requesting that Schulz be enjoined from continuing to play in the Federal League. Schulz was able to evade service in the lawsuit, however, by quickly returning to Buffalo; as a result, no injunction was ever issued in the suit.[21]

Meanwhile, the White Sox readied an injunction in Buffalo to block Chase from making his home debut on June 26, during what was being dubbed "Hal Chase Day." Anticipating that the major leagues would seek to stop Chase from playing, the Federal League arranged for him and his wife to stay at a resort just across the Canadian border, where he could not be served with legal papers. On the morning of his debut, Chase crossed the Niagara River by boat, and then reportedly wore his wife's clothes into the ballpark to avoid being detected by the process servers. The *Buffalo Express* would later opine, "Hal made a very pretty looking girl—heavily veiled."[22]

Upon reaching the stadium, Chase was directed toward an empty tool shed just off the field, where he hid until the start of the game. To make sure he would not be served with the injunction papers prior to his first at-bat, the BuffFeds arranged for the home team to lead off the game by batting first. Once the game had started, Chase—scheduled to bat second—emerged from

A pensive looking Hal Chase photographed in his Buffalo Federals uniform (Library of Congress, Prints & Photographs Division, LC-DIG-ggbain-17006)

the tool shed and strode to the on-deck circle. After sitting in the dark for two hours, however, he was unable to adjust to the bright light and quickly struck out on three pitches, which the Buffalo fans greeted with "a laughing cheer."[23] Chase was then served with notice of the injunction while walking off the field at the end of the inning.

The Federal League immediately filed a motion asking the court to dissolve the temporary injunction. The Federals had hoped to have Chase's case heard by local Buffalo judge Harry Taylor, a former major league player and one-time counsel to the Players Protective Association, an ill-fated union in 1900. The Feds believed Taylor's background would make him sympathetic to their case. However, Taylor—who had also subsequently served as president of the International League—declined to hear the case, believing it would be best to have a more impartial judge decide the matter. As a result, Judge Herbert Bissell would preside over the case.[24]

In his motion to dissolve the injunction, Chase asserted that he had properly repudiated his contract with Chicago by providing the club with ten days' notice. More significantly, Chase also argued that every team within organized baseball had unclean hands because of their alleged violations of federal and state antitrust law, disentitling them to injunctive relief.[25] Although no copies of his motion remain, based on the discussion in Judge Bissell's opinion, it appears that Chase focused his antitrust allegations on the National Agreement. In particular, he apparently asserted that by rigidly enforcing the reserve clause, the National Agreement had enabled organized baseball to control the services of nearly every highly skilled player in the country, thereby giving the major leagues a monopoly over the industry.[26]

After Chase's motion was filed, August Herrmann quickly issued a statement trivializing his antitrust claim: "The Federal League leaders probably have forgotten that we invited investigation along that line, and did so long before the present condition was thought of. We would welcome such an investigation at any time."[27]

Although Herrmann publicly invited antitrust scrutiny, organized baseball's attorneys did their best to argue that antitrust law was wholly inapplicable to professional baseball. Chicago filed a formal Brief in Opposition to Chase's motion to dissolve the injunction, asserting that the industry was not governed by either federal or state antitrust law because those laws only regulated "commerce," and not a mere "sport" like baseball. Specifically, the attorneys argued that the game did not fall within the contemporaneous definition of commerce, which they contended meant only the production or sale of tangible goods and property. The lawyers asserted that baseball teams did not produce anything of lasting value, but instead merely performed "a series of acts that are witnessed by a spectator and pass into oblivion."[28] In so arguing, organized baseball sought to categorize its business along with fields like law, medicine, professional theater, and insurance, all of which prior courts had concluded were not engaged in commerce because they did not produce tangible goods.

Moreover, Chicago's brief asserted that the entire idea that federal law regulated baseball was absurd. Baseball's legal team stated that congressional regulation of any sport was "obviously contrary" to the United States Constitution, and stressed that no court had ever held that baseball was governed by federal law. Instead, the brief contended that baseball had always been regulated under state law, pointing to various local restrictions such as those prohibiting the playing of baseball on Sundays in certain communities. Apparently hoping to intimidate Judge Bissell, the attorneys cautioned that a court would have to be quite self-assured to apply federal law to the sport: "[A]t this late day the judge must be extremely confident of his learning and his authority and his legal foundations, to be the one to pronounce for the first time a decision holding that baseball is interstate commerce, and is governed by Federal rather than state law."[29] Chicago further argued that the National Agreement had benefited the public by providing good quality baseball to fans, which had in turn increased the popularity of the game, to the benefit of the players. In other words, the club asserted, even if organized baseball was a monopoly, it was a benevolent one that should not be challenged under antitrust law.

Finally, the White Sox rejected Chase's contention that he had validly terminated his contract pursuant to the ten-day release provision. The brief argued that the provision clearly allowed only the team, and not the player, to terminate the contract, while also noting that Chicago had in fact offered to remove the provision from Chase's contract, but that he refused. The lawyers further justified the provision by arguing that the clause was necessary to maintain the obedience and loyalty of the players.[30]

Judge Bissell heard oral arguments in the case in Buffalo on July 9 and 10, 1914. Chase was represented by Chicago attorney Keene Addington, whom he had first met while attending college in Santa Clara, California. Addington emphasized the antitrust issue in his argument, citing various clauses from the National Agreement and asserting that they rendered organized baseball's hands unclean, leaving it undeserving of injunctive relief. Addington closed his argument by intimating that additional antitrust proceedings could be forthcoming against organized baseball under Section 4 of the Sherman Act, a provision that empowers federal attorneys to institute antitrust lawsuits.[31]

Chicago's counsel in the case, Ellis Kinkead, later described Addington's argument as "elaborate and forceful," noting that despite speaking "for some five hours on this subject, he had the good attention of the judge, who made frequent and copious notes." For his part, Kinkead stressed the argument that playing baseball did not constitute commerce under the Sherman Act. Although Kinkead remained "confident that Mr. Addington's position is not sound," he feared that because "Judge Bissel [*sic*] has not had any considerable experience in federal questions . . . there is danger of his going astray on the Sherman act." "The situation is an unfortunate one," Kinkead concluded, "but all we can do is to meet it and thrash the question out."[32]

At the close of the hearing, Judge Bissell promised to decide the case within a week, stating that if the "injunction is to be dissolved, it should be done promptly." However, owing to the importance and complexity of the questions involved, the judge allowed the parties to file additional briefing on the antitrust issues.[33]

Meanwhile, as the Federal League and organized baseball were battling in court over Marsans and Chase, the Federals' appeal in the *Killefer* case was moving forward. The ChiFeds filed a brief with the United States Court of Appeals for the Sixth Circuit arguing that the district court had erred by not enjoining Killefer from playing for Philadelphia. In particular, the brief emphasized the unclean hands issue, asserting that the Federals had not acted improperly because the reserve clause in Killefer's 1913 contract allegedly lapsed after the Phillies had waited until late January 1914 to begin negotiating with the player. Moreover, the ChiFeds argued, any harm they may have inflicted on Philadelphia by inducing Killefer to disregard his reserve clause—the basis of the district court's unclean hands finding—was wholly irrelevant because they were seeking an injunction against the player, not the team.[34] In other words, the Federals believed that only their dealings with Killefer himself were relevant to determining whether the ChiFeds' hands were unclean. Philadelphia effectively rebutted this contention in its brief by arguing that because the team had itself become a defendant in the case, any inequitable conduct by the ChiFeds toward either the Phillies or Killefer was relevant when deciding whether to grant injunctive relief. The team also contested the Federals' assertion that the reserve clause had lapsed as a result of its delay in beginning negotiations with Killefer, insisting that the clause bound Killefer until he himself had initiated contract discussions with another team.[35]

The Sixth Circuit heard oral arguments in the case on June 10, 1914, with George Wharton Pepper again appearing on behalf of Philadelphia. Although no transcript of the hearing exists, Pepper reportedly emphasized the unclean hands issue during his argument by appealing to the greater moral issues at stake in the case:

> There is hardly a boy or man in this whole country who does not follow the great national game of base ball with as much eagerness as he awaits his breakfast in the morning. The influence it wields is tremendous. For this reason, if no other, fair play should at all times characterize the methods of conducting the game. If we permit one team to seize upon players of another without regard to moral or legal obligations we are going to undermine the whole structure and the game will lose its hold upon the public and cease its existence as a national sport.[36]

Pepper's argument persuaded the appellate court, which affirmed the lower court's decision on June 30, 1914. In its opinion, the Sixth Circuit concluded that the reserve clause imposed a duty on Killefer to negotiate in good faith with Philadelphia for the 1914 season. By interfering with that process, the court believed that the Federals had acted inequitably, and therefore did not deserve injunctive relief.[37]

Despite the adverse ruling, Federal League president Jim Gilmore insisted that his organization was not discouraged, arguing that the decision did not implicate the validity of either the ten-day release provision or the reserve clause, the two most important issues to his league. Gilmore said he remained confident that higher courts would sustain the Federals' position on these issues.[38]

Gilmore's faith would be rewarded two weeks later, on July 16, when the Appellate Court of Illinois gave the Federal League its first clear legal victory by reversing the lower court's preliminary injunction in the *Chief Johnson* case. In a split, two-to-one decision, the majority reasoned that the ten-day release provision rendered Johnson's contract with Cincinnati so one-sided that it could not be enforced via injunctive relief because of a lack of mutuality. Even though the court believed an injunction was unwarranted, it did note that the contract was not wholly unenforceable, meaning that Cincinnati could continue to pursue its case for monetary damages against the pitcher.[39] Nevertheless, Johnson was allowed to resume his Federal League career.

Publicly, the Federals were jubilant. Edward Gates stated that "[t]he reversal of Judge Foell's opinion by the appellate court of Illinois is a complete vindication of our position," predicting that the precedent would carry great weight in the *Marsans* and *Chase* cases.[40] However, in private the Federals recognized that the decision came too late to revive their plans for a large-scale raid of the major leagues, as the lower court's initial ruling in the *Johnson* case had deterred most of the targeted players from jumping to the new circuit.[41]

Meanwhile, August Herrmann vowed to immediately appeal the decision to a higher court. However, under Illinois judicial procedure, Cincinnati was unable to appeal the decision to the state Supreme Court until a full trial had been held in the case.[42] As a result, the best that the club could do was to ask the appellate court to reconsider its decision, an unlikely and ultimately fruitless exercise. Instead, organized baseball's counsel recommended that the team file additional injunction proceedings against Johnson in other Federal League cities, and accordingly prepared to initiate such a suit in Buffalo pending the court's decision in the *Chase* case.[43]

Organized baseball's plans to enjoin Johnson in New York never materialized, however, after Judge Bissell issued a decision vacating the preliminary injunction against Chase several days later. Bissell began the opinion by stating that the dispute required a close examination of the various provisions contained in the National Agreement. Specifically, he discussed the ten-day release provision and reserve clause, noting that teams possessed complete control over their players and could release, trade, or even send them to the minor leagues whenever the club desired, without any recourse for the players. Because the National Agreement mandated that all player contracts include the reserve clause—and enforced the provision through the threat of banishment—players had no way to escape the clause. "Thus the baseball player is made a chattel,"[44] Bissell observed, forced to either accept the terms of employment offered by his existing team or else enter another profession entirely. Factoring in the one-sided ten-day release provision as well, the judge determined that Chase's contract was legally unenforceable because of a lack of mutuality.

Next, Judge Bissell turned his attention to Chase's antitrust claims. He started off by agreeing with the Chicago club that baseball was sport, not commerce, and thus was not governed by federal law or the Sherman Act. Nevertheless, Judge Bissell decided that organized baseball had violated New York's state common law governing monopolies by illegally controlling the entire industry pursuant to the National Agreement. "'Organized baseball' is now as complete a monopoly of the baseball business for profit as any monopoly can be made," he observed.[45] In particular, Bissell believed that through the reserve clause, the teams comprising organized baseball had conspired to violate their players' intrinsic right to freely market their own labor, a form of "benevolent despotism" he considered "contrary to the spirit of American institutions, and . . . to the spirit of the Constitution of the United States." Consequently, he ruled that by violating New York state antitrust law, organized baseball had come to his court with unclean hands and thus was not entitled to a preliminary injunction.

The Federals immediately praised Judge Bissell's decision. Jim Gilmore stated that he had never doubted his league would prevail in the case, and proclaimed that the decision invalidated all of organized baseball's player contracts.[46] The Federal League's general counsel, Edward Gates, also predicted that the decision would have far-reaching effects, benefiting all players within organized baseball: "This indeed, is a victory and one which means a great deal to the ball players who have for years been tied up to the national agreement and restrained in their free right to contract. This decision is by far the most far reaching that has been decided against organized baseball. It will result in great and much needed reforms in the national game."[47] In particular, Gates applauded Judge Bissell's finding that the National Agreement had created an illegal monopoly under state common law, declaring that the holding "opens up the field for the Federal League."[48]

Not surprisingly, the baseball establishment was less enamored with the decision. The *Sporting News,* which by this point had become an unabashed supporter of organized baseball in its war with the Federals, condemned the decision: "This unlawful monopoly raised a sport that was a medium for gambling and fraud . . . to the stage where millions are proud to declare their allegiance to it as the 'Only Game.' . . . This is the system that is indicted by Judge Bissell from the bench because it sought before him to compel a conscienceless creature named Chase."[49]

Meanwhile, organized baseball's attorneys prepared to appeal the decision. Ellis Kinkead believed that Judge Bissell's reliance on the state common law of monopoly was unjustified, as the issue had not been fully argued in the case. Moreover, Kinkead asserted, "What little there is of Common Law on the subject of monopoly clearly relates to the same kind of monopoly as that covered by the Sherman Act,"[50] which Judge Bissell had concluded did not apply to baseball. Indeed, because both federal and state antitrust law only regulated "commerce," if baseball was merely sport and not commerce as Judge Bissell believed for purposes of the Sherman Act, then the state common law also should not apply.

Organized baseball's lawyers secretly reached out to Judge John Samuel Lambert of the New York appellate court, asking if he would be willing to reinstate the injunction against Chase and stay Judge Bissell's decision pending an appeal. Lambert declined, explaining in a private letter to baseball's counsel that he did not believe the lower court's decision was so clearly erroneous that it warranted an immediate reversal before an appeal had been fully briefed.[51] The Federals apparently never learned of organized baseball's behind-the-scenes maneuvering.

Despite its recent setbacks, organized baseball pressed on, preparing for the eventual trial in the *Armando Marsans* case. In particular, its local St. Louis counsel was concerned that the fact Marsans had signed his initial contract in Cuba could potentially render his 1914 contract void under the Alien Immigration Act, which prohibited the importation of skilled labor unless "labor of like kind . . . can not be found in this country."[52] Cincinnati held off on filing an affidavit from the team executive who signed Marsans specifically so as not to tip off the court or opposing counsel about the issue.

This caution turned out to be for naught, however, as Marsans's attorneys had identified the issue themselves. When Marsans filed his answer in the lawsuit on July 24, 1914, it included an allegation that his contract was null and void under the Alien Immigration Act.[53] In addition to the immigration issue, Marsans also asserted a number of other defenses against the Reds. For example, he argued that Cincinnati was precluded from filing suit against him in Missouri because the club was not registered to do business in the state. The team was already well aware of this fact, having previously decided not to seek an injunction against another defector in Missouri state court for this very reason.[54] Perhaps as a result of the news reports generated by the *Marsans* case, the Missouri secretary of state sent a letter to Cincinnati a few weeks later notifying the club that it had failed to register to do business as required under state law, and threatening to prosecute if the team did not immediately apply for a license.[55]

Next, Marsans asserted that his contract was unenforceable because of a lack of mutuality, insofar as he was bound to the club for life pursuant to the reserve clause, while Cincinnati could terminate the agreement at any time simply by providing ten days' notice. Finally, Marsans hoped to invoke the recent decision in the *Chase* case by asserting that organized baseball had illegally monopolized the industry in violation of state and federal antitrust law. Specifically, he argued that organized baseball had monopolized the sport under the National Agreement and reserve clause by effectively controlling the entire labor market for professional baseball players. Players had no recourse, he alleged, because any player or team that violated the reserve clause would immediately be banned from organized baseball. Meanwhile, Marsans contended that contrary to Judge Bissell's holding in the *Chase* case, organized baseball was engaged in interstate commerce, and thus was subject to federal antitrust law because the major league teams resided in various states and routinely transported their players across state lines.[56]

Cincinnati's attorneys John Galvin and Ellis Kinkead would later characterize Marsans's answer as "elaborate," viewing the antitrust allegations in particular as "a serious menace." The attorneys had become less concerned with Marsans's defense under the Alien Immigration Act, however, believing that Cincinnati could defend itself against this claim by arguing that Marsans's current contract had been executed in the United States, even if his initial contract had not. Moreover, they doubted whether Congress intended for the law to apply to baseball players in the first place.[57] Nevertheless, they recommended that Marsans's case be delayed as long as possible, given that the player was already enjoined from playing until it proceeded to trial.[58]

At the same time Marsans's case was progressing, organized baseball formulated a new legal strategy to counter Chief Johnson's defection to the Federal League. Shortly after the Illinois appellate court overruled the trial court's injunction in Johnson's case, baseball's lawyers had planned to file for a new injunction in New York, only to have those plans derailed by Judge Bissell's decision in the *Chase* case. Instead, Cincinnati elected to file a new injunction suit against Johnson in Pittsburgh on July 27, 1914, in hopes of preventing the pitcher from appearing in the Kansas City Federals' upcoming series in the city.

Judge Joseph M. Swearington of the Court of Common Pleas of Allegheny County temporarily enjoined Johnson on July 30.[59] The judge issued the injunction on the basis of the Pennsylvania Supreme Court's decision in *Lajoie,* which he felt was binding precedent in the case. However, under Pennsylvania judicial procedure, a temporary injunction could only last five days before the court had to hold an evidentiary hearing to decide whether to make the injunction permanent. Judge Swearington proposed holding the hearing on August 3, a date on which Cincinnati's attorney John Galvin knew his key witnesses were unavailable. As a result, Galvin feared that the court would be forced to let the injunction lapse after five days. However, just when Galvin was about to speak up, he overheard the Federal Leagues' attorneys privately discussing their own unavailability on August 3. Galvin remained silent while Edward Gates unwittingly asked the court if the hearing could be postponed. Judge Swearington agreed, so long as the Federals would consent to have Johnson abide by the injunction during the interim. Gates agreed, and the hearing was postponed until September 1.[60]

Following the hearing, Galvin wrote to August Herrmann predicting that the Federal League would honor the injunction outside Pennsylvania, reasoning that by permitting Johnson to appear in a game anywhere in the country, both the player and league would be in contempt of court, thus hindering their ability to get the injunction dissolved.[61] Contrary to Galvin's intuition, though, the Federals did not hesitate to violate the injunction after Johnson's team left Pittsburgh, allowing him to pitch in Baltimore, Brooklyn, and Kansas City despite the court's order.[62]

As the September 1 court date approached, attorneys for the Federal League reached out to organized baseball's counsel asking if they would agree to delay the hearing. Galvin refused, arguing that any delay would further compromise the interests of his client, who he asserted was being harmed each time Johnson violated the Pennsylvania court's injunction. As a result, the Federals went to the Illinois trial court, where the initial case against Johnson was still pending, and asked the court to enjoin Cincinnati from further pursuing its case in Pittsburgh. The day before the scheduled hearing in Pittsburgh, the Illinois court issued an order restraining Cincinnati from continuing to prosecute the Pennsylvania suit.[63]

Nevertheless, Galvin traveled to Pittsburgh on September 1 to inform Judge Swearington of the recent events and notify him that Cincinnati would be unable to proceed with the hearing. Galvin also read from a story in that morning's *Pittsburgh Post,* quoting a Pittsburgh Federals official boasting that the Illinois court order had effectively ended Cincinnati's Pennsylvania suit, and announcing that Chief Johnson would thus pitch in Pittsburgh the next week.[64] The news did not sit well with Judge Swearington, who vowed that "such further steps would be taken against the Kansas City Club and

Johnson as might be considered necessary to uphold the dignity of the local courts."[65] Shortly thereafter, the judge issued an opinion permanently enjoining Johnson from playing in the Federal League, contending that notwithstanding the Illinois court's order, the case was properly before him and that he was obliged to maintain his court's authority.[66]

As the summer of 1914 wore on, the baseball press began to grow tired of the litigation between organized baseball and the Federal League. The *Sporting News* declared in July that "[t]here is no real reason for either side in all this lawing [*sic*] to enthuse over any decisions as yet given. It is a mere matter of courts disagreeing."[67] Indeed, the final tally for the 1914 court cases revealed that organized baseball and the Federals had battled to a draw, with the major leagues coming out on top in the *Killefer* and *Marsans* decisions, while the Federal League had ultimately won the *Chase* and *Chief Johnson* cases (at least the more highly publicized Illinois phase of the latter). Nevertheless, the *Sporting News* could not pass up the opportunity to take a shot at the Federal League, opining, "Least of all should the Federals rejoice, for ultimate victory for their contention would mean only defeat for a system of contracts that even they admit must be maintained if there is to be any regulation of the game."[68]

Baseball Magazine concurred, stating in August that the public had grown tired of the baseball war, and that the players' disloyalty left fans to wonder whether they would be equally willing to throw games.[69] Even the *Washington Post* issued an editorial declaring that most baseball fans were tired of the lawsuits and did not care about issues of contractual validity. The editorial praised the Federals for putting up a good fight, though, and suggested that organized baseball consider making peace.[70]

Initially it appeared that the baseball media might get its wish. Beginning in July, the National Commission began receiving informal suggestions that the Federals were ready to settle. For example, August Herrmann reported that he had heard Charles Weeghman, one of the major financial benefactors of the league, was willing to capitulate on the condition that he receive a minor league franchise in Chicago in the American Association.[71] Ban Johnson said that he had similarly heard that Brooklyn Federals owner Robert Ward—another significant financial backer of the league—was trying to begin negotiations to purchase the Boston Red Sox.[72] Then in late September, the *Chicago Tribune* reported that the general opinion within the Federal League was that it should seek a truce ending the war.[73]

That the Federals' strongest financial supporters were growing weary of continuing the fight against organized baseball should have come as no surprise. Several news sources reported that the league's franchises in Pittsburgh,

St. Louis, and Indianapolis each lost between $60,000 and $100,000 in 1914. Meanwhile, the admittedly hostile *Sporting News* estimated that the Federal League as a whole had run a deficit of over $670,000 for the season.[74]

The war had taken a financial toll on organized baseball as well, however. In addition to paying players much higher salaries, major league teams also had to shoulder significant legal fees likely running into the tens of thousands of dollars. Tellingly, the National Commission's war chest had dwindled from $27,709 at the start of 1914 to $1,486 one year later.[75] As a result, Ban Johnson wrote August Herrmann in late-October 1914, stating that he did not "favor the plan to push the cases now pending in the courts," in no small part because "[t]he funds are not available for any additional expense." Instead, Johnson recommended that "it would be well to get our bearings before we proceed any further."[76]

Not only was there reason to believe that both sides would be amenable to negotiating a truce, but organized baseball's attorneys were also encouraging a peace settlement. John Galvin and Ellis Kinkead wrote a letter to August Herrmann on October 7, updating him on the status of the year's litigations. In the letter, the lawyers cautioned that the pending cases could result in the National Agreement and related player contracts being declared legally unenforceable: "[T]here are elements in the litigation now pending between the Commission's clubs and the clubs of the Federal League which may result in a finding by some court, perhaps a Federal court of weight, that the National Agreement is an inequitable instrument and that any rights exercised under it or contracts made pursuant to it will be denied the aid of a court of equity in whatever form they may be presented in litigation. . . ."[77]

Meanwhile, the attorneys also feared that the Federal League's antitrust allegations could spur a potential government investigation: "[W]e see also the possibility in the event of such a decision of some United States District attorney or of some State's attorney undertaking a prosecution against the National Commission as in contravention of the Sherman act, which prosecution we do not believe would finally succeed but would doubtless be of great prejudice to the welfare of baseball and entail enormous financial loss." As a result, the lawyers urged Herrmann to resolve the Federal League war in order to "remove from litigation the questions which we feel [are the] most serious."[78]

Perhaps motivated by his attorneys' counsel, August Herrmann agreed to meet with Charles Weeghman on several occasions in October and November 1914 to discuss a potential settlement. During these meetings, Weeghman informed Herrmann that—contrary to earlier reports—he wanted to obtain a major league club in any peace agreement, as did the owners of the Brooklyn, Pittsburgh, and St. Louis Federal League squads. Weeghman also demanded assurance that the BaltFeds and BuffFeds would be financially compensated by organized baseball. Though the purchase of four big league clubs by Federal League owners was a nonstarter, Herrmann and Weeghman did meet at one point with Charles Taft—the owner of the Chicago Cubs, and half-brother of former President William Howard Taft—to discuss Weeghman's possible purchase of the team.[79] Herrmann eventually put together the framework of a more modest deal in which Weeghman and the Brooklyn Federals would be allowed to buy major league teams, while the other Federal League squads would be merged with existing clubs in the International League or American Association. Herrmann presented the tentative proposal to his fellow National League owners, but acknowledged that Ban Johnson and some of the American League magnates were not "keen for peace. They are firmly of the opinion that the Federal League has been licked and they cannot go on next year."[80]

Indeed, during the course of the settlement negotiations, organized baseball reportedly received confidential information regarding the Federals' financial condition, leading many within the major leagues to believe their rival would not be able to survive the 1915 season. As Ban Johnson declared to the press, "[t]here is not a chance [the Federal League] will start another season if left alone."[81] Organized baseball was also emboldened by the knowledge that by early September, more than 60 percent of its players had already signed new, more legally binding contracts for 1915—in which the ten-day release provision was omitted—severely limiting the Federals' pool of potential targets for defection that off-season.[82]

Any remaining hope for peace collapsed when several of the smaller market Federal League teams rejected Herrmann's proposal and demanded that their circuit be recognized as a third major league. Stockholders in the league's Baltimore, Buffalo, Indianapolis, and Kansas City franchises strongly desired "big league" status for their cities, but this was a concession that the existing major leagues were simply unwilling to make. Consequently, Jim Gilmore declared in mid-November that "[t]here will be a third major league next year and peace can not come except by Organized Ball accepting that as a premise on which to reach the conclusion and bring about a settlement of the war."[83]

Even though the peace talks had collapsed, on December 7, 1914, Boston's National League franchise nevertheless decided to withdraw the suit it had filed in Baltimore against the Federal League in April seeking damages for the defection of pitcher Jack Quinn. The team admitted in court that it would be difficult to establish any financial injury from the loss of the player considering the club's successful 1914 campaign.[84] Indeed, the team had just completed one of the most miraculous comebacks in baseball history, sweeping Philadelphia in the World Series after finding themselves in last place as late as July 18.[85]

Meanwhile, with the prospects for peace having faded, the Federals decided to go on the offensive. In early December, Weeghman's ChiFeds made their biggest splash yet, signing future Hall of Famer, and arguably the greatest pitcher of the era, Walter Johnson to a three-year contract worth $17,500 per season. The American League quickly responded by announcing it would file for an injunction against the pitcher, while Johnson's former team, Washington, threatened to sue Weeghman personally for tampering with its player.[86] To lay the foundation for its case, the team sent Weeghman a telegram stating: "Washington Club notifies you that it paid Walter Johnson the sum of twenty-five hundred dollars for an option for his services for season of nineteen fifteen, and that Johnson [h]as heretofore been notified Washington Club will exercise this option."[87] Organized baseball believed that Johnson's prior contract would stand up in court because it did not include the ten-day release provision. Conversely, the Federals believed that Johnson had fulfilled his obligations to Washington under the reserve clause after the club withdrew its most recent contractual offer, freeing the pitcher to sign with the ChiFeds.[88]

At the same time Washington was threatening legal action, organized baseball worked behind the scenes to convince Johnson to return. Nearly two weeks after he had signed with the Federals, Johnson was persuaded that his prior option contract with Washington was legally binding. As a result, he announced he was repudiating his Federal League agreement and returning to Washington on December 20, 1914. The news shocked Weeghman and Gilmore, who implored the pitcher to meet in Chicago with three neutral attorneys to get a second opinion.[89] Johnson declined, later explaining his decision to *Baseball Magazine*: "I did not treat the Federal League right. I broke my contract with them. But . . . only because I was convinced that by not doing so I would be doing a greater injury to Washington. Perhaps I was wrong, but I at least acted for what I considered best. . . . I bungled it, no doubt, but it is done."[90]

The Federals vowed to pursue legal action against organized baseball to enforce Johnson's contract with the ChiFeds.[91] Ultimately, however, they would opt for a more momentous course of action.

4
The Landis Case
January 1915

"We're going to break up organized baseball," Federal League president Jim Gilmore excitedly exclaimed to a reporter from *Baseball Magazine* on the morning of January 5, 1915. "I have just come from my lawyers. We filed this bill with Judge [Kenesaw Mountain] Landis," he explained. Gilmore then described his bold aims for the lawsuit: "We'll sue them for conspiracy and for restraint of trade. We'll break up the baseball trust and the National Commission. We'll free every ball player in the United States. We'll have the courts declare them free agents and we'll put a stop once and for all to this calling us outlaws and making libelous remarks about our financial standing and all that kind of business. . . . And we'll win, too. Our cause is just, our arguments are sound."[1]

The Federal League's ninety-two-page complaint was as ambitious as Gilmore described. Formally captioned *Federal League of Professional Base Ball Clubs v. National League of Professional Base Ball Clubs,* the suit was filed in federal district court in Chicago, naming both the American and National Leagues as defendants, along with the sixteen major league franchises, and each of the three members of the National Commission: August Herrmann, Ban Johnson, and John Tener.[2] The complaint asserted three primary legal claims against the major leagues: (i) that they had formed an illegal monopoly in violation of federal antitrust law, (ii) that their illegal monopoly also violated state antitrust law, and (iii) that they had conspired to injure or destroy the Federal League.

Specifically, the complaint began by describing the Federal League, noting that it had been formed in Indiana in 1913, and that the league and its "constituent members" (that is, teams) were all engaged "in the business of baseball" with more than $3 million invested to date. The document further explained that the league had always operated outside the National Agreement, and had never attempted to join organized baseball. Next, it discussed the history of the formation of both the American and National Leagues, in the process identifying the official state of residence of each of the defendants.[3] This latter, seemingly innocuous information would become a particularly important aspect of the Federals' case, providing them with an additional basis on which to maintain the suit in federal court. Although federal courts typically preside over cases involving federal law, pursuant to the doctrine of "diversity jurisdiction" they will also entertain lawsuits brought under state law if (i) the plaintiff(s) and defendant(s) reside in different states, and (ii) a sufficient amount of money is at stake in the suit ($3,000 in 1915). The Federals would rely on diversity jurisdiction to keep their suit in federal court if the judge held that their federal antitrust claims were inapplicable. Later in the complaint, in fact, the Federal League explained that its eight teams did not formally appear as parties in the case on account of potential "technical questions of jurisdiction. . . ."[4] The league offered to include the teams in the suit, however, if the defendants agreed to waive these jurisdictional objections. The parties would ultimately debate this issue in court.

From there, the complaint launched into a lengthy discussion of the business of baseball. It characterized each of the major leagues as a circuit consisting of eight teams in different cities, with the teams having to travel across state lines to play games in front of paying audiences. The Federals also explained that each major league employed a number of umpires, who themselves traveled from state to state to preside over the league's games.[5] These activities provided the basis for the Federals' claim that organized baseball was engaged in interstate commerce and thus was subject to federal antitrust law.

The Federal League argued that organized baseball had monopolized the supply of professional baseball players, preventing new leagues—such as its own—from vigorously competing with the established circuits. The complaint stated that all but three hundred of the nearly ten thousand professional players in the country were effectively "under the domination and control of the National Agreement . . . and the National Commission," with mechanisms such as the reserve clause and blacklisting used to bind players to organized baseball from the time they signed their first professional contracts until the end of their careers.[6] Moreover, the league asserted, these contracts were not truly voluntary agreements because the National Commission had mandated the specific terms of every professional player's contract since 1903.

The Federals then took aim at the National Agreement. The complaint argued that the stated purposes of the agreement—including the promotion of the national pastime and betterment of ballplayers—were "mere pretenses, shams, subterfuges and disguises."[7] Instead, the Federals asserted that the agreement was designed to perpetuate the American and National Leagues' control over professional baseball and their domination of professional players and their salaries. The two major leagues were accused of centralizing their control over the sport via the National Commission, a body the Federal League characterized as not only baseball's "highest legislative body, as to whose law there is no veto," but also its "supreme judicial tribunal from whose decrees there is no appeal."[8] The complaint argued that this arrangement injured not only the players but also the public, rendering it unlawful both under the "anti-trust and anti-monopoly statutes of the United States of America" and state common law.

The Federals next accused the major leagues of "conspir[ing] and confederat[ing] together to injure or destroy" their organization.[9] In particular, the complaint identified a number of practices allegedly intended to deter players from signing with the rival circuit as well as to drive down its attendance. For example, the document contended that officials of the two major leagues had frequently told players and the press that the Federal League was financially irresponsible and would not be able to honor its contracts. Similarly, the complaint charged that the established leagues had threatened to blacklist any player who signed with a Federal team, and derisively referred to such players as "contract jumpers" while characterizing the Federals as an "outlaw" league.[10]

More significantly, the Federals argued that organized baseball had conspired to tie up in court any player defecting to the league, recounting the past year's litigation involving Chief Johnson, Hal Chase, and Armando Marsans. The complaint alleged that the major leagues intended to file similar suits against thirteen additional players who had recently signed with the rival circuit, citing a suit filed just two days earlier in federal district court in Cincinnati against new Brooklyn Federals manager Lee Magee. Finally, the Federals noted that in addition to seeking to enjoin their players, the American and National Leagues had also relentlessly worked to recruit any defecting players back to their side. In particular, they emphasized the recent case of Walter Johnson, contending that the player signed a binding contract with the ChiFeds only to be persuaded to repudiate the agreement and rejoin the Washington Senators.[11]

The Federals closed their complaint with eleven "prayers for relief." The first three requests delineated the primary accusations against the major leagues, asking the court (i) to declare both the National Agreement and National Commission illegal and void, (ii) to affirm that organized baseball was an illegal monopoly in violation of federal and state antitrust law as well as "in derogation of the constitutional right of contract," and (iii) to rule that the defendants had conspired to destroy the Federal League.[12] The Federals then urged the court to issue an injunction preventing the major leagues from continuing to operate under the National Agreement, or from making any further disparaging remarks about the rival league's financial condition or its players. The complaint also asked the court to declare that all existing player contracts entered pursuant to the National Agreement were null and void, thereby freeing any professional player to sign a contract with the Federal League. In addition, it requested that organized baseball be ordered to dismiss all pending court actions against Chief Johnson, Chase, Marsans, and Magee, as well as forgo filing any additional lawsuits against other Federal League players. Along with a preliminary injunction, the Federals also sought an award of damages as well as any other relief the court deemed appropriate.[13]

As Gilmore had indicated in his interview with *Baseball Magazine,* the Federals filed their suit with federal district court Judge Kenesaw Mountain Landis of the Northern District of Illinois. Appointed to the bench by President Theodore Roosevelt in 1905, Landis first rose to national prominence in 1907 when he issued a then-record $29,240,000 judgment against the Standard Oil Company for various anticompetitive practices (a fine that was later overturned on appeal). Many have speculated that Landis's subsequent reputation as a "trust-buster" motivated the Federal League to file its suit in his court. Also known for his theatrical flair in the courtroom, the judge was described by one newspaper reporter as "an irascible, short-tempered, tyrannical despot" who was "more arbitrary than . . . any jurist I have ever seen before or since."[14]

Named in honor of the 1864 Civil War battle in which his father suffered a severe leg injury—at the time both "Kennesaw" and the judge's "Kenesaw" were accepted spellings—the forty-eight-year old Landis was a devoted baseball fan. Although some subsequent commentators have surmised that his love for the game must have taken the Federals by surprise,[15] this likely was not the case. With its Chicago-based leadership, the Federal League almost certainly would have been aware that a high-profile individual like Landis was a baseball fan. In fact, the judge was known to frequently attend games throughout his years on the bench, and had developed a reputation for being a particularly rowdy Chicago Cubs booster during the team's championship years from 1906 to 1910.[16]

Judge Kenesaw Mountain Landis presided over the Federal League's antitrust lawsuit against the major leagues, and would later become major league baseball's first commissioner (Library of Congress, Prints & Photographs Division, LC-DIG-ggbain-07125)

Indeed, in the days following the initiation of the Federals' lawsuit, the press reported that Judge Landis was a well-known baseball enthusiast who was expected to use his personal knowledge of the game to help decide the case, with the *Sporting News* noting in particular that the judge would enter the case with "clean hands" after refusing to accept free passes from the Chicago Cubs, White Sox, or ChiFeds in 1914.[17] Rather than taking the Federals by surprise, the league most likely either believed that Landis's baseball fandom would be a nonfactor in the case, or perhaps even viewed it as beneficial, insofar as he would approach the suit with a more nuanced understanding of the system they were challenging. It was likely no coincidence then that the Federals ultimately filed affidavits in the case from both Joe Tinker and Mordecai Brown, two of Landis's favorite former Cubs.

Nevertheless, the Federals were almost certainly unaware of the personal interest that Landis appeared to have taken regarding one aspect of their complaint. On the day the suit was filed, National Commission chairman August Herrmann wrote a letter to Washington manager Clark Griffith inquiring whether there was any truth to a rumor that Landis had confidentially written to Walter Johnson in December encouraging him to return to organized baseball.[18] Griffith promised to look into the matter, but cautioned that the existence of any such letter should remain private, as he believed "our interests are safe in Judge Landis's hands."[19] Several days later, Herrmann received a letter from Benjamin Minor, president of the Washington franchise, cryptically suggesting Herrmann ask National Commission secretary John E. Bruce about the Landis letter.[20] Unfortunately, there is no evidence confirming whether Landis had in fact contacted Johnson.

After the league filed its lawsuit, Jim Gilmore released a public statement explaining the action: "By bringing this suit at this time we hope to determine all legal controversies between organized baseball and the Federal league before the start of the playing season. The Federal league claims the right to litigate and is willing to submit to the court all of its rights and differences for determination in order to relieve the national pastime from any detracting influences, such as court proceedings during the playing season, and I hope that organized baseball will not resort to any means to prevent that result."[21]

Meanwhile, Federal League general counsel Edward Gates sought to assure the public that the league did not wish to destroy the national pastime, telling the press "[w]e do not want to injure the game of baseball and we do not seek to benefit ourselves from the decision of the court, should it be in our favor." He also hinted that the Federal League's aims in the lawsuit were not as broad as its complaint suggested: "We have not brought the suit with the anticipation of getting all the players of organized ball set free by court action. In order to grab them for our own use. We simply wish to protect what we have."[22]

In public, organized baseball's leadership responded confidently to the news that they had been formally charged with violating antitrust law. American League president Ban Johnson reportedly laughed when asked whether he was worried about the suit, stating, "The Federal league is simply trying to get a little more publicity."[23] "Of course we will fight the suit," he continued, "[w]e have no fear of the result, and I am sure it will put us right before the public."[24] Johnson then took another shot at his rivals: "I am afraid of only one thing, and that is that the Federal league will blow up before the suit can be heard."[25] Johnson also professed to take comfort in the fact that the case would be tried before Landis: "It is gratifying to know that this suit will be heard by Judge Landis. . . . Judge Landis is one of the best informed legal authorities as to baseball affairs in this country. He is eminently fair and there is not a doubt in my mind that the Federal's [*sic*] suit will be capably dissected by him. We will come out with flying colors."[26]

Similarly, August Herrmann stated that the major leagues had "nothing whatever to fear" from the lawsuit, noting that baseball had been inviting antitrust scrutiny from either the courts or Congress for years. "Our acts . . . [are] an open book and a matter of record," he confidently declared, adding that organized baseball's defense in the case would be "astounding and surprising." "Charging that the rules of organized baseball and the national agreement are a violation of the common law and the anti-trust statutes of the country, as made by the Federal league, is a mild one as against the charge which we will present of fraud, conspiracy, and bad faith."[27]

National League president—and still sitting governor of Pennsylvania—John Tener responded even more forcefully to the charges levied against him and his colleagues: "Did I think for a moment that the conduct of organized baseball under the national agreement was a violation of the law and in restraint of trade and a harmful influence in any respect, I would voluntarily advocate its annulment and withdraw from the National Commission."[28] Tener then emphasized the beneficial aspects of the organization: "But to the contrary, I am convinced that the players advance more speedily in their profession, their earnings, are greater, and better secured and the national game better promoted and protected by reason of compliance by all of the clubs with the terms of the national agreement than with it not in effect."[29]

In private, however, organized baseball recognized that the Federals' suit posed a significant threat. The day after the complaint was filed, August Herrmann sent a confidential bulletin to all major league owners, stating: "The charges made by the Federal League in Chicago, in my judgment, are of such a character that their falsity must be absolutely proved to the baseball public. The issue as now presented had to be met sooner or later, and I believe it is better to meet it now than to have further delay in the matter."[30] Herrmann also urged the clubs to submit any information they had regarding the Federal League's attempts to induce their players to defect. The National Commission had begun collecting this information in December for use in a possible conspiracy lawsuit of its own against the Federal League.[31] Now the commission's lawyers were stressing its importance in organized baseball's defense.[32]

Writing to John Tener, Herrmann emphasized the importance of quick action, arguing that organized baseball must be ready to defend itself in court on the merits of the charges as soon as possible, and suggesting that the defendants defer any potential jurisdictional or other technical legal defenses. Herrmann also speculated that the Federals filed the suit simply to stop the major leagues "from interfering with players that the Federal League Clubs have stolen," analogizing the rival circuit to a purse thief who "turns around and begins to yell at the top of his voice 'Stop, thief,' for the purpose of diverting attention from himself and directing it towards innocent persons."[33]

The press shared Herrmann's belief that the lawsuit presented a serious challenge to the baseball establishment. The *New York Times* reported that "[t]he action is regarded by baseball men as a most threatening attack on organized baseball," one that could potentially result in "a most intricate organization, built upon the experiences of years, [being] shattered. The action brings the baseball war to its most acute stage."[34] Similarly, the *Chicago Tribune* predicted that a victory by the Federals "would hurl the baseball world into a state of chaos, for it . . . would mean that every contract made under its provisions would immediately become illegal."[35]

Meanwhile, the consistently partisan *Sporting News* did not attempt to hide its feelings, announcing in its page-one headline, "Feds Pull Greatest Bone in All Their Erratic Career," while publishing an editorial in the same issue declaring—in all caps no less—that the paper was "DEVOTED TO ORGANIZED BASE BALL."[36] In particular, it charged that the Federals were hypocritical to accuse the major leagues of being an illegal trust after the rival league had tried to join organized baseball during the November peace negotiations. The paper viewed the suit as an admission of weakness on the part of the Federals, predicting that "[t]rue lovers of base ball the world over will not back the Federal leaguers in this wild and wooly method."[37]

Judge Landis quickly scheduled a hearing in the case for January 20—just fifteen days after the complaint was filed—to decide whether to grant the Federal League the preliminary injunction it had requested. He also issued an order requiring the defendants to file any affidavits they wished to submit in their defense by January 16.[38] As a result, both sides quickly went to work preparing their respective cases. Organized baseball scheduled a meeting in Chicago for its executives and attorneys to plan the defense, with Herrmann sending a telegram to every major league owner requesting his presence at the hearing to ensure that organized baseball presented a strong, unified front. Meanwhile the Federals conferred in Indianapolis to prepare their own supporting affidavits.[39]

As part of the preparatory efforts, the National Commission announced that it would be financing the defense of the antitrust suit on behalf of all twenty-one named defendants. August Herrmann urged the commission not to let "the question of fees . . . stand in the way at this time. It is too important. We must win this fight."[40] Ultimately, the commission agreed that the National League would hire George Wharton Pepper, the prominent

Philadelphia attorney who had successfully defended organized baseball in the *Killefer* case, while the American League would be represented by local Chicago attorney George W. Miller. In addition, the commission retained three of the attorneys who had represented organized baseball in several of the 1914 litigations, namely Cincinnati-based lawyers John Galvin and Ellis Kinkead, and St. Louis attorney George Williams, who had helped represent the Reds in the *Marsans* case.

Soon after organized baseball selected its counsel, Kinkead sent letters to both Pepper and Miller providing his initial impressions of the complaint. In the letters, he noted that the Federal League's failure to include its individual teams as plaintiffs raised a potential standing issue because the entities that truly stood to benefit from the case were not parties to the litigation.[41] He also suggested that the recently enacted Clayton Act could provide a potential defense for organized baseball, insofar as Section 6 provided that "[t]he labor of a human being is not a commodity or article of commerce."[42] Although originally intended to prevent management from suing labor unions under the Sherman Act, Kinkead believed that organized baseball could use this language to argue that federal antitrust law did not apply to the case, as the Federals were asserting the major leagues had monopolized the labor market for baseball players. Finally, he noted that the National Commission wanted to have the case tried on its merits rather than rely on any potential technicalities, such as the argument that many of the defendant teams were not subject to the court's jurisdiction as out-of-state corporations.[43]

While organized baseball was busy preparing its defense, the Federal League submitted twenty affidavits setting forth the testimony it would rely upon during the upcoming hearing before Judge Landis. The most newsworthy of these statements was undoubtedly that submitted by Landis favorite Mordecai "Three-Finger" Brown, who made headlines by asserting that professional baseball players had been traded for dogs on at least two different occasions. Specifically, Brown alleged that Joe Cantillon of Minneapolis' minor league franchise had once traded a player for a bulldog, while Roger Bresnahan, the manager of the St. Louis Cardinals, had bartered a minor league player for a bird dog.[44] Both men fiercely denied the allegation, with Bresnahan submitting his own affidavits explaining that the dog had merely been a gift and was in no way related to the player transaction in question.[45]

Brown also discussed his demotion from the Chicago Cubs to a minor league team in Louisville in 1912, after sustaining a serious knee injury earlier in the season. He alleged that as a result of the demotion, his salary was automatically cut from $5,500 per year to $300 per month. He also contended that Louisville officials had told him that he would not be allowed to return to the major leagues without Chicago Cubs president Charles Murphy's consent.[46] While most of the media sensationalized Brown's allegations, the *Sporting News* trivialized the affidavit, stating, "Perhaps nothing better was to be expected from simple-minded Mordecai Brown."[47]

Although not as colorful, the Federal League's most substantive affidavit was filed by William Watkins, a former player and manager within organized baseball. Watkins formally accused the major leagues of blacklisting players who disregarded the reserve clause, and described various other ways in which organized baseball abused its players. He alleged, for instance, that despite the National Agreement's formal prohibition of "farming"—a procedure in which a major league team would retain the rights to a player demoted to the minor leagues—big league squads nevertheless frequently sold their players to minor league clubs via secret agreements whereby they were guaranteed the right to repurchase the player's contract at a later date.[48] This practice prevented otherwise meritorious players from reaching the major leagues.

Similarly, Watkins explained that minor league teams routinely protected their players during the annual fall draft—in which major league teams selected minor league players—by temporarily selling a player to a friendly major league team shortly before the draft, with an assurance that the player would later be returned. This practice was colloquially known as "covering up." Finally, Watkins accused major league franchises of violating the waiver process, a mechanism in which teams were required to make their players available to all other big league squads before assigning the player to a minor league club. Watkins asserted that the major league teams regularly agreed not to claim each other's players via waivers to ensure that the player's original club would continue to control his rights at the minor league level, thus depriving the player of a chance to continue to compete at the highest level.[49]

The *Sporting News* took particular offense to Watkins's affidavit, arguing that he had overstated the frequency with which these abusive practices were used: "There are many things in the Federal affidavits that are ridiculous, trivial and irrelevant, but this sworn statement of Watkins is vicious and unjust, and in lending himself to it, Mr. Watkins indicates how a man can become contaminated by bad company."[50]

In addition to the Brown and Watkins affidavits, the Federals also submitted sworn statements from several of their league's other notable players, including Ennis "Rebel" Oakes, Otto Knabe, and Landis favorite Joe Tinker. These players discussed how they had been traded or sold from club to club throughout organized baseball without ever being consulted, and argued that although they had objected to the inclusion of the ten-day release provision in their contracts, they—and most of their colleagues—knew that any such objections were futile.[51] Several of the players also discussed how organized baseball had pressured them to return to their major league teams even after they had formally signed with the Federal League.

The defendants responded to the Federals' allegations with their own set of thirty-seven affidavits. The most significant of these was the thirty-one-page statement provided by August Herrmann rebutting many of the Federals' claims. Herrmann denied that the National Agreement and National Commission had ruthlessly monopolized the game of baseball, and attempted to justify several of the practices specifically attacked in the Federals' complaint. He argued, for example, that the reserve clause was necessary to maintain competitive balance between major league teams; without it, he contended, the most talented players would flock each year to the richest clubs located in the nation's most populous cities. Herrmann further stated that players generally approved of the provision, noting that the Federal League's own contracts also contained both a reserve clause and a ten-day release provision. Moreover, he disputed the assertion that organized baseball blacklisted players, although he acknowledged that some teams might be hesitant to re-sign a player who had previously repudiated his contract over concerns about his trustworthiness.[52]

Herrmann then denied that organized baseball had formed a conspiracy to injure the Federal League. He instead insisted that teams had simply made individual decisions to enforce their player contracts in court, and had not interfered with any lawful contract entered between a player and the Federal League. If anyone had formed a conspiracy, Herrmann contended, it was the Federals, whose teams were working together to harm organized baseball by inducing its players to breach their contracts.[53]

Finally, Herrmann appealed to Judge Landis's affinity for baseball by noting the sport's standing as a national institution, cautioning that any injunction issued in the case would damage the game by preventing the two major leagues from competing with one another in the World Series. He warned that such an outcome would most acutely hurt the more than 7,500 players relying on organized baseball for their livelihood.[54]

In addition to his primary affidavit, Herrmann filed several others rebutting specific charges leveled by the Federal League. For example, in one declaration he contested the Federals' claim that they had never sought to join organized baseball. Herrmann recounted the series of events that transpired during the previous fall's peace negotiations, contending that the rival league made several proposals under which it would agree to terminate its challenge if its owners were allowed to purchase teams within organized baseball.[55]

Along with the affidavits submitted by Herrmann, organized baseball also filed sworn statements by representatives of all sixteen major league teams. These declarations generally affirmed that no conspiracy had been formed to injure the Federal League, and recounted a number of occasions on which the Federals had interfered with each team's players, efforts that were alleged to have negatively affected the players' focus and discipline.[56] Some of the teams also contested the Federals' assertion that various players had objected to the ten-day release provision in their contracts, stating that they had never had a player complain about the provision. These officials further argued that the ten-day clause was essential, insuring that players would face the imminent loss of their job if they failed to give their maximum effort on the playing field.[57]

The submission of organized baseball's affidavits motivated the Federals to file six more of their own, rebutting the charges that the major leagues had levied against their organization. By far the lengthiest of these affidavits was submitted by Jim Gilmore, who spent forty-four pages contesting organized baseball's allegations. He denied that the Federals had conspired against the major leagues, arguing that his league had only signed players whose prior contractual obligations were invalid. In particular, he said that on the advice of legal counsel, his league targeted only those players whose prior contracts included a ten-day release provision, or those whose clubs had not exercised their reserve option before the end of the previous season. Gilmore further noted several instances in which his league had offered to terminate its contract with a player if his former team could produce evidence of a legally valid agreement.[58]

Although Gilmore acknowledged that the Federal League's own contracts included a reserve clause and—at times—a ten-day release provision, he explained that it only used the latter clause for unproven players, omitting it when signing a proven major leaguer. Along these same lines, Gilmore argued that the league in 1914 had refused to allow its Kansas City franchise to release a player pursuant to the ten-day provision. He also challenged organized baseball's claims that it never threatened to blacklist players, citing published statements attributed to Ban Johnson in early 1914. Finally, Gilmore contested August Herrmann's allegations that the Federals had sought to join organized baseball. First, relying on a technicality, he argued that neither the Federal League itself, nor any of its member teams, had ever formally applied for admission into organized baseball. More significantly, however, Gilmore recounted the various peace negotiations from the past fall, noting that an official from organized baseball instigated every meeting. He also stated that his league had always demanded that significant modifications be made to the National Agreement as part of any settlement.[59]

As the hearing approached, both sides anticipated a speedy resolution to the case, predicting that Judge Landis would render a decision well in advance of the start of the upcoming baseball season. "[T]here is nothing which might drag matters over an extended period," Jim Gilmore explained. "We are ready now, and there is no reason why the other side should want any delay. The sooner this fight is over the better it will be for the game."[60]

The public also anxiously awaited the start of the trial. According to the *Chicago Tribune*: "From the interest displayed about town in the row, one would judge it would be a good proposition to hold the trial at [Chicago's historic] Auditorium [Theater] or at one of the ball parks and charge admission. Enough might be taken in at the gates to pay the expenses of the show."[61] The *Tribune* later predicted that some twenty-five thousand fans would try to attend the hearing, a proceeding that was expected to "undoubtedly [be] the greatest contest in the history of the national sport and the outcome [of which] will be awaited by eager fans from coast to coast." Meanwhile, the *Christian Science Monitor* noted that the suit differed significantly from some of Judge Landis's prior celebrated antitrust cases insofar as tens of thousands of Americans were deeply concerned about the effect his ruling would have on the future of the sport. The paper urged the court not to rigidly apply the Sherman Act in the suit, but instead to take the public's interest in baseball into account with the goal of safeguarding and improving the national game.[62]

As expected, the federal courthouse in Chicago was teeming with activity prior to the start of the hearing on the morning of Wednesday, January 20. The *Sporting News* described the scene as "the greatest array of base ball magnates ever assembled at one time." Among those in attendance were most of the significant officials from the three major leagues, along with various players, umpires, and even the wives of Charles Weeghman, Jim Gilmore, and Judge Landis. In the courtroom, the league executives sat in front with their counsel, while the remaining owners assembled within the first few rows of seating.[63]

More than six hundred spectators crammed into a courtroom intended to hold no more than two hundred, with at least another one thousand turned away at the door. Ten bailiffs were assigned to the proceedings to maintain order, with many of the fans that were lucky enough to get into the hearing skipping lunch that afternoon to ensure that they did not lose their seat. The

John Tener and Ban Johnson in Chicago at the time of the Landis suit (Chicago History Museum, SDN-060107, photo by the Chicago Daily News)

general mood of much of the audience was summed up when, just before the hearing began, one spectator responded to the bailiff's call for order in the courtroom by shouting "Hey, boy, gimme a bag of peanuts!"[64]

Judge Landis officially convened the proceedings by asking each side's attorneys to identify themselves. While a team of eight attorneys represented organized baseball, the Federal League would rely on only three lawyers: its general counsel Edward Gates, his law partner Quincy Myers, and Chicago-based Keene Addington, the attorney who successfully defended Hal Chase in Buffalo the previous July.[65]

Gates began the hearing by announcing that each of the Federal League's eight teams was prepared to formally enter the suit as a plaintiff, so long as the defendants were willing to waive any jurisdictional questions that their intervention might raise. American League counsel George Miller responded on behalf of all the defendants that his clients were willing to waive any objections on personal jurisdiction grounds (that is, any argument that the out-of-state defendants were not properly within the Illinois court's power). However, Miller argued, the defendants could not waive all jurisdictional issues in the case, as the court would have to decide for itself whether it possessed subject matter jurisdiction over the suit (that is, whether a legitimate claim had been raised under federal law, or alternatively if the requirements for diversity jurisdiction had been satisfied). After some debate between the attorneys, Judge Landis ultimately agreed that the question of subject matter jurisdiction was for him to decide, and with that the substantive portion of the hearing began.[66]

Keene Addington led off for the Federals, launching into a detailed discussion of the National Agreement. Walking through each section of the pact, he argued that it enabled the major leagues to control practically the entire supply of professional baseball players and, in the process, effectively prevent any serious rival league from forming. Quoting Article I, Section 1, he noted that the agreement explicitly declared that any non-signatory team or league was an "enemy of organized baseball," wording that the attorney contended was "no idle phrase."[67]

Addington next attacked the reserve clause, insisting that contrary to an assertion in August Herrmann's affidavit, the practice was not grounded simply in a single provision in each player's contract, but rather was ingrained throughout the entire National Agreement. Quoting various sections of the agreement, he pointed out that all signatory clubs must "pledge themselves to recognize the right of reservation," with any team or league not respecting the practice "considered an outlaw organization." Furthermore, he contended that Article VI, Section 3, stating that "[t]he right and title of a Major League Club to its players shall be absolute," effectively "reduce[d] the player to a chattel."[68]

Addington also contested organized baseball's assertion that it did not blacklist players who violated the reserve clause, noting that the National Commission's own rules stated that a player who breached his contract "shall be declared and promulgated to the disqualified to play" list, after which he must wait a full three years before applying for reinstatement. As a result, the attorney argued, the player's actual contract was itself largely superfluous, with the National Agreement guaranteeing teams the perpetual right to their players' services. The only purpose of a player's contract, he contended, was to provide the defendants with a legal basis upon which they could go to court to enjoin the player from leaving for a competing organization.[69]

Continuing his assault on the National Agreement and reserve clause, Addington emphasized that the defendants' control over players was not limited to those competing in the major leagues, but extended to the minor leagues as well. He explained that the agreement established an annual draft—a practice never mentioned in a player's contract—in which teams from higher-ranked leagues were allowed to select players from circuits of lower classification. Addington argued that contrary to what the defendants may claim, the draft actually impeded players' career progression insofar as limitations were placed on the number of men that could be selected from a single minor league team. For example, only one player could be drafted per year from a Class AA team, while only two could be selected from a Class A team. Once these limits had been met, all remaining players on the team could not be promoted without their club's consent.[70]

The *Chicago Tribune* described Addington's attack on the reserve clause as "a fiery summary . . . emphasizing the point of the 'system' which controls the destiny, the salary, and the abode of the player throughout his career."[71] Indeed, throughout this portion of the argument, Addington referenced particularly harsh decisions issued by the National Commission in cases where players had appealed the way they were treated by their teams.[72] By emphasizing organized baseball's mistreatment of professional players, rather than simply dwelling on how the defendants had made it more difficult for the Federal League to compete, he elevated the stakes of the case from a simple dispute between business rivals to a matter of fundamental fairness affecting thousands of ballplayers, thereby characterizing organized baseball as a harmful monopoly in need of regulation. The presentation did not impress everyone, however, as organized baseball's de facto mouthpiece, the *Sporting News,* described the argument as "not only unconvincing but dull as well. The audience was 'walking out' on Addington and those who came to see a display of verbal fireworks wanted their money back."[73]

Addington closed the first day of the hearing by emphasizing the dictatorial power of the National Commission: "[S]ee the exercise of power here, see these three men, standing at the head of this great organization, with all of the power back of them, with this agreement back of them, with their power to construe it and enforce it, and to construe it according to the letter, and according to the spirit, as they see it, with nothing beyond. . . ."[74] Organized baseball's leaders brushed off Addington's criticisms after court adjourned that evening, declaring that none of the day's events had been a surprise. In particular, John Tener stated, "We have nothing to fear from what was brought up today."[75]

Day two of the hearing began with a noticeable drop-off in attendance, not only among baseball fans but the magnates as well.[76] One of those not in attendance was Chicago White Sox owner Charles Comiskey, who reportedly had a representative ask Judge Landis early in the hearing, and off the record, whether he could be excused from court to head to Wisconsin on vacation. The judge allegedly responded, "You tell Mr. Comiskey to go up there by all means and that I hope he'll have a fine time."[77]

Keene Addington picked up where he had left off the previous day, continuing his review of the relevant provisions of the National Agreement. He first focused the court's attention on Article VIII of the agreement, which

Keene Addington forcefully represented the Federal League before Judge Landis (Library of Congress, Prints & Photographs Division, LC-DIG-ggbain-18294)

mandated that "[a]ll contracts between Clubs and players in the Major Leagues shall be in the form prescribed by the Commission."[78] Addington noted that the document required each player's salary to be divided so that 25 percent compensated him for the reserve clause, with the remaining 75 percent for "service rendered." Moreover, teams were specifically forbidden from entering a "non-reserve contract" without the prior permission of the National Commission. Taken together, these revelations undermined organized baseball's assertions that their player contracts were voluntary agreements in which players consensually agreed to accept a portion of their compensation in exchange for the reserve option.

After completing his review of the National Agreement, Addington began an exposition of Judge Bissell's decision from the *Hal Chase* case. Judge Landis appeared to grow impatient with the Federals' counsel for the first time during this discussion, at one point cutting him off to suggest that "unless there is something in that opinion that you consider a little more pointed than what you have already read, I do not believe that it is necessary to go on."[79] Addington transitioned into a consideration of whether baseball players were subjected to "involuntary servitude within the meaning of the Constitution of the United States." He cited several cases, including a recent decision in *United States v. Reynolds*,[80] in which a man had been required to provide more than nine months of farm labor to pay off a $15 debt. Here again, Landis interrupted Addington to inform him that there was no need to recite the facts of several cases with which he was already quite familiar.[81]

Likely sensing that the judge was becoming annoyed, Addington offered to begin an analysis of the Federal League's complaint. Judge Landis cut him off, however, stating that he wanted to ask a question or two regarding the matter of jurisdiction. The press would later characterize Landis's interjection as a "staggering blow" to the Federals. In reality, however, Addington appeared well prepared to address the issue, discussing the question of diversity jurisdiction at length by citing a number of relevant legal precedents.[82]

Specifically, Addington asserted that the offer by the eight Federal League franchises to intervene in the suit had no bearing on the court's jurisdiction over the case. He argued that at the time the complaint was filed, a complete diversity of jurisdiction existed, because the Federal League itself was an Indiana corporation, while all of the defendants resided in other states. Citing several precedents, he contended that any subsequent intervention thus did not disrupt the court's jurisdiction. Moreover, Addington noted, the question of diversity jurisdiction was only relevant if the complaint did not assert a claim under federal law, which was not the case here because the plaintiff had asserted allegations under the Sherman and Clayton Acts. Before the Federals' attorney could provide an extended analysis of this issue, however, Judge Landis said he wanted to hear from the defense attorneys on the point, because they carried the burden of proving that federal antitrust law did not apply to baseball.[83]

National League counsel George Wharton Pepper began the defense by noting that his present duty was not to convince the court that his clients should ultimately prevail on the merits of the case, but simply to raise enough doubt to render a preliminary injunction unwarranted. Speaking in what the *Chicago Tribune* described as "musical and pleasing tones," he claimed that this case was "the only occasion that I recall in the course of [my] professional experience in which I have reason to oppose a motion for a preliminary injunction under the embarrassment of having heard from the plaintiff not so much as one word respecting either the thing which he wishes to enjoin, or the reason why the court should . . . enjoin it."[84]

Pepper argued that the court must distinguish between the defendants' past conduct and their present practices when determining whether to grant injunctive relief. In particular, he alleged that under the recently revised player contract, organized baseball did not control its players' services in perpetuity, but merely for a single additional year. This revelation reportedly "shocked" Judge Landis, who interrupted to make sure that he had understood Pepper correctly. The implication of Pepper's assertion was that even if organized baseball's practices had harmed the Federals in the past, there was no need for the court to issue an injunction now because the rival league would no longer be injured in the future. This was especially true here, Pepper contended, when the Federal League did not merely seek to enjoin organized baseball "but to guillotine, to decapitate" it.[85]

Pepper next acknowledged the seemingly harsh decisions rendered by the National Commission that Keene Addington had emphasized the day before, admitting that some players appear to have been treated poorly by organized baseball. "I guess my client won't like it if I say what I am going to say now: I think Mr. Murphy treated Mr. Mordecai Brown in a way in which I should never have treated him." Nevertheless, he asserted, the benefits of the National Agreement had outweighed its demerits. Pepper contended that the agreement was formed to bring order to the game and, rather than stifle competition, sought "to give the public all the ball it could stand."[86]

In contrast, he painted the Federal League as unscrupulous and immoral, emphasizing a statement in Jim Gilmore's affidavit asserting that the rival circuit was legally entitled to induce the breach of organized baseball's player contracts. "[T]hat little statement . . . I should like to keep like a fly in amber so that you can look at it from time to time during the consideration of this case," Pepper suggested. He argued that rather than train its own players, the Federals simply wanted to steal men that organized baseball had spent many seasons developing, using antitrust law to obtain advantages that the major leagues had taken years to attain. He further emphasized the apparent hypocrisy of the Federal League's position, given that it included both the reserve clause and ten-day release provision in its own player contracts.[87]

Throughout his criticism of the Federals, Pepper never missed an opportunity to add a little levity to the proceedings. At one point he referenced a prominent piece of art hanging on the courtroom wall, teasing that while "it seems to me that that is a picture of King John confronted by [the Magna Carta] . . . I have no doubt that Mr. Addington thinks that is an allegorical picture of President Gilmore shrinking in horror from the National agreement." Later, he characterized the plaintiff's complaint as a "bill more richly deserv[ing] the title of a 'complaint' than almost any pleading that I ever read. It is a sort of outpouring of the soul of the plaintiff. . . ."[88]

Finally turning to the issue of jurisdiction, Pepper began by stating that his clients would be more than happy to have Judge Landis preside over the suit: "we would like your Honor to decide this case if anybody has to do it." Nevertheless, he believed that serious questions existed regarding the court's jurisdiction. He asserted that the intervention of the individual Federal League teams had destroyed any diversity jurisdiction in the case—because the suit now featured plaintiffs and defendants from the same state—leaving only the question of whether a valid claim had been asserted under federal law.[89]

Pepper argued that the recently enacted Clayton Act was dispositive on this latter issue. Relying on the argument that Ellis Kinkead had identified shortly after the suit was filed, he recited the opening passage of Section 6 of the statute: "The labor of a human being is not a commodity, or an article of commerce."[90] Pepper contended that this language foreclosed the possibility of federal antitrust liability in the case because the Federals were asserting that organized baseball had monopolized the services of professional baseball players. In other words, based on Section 6, Pepper asserted that the monopolization of the labor of human beings was not subject to federal antitrust law.

At one point during the discussion of jurisdiction, Judge Landis interrupted to say that he was surprised by how Pepper characterized the playing of baseball: "I might as well be frank with you gentlemen about this. As the result of thirty years' observation . . . I was somewhat shocked to hear you call it labor." Although commentators have traditionally viewed this as an attempt by Landis to inject some humor into the proceedings, he was also raising a legitimate legal concern. Indeed, at the time of the hearing, the term "labor" was frequently used legally to refer only to menial, physical work, and not the efforts of skilled employees (such as those of professional baseball players). Pepper's response treated the judge's statement as a serious question, acknowledging that he was assuming Congress was referring to both skilled and unskilled labor.[91]

Even without this statutory language, however, Pepper believed that federal antitrust law did not apply to baseball because it was not "commerce." Although the attorney acknowledged that the game might appear to be commerce at first glance, upon closer examination he was confident the court would agree that it was merely "sport" or "amusement."[92] He emphasized a recent decision from a New York state court in *Metropolitan Opera Co. v. Hammerstein,*[93] in which the judge—relying on the traditional definition of commerce as the production or sale of tangible goods—held that theatrical exhibitions were not commerce and thus not subject to the Sherman Act. As in *Hammerstein,* Pepper argued that baseball teams simply produced intangible exhibitions, with any transportation of players or equipment across state lines merely incidental to the true, fundamental nature of the endeavor.[94]

Before concluding for the day, Pepper offered one final analogy, comparing the business of baseball to that of insurance, which the U.S. Supreme Court had previously held was not interstate commerce even though policies were routinely sold across state lines. Pepper thus urged that baseball games, like insurance agreements, were "matters of purely local concern," and not subject to the Sherman or Clayton Acts.[95]

Day three of the hearing began with Pepper continuing his argument that baseball did not constitute commerce. In particular, he asserted that if baseball was not commerce for purposes of federal law, then it also stood to reason that it was not commerce under state law either, rendering the Federal League's common-law antitrust claims inapplicable.[96] That left the Federals with only their conspiracy charge, a claim that Pepper asserted had not been pled with enough specificity in the complaint to support a preliminary injunction.

Having dissected the Federals' three primary legal claims, Pepper turned his attention to the league's specific requests for relief. Emphasizing the breadth of the injunction sought by the plaintiffs, he asserted that even the federal government would never seek to wholly enjoin a defendant's practices on a preliminary basis in the manner requested here. Instead, he noted that government antitrust prosecutions typically gave the defendant a chance to modify its practices to comply with the law.[97]

At this point, Federal League counsel Edward Gates interrupted to clarify that the only preliminary relief his clients were seeking was an injunction covering clause fourteen of the complaint, the allegation that organized baseball was conspiring to destroy the rival league. Gates thus contended that the Federals were really only asking the court at present to prohibit organized baseball from doing two things: (i) interfering with its players, including the initiation or continued prosecution of any court actions, and (ii) denigrating the league in the press by questioning its financial condition or referring to it and its players as "outlaws" or "contract jumpers." The remaining relief, Gates suggested, could wait until after a full trial on the merits of the case. Pepper seized on this concession, arguing that if that was all the Federals sought, then the case truly did not belong in federal court because they were merely litigating a state law conspiracy claim.[98]

Before moving on to the Federal League's remaining requests for relief, Pepper warned Judge Landis, "really, your Honor, this thing gets worse as you go on. As was said of the baboon climbing a pole, the higher he gets the worse he looks." For instance, he argued, the court could not grant the plaintiffs one portion of the relief they were seeking because federal courts were prohibited from enjoining state court litigations in the manner that the Federals requested. Meanwhile, he ridiculed the complaint's request for the court to declare all of organized baseball's player contracts null and void, noting that this would affect even those players who did not object to their current agreements.[99]

Pepper wrapped up his portion of the defense with a personal appeal, leading to perhaps the most famous exchange of the entire hearing:

> MR. PEPPER: Just before I take my seat, sir, I want to say something to your Honor which is almost personal. I do not want your Honor to suppose in this case that the only interest that I have is in the magnates, club owners and leagues. I love this game, and I believe your Honor does.
>
> THE COURT: Well, we will have to keep affection, love and affection, out of this lawsuit.
>
> MR. PEPPER: Let us keep it out; but I, sir, for one, cannot concede and will not concede to Brother Addington any monopoly of interest in the individual ball player, sir.
>
> THE COURT: Well, you gentlemen need none of you spend any time on that in talking to me.
>
> MR. PEPPER: I am very, very glad to hear that, sir, because if I recollect right—

THE COURT: I think you gentlemen around here all understand that a blow at this thing called baseball—both sides understand this perfectly—will be regarded by this court as a blow at a National institution. Therefore you need not spend any time on that phase of this subject.

MR. PEPPER: I very, very gladly defer to your Honor's suggestion, and just because that is so clearly in your Honor's mind I leave this case, sir, in your Honor's hands. . . .[100]

Based on abbreviated reports of this exchange, commentators have historically interpreted Landis's "a blow at this thing called baseball" line as a sign that he was predisposed to rule against the Federal League.[101] This interpretation effectively conflated any attack on organized baseball as an attack on the sport itself. However, when viewed in its entirety, the exchange can be read quite differently, with the judge instead saying that any affinity for the game of baseball had to be kept separate from the issue of whether the defendants had violated the law. Indeed, contemporaneous accounts suggest that the Federal League's officials joined in the courtroom audience's applause following Landis's pronouncement.[102]

Having finished his argument, Pepper handed the floor over to the American League's counsel, George Miller. Miller focused his presentation on the proposition that the Federal League was not entitled to injunctive relief because its hands were unclean. Speaking in "an impressive and forceful style, which stamped every argument set forth," he picked up on the theme that Pepper had established the day before, arguing that the Federals were an unscrupulous organization.[103]

Miller began by discussing at considerable length the Federal League's inducement of eighteen different players under contract to organized baseball. At one point, he joked that he should "express [his] appreciation to" Jim Gilmore for having supplied the defense with such a "magnificent" affidavit, focusing in particular on his admission that the league's policy was to induce players under contract to major league teams. He argued that even if Judge Landis agreed with the Federals' contention that the major league player contracts were themselves legally void, the rival circuit's interference with the agreements nevertheless rendered its hands unclean, undermining its request for injunctive relief. On this point, Miller emphasized the ruling of the federal court of appeals the year before in the *Killefer* case, in which the court had held that the Federals' inducement of major league players disentitled them to an injunction, even though the players' underlying contracts were not legally enforceable.[104]

He then stressed that the Federal League's own player contracts included the very same provisions—namely the reserve clause and ten-day release provision—that it attacked in organized baseball's agreements. In fact, Miller argued, the rival league's reserve clause was even more restrictive than the major leagues,' insofar as it bound players for ten years, while organized baseball's allegedly now only obligated them for a single additional season. He also pointed out that the Federal League's rules reinforced its reserve clause, prohibiting teams from negotiating with each other's players and providing that any player failing to obey his contract would be suspended. Miller contended that the league could not rightfully challenge organized baseball's contracts and rules when its own were equally restrictive. Therefore, he asserted, the Federal League had not filed its complaint in good faith, also rendering its hands unclean.[105]

Next, Miller focused the court's attention on the Federal League's recent peace negotiations with organized baseball. Noting that the plaintiffs admitted they had conferred with the major leagues, he pointed out a number of occasions where, contrary to the assertion in Gilmore's affidavit, the league had proposed peace terms that would not have required any reformation of the National Agreement. As a result, he argued, injunctive relief was not justified in a case where the plaintiff had tried to join the alleged wrongdoer, insisting that the Federals would have been laughed out of court if they had candidly admitted they raided major league rosters for more than a year in hopes of joining organized baseball, but now were suing because they had failed to succeed.[106]

Miller wrapped up organized baseball's defense by asserting that any injury the Federal League would sustain if a preliminary injunction were denied was more than outweighed by the damage that the issuance of an injunction would inflict on organized baseball:

> What will happen to us if you issue this writ, and go the length of the prayer of relief of their bill? Our organization will be temporarily destroyed. The plan, which has made the American game of baseball what it is, will have been destroyed by the stroke of your Honor's pen, and if in the end you [reach] the conclusion that you have improvidently granted the writ, we can only gather together the scattered pieces of an organization which we have spent forty years in building up, and which you have stricken down in the single stroke of your pen.

He contended that even the Federal League did not truly want to see organized baseball destroyed, rendering its suit "a sham and a pretense." Miller thus urged Judge Landis to refrain from issuing a preliminary injunction, and instead encouraged him to hold a full trial on the merits of the case, after which the defendants would be content to "go up or down as the conscience and right of our position demands."[107]

By the time organized baseball's attorneys had finished their presentation, the *Christian Science Monitor* declared that they had removed every smear "of discredit placed upon their clients by the independent league and left the older organizations standing in polished splendor." In particular, the *Chicago Tribune* praised George Pepper's presentation of the case, reporting that he had taken each of the Federals' charges and successfully left them "torn beautifully into small bits."[108] Following Miller's summation, the court adjourned for the evening, with the major league magnates reportedly leaving the courthouse confident they would be completely vindicated thanks to the eloquence of their attorneys.

The final session of the hearing was held on Saturday, January 23, and would prove to be "one of the best attended and most intense of the four."[109] The morning began with Edward Gates's law partner, Quincy Myers, launching into a discussion of the jurisdictional issue. Before he could begin, however, Judge Landis interrupted to inquire "just what you have in mind, if you get a restraining order in this case, [what] the provisions of that order should be?" Gates stepped in to answer the question by reaffirming the clarification he had provided the day before. He stated that although the complaint sought a broad array of potential relief, the plaintiffs were currently only asking for a preliminary injunction preventing the defendants from continuing their harassment of the Federal League.[110]

In particular, Gates stressed that his clients did not seek to prevent the defendants from continuing their usual course of business or from sending their teams to spring training camps. Instead, he maintained, the league just wanted to protect itself. This led the *Sporting News* to later question why it was that if the Federals were only seeking to prevent organized baseball from interfering with their players, they nevertheless asked for ten times more relief in their complaint.[111]

With his preliminary inquiry out of the way, Judge Landis returned to the question of jurisdiction, noting that it "is by no means plainly settled here yet," although confessing that he "would not be displeased to see [my] jurisdiction clearly established, because this is a mighty attractive controversy that you gentlemen have brought in here." Myers began what the *Chicago Tribune* characterized as a "most forceful and impressive" argument by addressing the issue of whether baseball was commerce. He started by highlighting the fact that both the American and National Leagues earned $20,000 per season from equipment manufacturers in exchange for the right to produce each league's official baseball.[112] He also noted that the

American League received another $10,000 per year from Western Union for the right to transmit its game results across the country via telegram.

Perhaps more significantly, though, Myers cited a series of precedents holding that the transportation of supplies or persons across state lines constituted commerce. Emphasizing the fact that the two major leagues routinely sent both players and umpires between states, he argued that this activity subjected organized baseball to the Sherman and Clayton Acts.[113] Throughout this discussion, however, Myers never directly addressed George Pepper's argument that such transportation was merely incidental to the actual business of baseball, which was fundamentally premised on games played in a single state. In other words, because the Federals did not allege that baseball's transportation practices themselves violated antitrust law, the precedents Myers cited holding that the act of transporting people across state lines constituted commerce did not directly undermine the defendants' argument. Instead, the precedents merely served to verify what organized baseball believed was an irrelevant point of law.

Myers then addressed the defense's assertion that the opening phrase of Section 6 of the Clayton Act—declaring that labor was not an article of commerce—precluded the application of the Sherman Act in the case. Specifically, he contended that the provision was intended to protect unions from antitrust law, and thus did not entirely withdraw all labor from the scope of the antitrust laws. Moreover, he argued, even if Pepper's interpretation of the provision was correct, that did not mean that any business relying on labor was no longer engaged in commerce, but simply that the labor in and of itself would not fall within the bounds of the Sherman Act.[114]

Next, the attorney disputed organized baseball's assertion that its reserve clause now bound a player to his team for only a single additional season. He argued that despite what the defendants might have alleged, the National Agreement still tied players "hand and foot" by forbidding teams from entering contracts without a reserve clause. Myers then handed the floor over to Keene Addington, who argued that organized baseball had refused to produce several recent contracts signed by players whose options had been renewed under the reserve clause. This gave rise to the most prolonged and heated exchange between counsel of the entire hearing. Addington believed that these most recent contracts would undermine the major leagues' new interpretation of the reserve clause, proving that in reality organized baseball continued to re-sign players to new agreements themselves containing a reserve option. Tacitly admitting that their current form contract still contained the reserve provision, George Miller responded on behalf of the defense by acknowledging that if a player agreed to renew his contract by entering a new agreement itself containing a reserve clause, then his clients were more than happy to accommodate him.[115]

Finally, Edward Gates took the floor to conclude the Federal League's case. He began by launching into a "fervid," two-hour attack on organized baseball's unclean-hands argument. Walking through the various affidavits that had been filed in the suit, he contended that the plaintiffs had not engaged in any wrongful conduct, but instead had only negotiated with players who they believed had invalid contracts or whose options had not been picked up prior to the end of the season. In fact, at one point Gates suggested that the Federal League would return every ballplayer it had signed from organized baseball if the court determined that the players had not been lawfully acquired. He also justified and differentiated the Federals' own use of the reserve clause and ten-day release provision by explaining that the former was more than fair because it guaranteed players an annual 5 percent raise, while the latter was only used in cases of untested players.[116]

Gates also challenged organized baseball's claim that it did not blacklist players who repudiated the reserve clause, citing an affidavit filed in the case by Federal League player James "Runt" Walsh. Included in the Walsh affidavit were letters sent to the player by Sam Lichtenhein, the president of Montreal's minor league franchise, in which Walsh was warned, "if you start to play with [the Federals], you are black-listed from organized baseball for three years." August Herrmann later privately admonished Lichtenhein for sending the damaging letters, claiming they were one of the most harmful revelations brought out against organized baseball during the hearing.[117]

Next, Gates rejected the defendants' contention that the Federal League was precluded from receiving injunctive relief because it had attempted to negotiate a settlement with the two major leagues. "If they want to talk peace, if they want to modify their agreement and make this thing legal, why shouldn't you listen to their proposition," he asked rhetorically. Gates insisted that officials from organized baseball had initiated every settlement discussion, making it disingenuous for the major leagues to now claim that the Federals were acting in bad faith by filing suit. He also cited several cases holding that even if a plaintiff had acted inequitably, injunctive relief could still be granted to protect the public from an injurious monopoly.[118]

The *Chicago Tribune* praised Gates's performance, reporting that he "proved to be as impressive a talker as his adversaries." Indeed, at one point during the argument Gates tried to match George Pepper's wit by himself referring to the courtroom's painting of King John and the Magna Carta. He noted that the "handwriting on the wall" declared that no free man shall be denied justice, in stark contrast to the National Agreement, which he pointed out claimed that the "right and title of clubs to players shall be absolute."[119]

In the summation of his argument, Gates praised baseball as "an honest, moral, uplifting, healthy entertainment and recreation of a nation, a thing which is as necessary to a people as life or law itself." Nevertheless, he asked, "Was there ever, your Honor, a combination that declared itself to be a trust in its papers? Was there ever a trust that stated openly that its purpose was to monopolize a business and stifle competition? As in other cases, so here." Gates then applied a metaphor frequently used at the time to describe monopolies in other industries, contending that the Federal League simply desired to be "unrestricted by the tentacles of an octopus which has endeavored . . . to fasten itself upon guileless people under the guise of an appeal to the public fancy for entertainment."[120]

Gates closed by urging the court to conclude that baseball was subject to federal law: "Here is a business, a modern business, exercising and using all the means and methods known in modern interstate communication, intercourse and publicity; and it is as certainly, if your Honor please, commerce and intercourse within the meaning of the commerce clause of the Constitution of the United States, and as much within the Sherman Act and the Clayton Bill, as the control of commerce is by the Constitution of the United States given to Congress."[121] And with that, the Federal League rested its case.

Before formally adjourning the hearing, Judge Landis granted organized baseball twenty days for each of the defendants to file their formal answer to the Federal League's complaint. He also told the plaintiffs' attorneys that they could wait until Monday to file a memorandum of the legal precedents they had cited in the case. "I will attempt to struggle along tomorrow without any legal authorities," he joked.[122]

After the hearing, August Herrmann summed up the proceedings to the press: "Attorneys Pepper and Miller made notable speeches for the defense. Judge Landis evidently took a warm interest in all the points brought out and he handled the trial admirably and speedily. Of course, it would be entirely out of place for me to express any opinion as to whether he will grant the order or not. He is not quite certain as yet as to his jurisdiction in the matter and it is possible that he may decline to render a decision, but I think that one will be handed down very shortly."[123] Meanwhile, Jim Gilmore stated that the Federals likely would not appeal the court's decision if it ruled against their league, adding, "Should Judge Landis grant a favorable decision to the Federal league, it will mean much to us. Should he decide in favor of organized baseball, however, it will not mean the end of the Federal league. We will have a league this season and the next, regardless of what happens."[124]

In the days following the hearing, the media was generally uncertain which side would prevail. The *Washington Post* believed that Landis's decision would hinge on the issue of jurisdiction, while even the *Sporting News* was forced to concede that it was possible the court would grant the Federals a temporary injunction of limited scope. Both the baseball magnates and fans eagerly awaited the ruling, which the press predicted would be released within three weeks.[125]

Judge Landis, however, would keep everyone waiting much longer than anyone could have anticipated.

5

The Long Wait

February 1915 to February 1916

Shortly after the Chicago hearing, organized baseball's attorneys began preparing formal answers to the Federal League's allegations on behalf of each of the twenty-one defendants. John Galvin and Ellis Kinkead, the National Commission's lawyers, took the lead on the project.[1] They drafted a comprehensive answer for the Cincinnati Reds, as well as a joint answer for the three members of the National Commission, each of whom had been individually named as a defendant in the suit.[2] These answers denied the Federals' various claims, reiterating many of the same defenses asserted during the hearing.

In addition, Cincinnati's answer set forth a counterclaim against the plaintiffs, alleging that the Federal League's teams had themselves formed a conspiracy to harm organized baseball by inducing the defendants' players to breach their contracts. The team noted a number of occasions on which the rival circuit had recruited its players, and argued that this interference had not only undermined discipline and created unrest among the players but also reduced the public's interest in baseball. Cincinnati requested that the court issue an injunction against the plaintiffs to prevent them from continuing to interfere with its players.[3]

The other defendant teams drew heavily upon Cincinnati's answer, adopting the Reds' responses by reference in their own replies and supplementing them with additional examples of the Federals' interference with their own players. With the sole exception of the New York Giants, each of the other major league teams also asserted a counterclaim similar to that of Cincinnati's, accusing the Federal League of having conspired to harm organized baseball. It is not clear why the Giants did not include such a charge in their answer, although attorney Galvin later speculated that the team might have been considering filing its own separate conspiracy lawsuit against the Federals in another court.[4] Meanwhile, although a plaintiff would typically be expected to file a written reply to a defendant's counterclaim, it does not appear that the Federal League ever formally responded to the major league teams' allegations. Once again, it is not clear why this was the case.[5]

With the answers filed, all that remained was for the parties to wait for Judge Landis to issue his decision. Starting in early February 1915, reports periodically surfaced that a ruling would be released shortly. For example, the *Atlanta Constitution* reported on February 4 that Landis would hand down an opinion within the week. Two days later, however, the judge contradicted these reports by announcing that he would not be ruling that week.[6] The *Sporting News* would later state that the initial report had been based on a bogus rumor passed along to American League president Ban Johnson, allegedly on behalf of Landis. Johnson subsequently sent word to the judge notifying him of the misrepresentation. Nevertheless, the reports continued. Two weeks later, the *Washington Post* announced that Landis would "probably give his decision this week,"[7] only to see the week come and go without a ruling.

While the parties anxiously awaited Judge Landis's opinion, the Federal League continued its preparations for the 1915 season. Specifically, after the prospects for peace with organized baseball had faded the previous fall, the Federals set out to find rich new investors to help strengthen the league's financial standing for the upcoming season. Federal League president Jim Gilmore was eventually able to recruit Harry F. Sinclair, a wealthy oil tycoon, to join the ownership ranks. The thirty-seven-year-old Sinclair appeared eager to invest his vast fortune in the new league, once bragging that "he would like to have [New York Yankees owner] Colonel Ruppert and the other magnates of the two big leagues on a boat on the ocean and that he would throw overboard two dollars for every one thrown over by the other sixteen."[8] Years later, Sinclair would serve six months in prison for his role in the Teapot Dome scandal, after his oil company bribed President Warren G. Harding's secretary of the Interior, Albert Fall, to obtain oil rights on government land in Wyoming.

The Federal League initially planned to sell Sinclair its Kansas City franchise, on the understanding that the oilman would then move the team to Newark, New Jersey. After the club's existing shareholders successfully fought the effort in court, though, the Federals instead opted to assign Sinclair the league's Indianapolis franchise. Despite winning the Federal League championship in 1914, the Hoosiers were reportedly more than $100,000 in debt. The oil magnate then moved the club to Newark as originally planned.[9]

Oil tycoon Harry Sinclair joined the Federal League in 1915 (Library of Congress, Prints & Photographs Division, LC-DIG-npcc-23788)

Meanwhile, by February 1915 the Federal League was also fighting off attempts by organized baseball to steal back more of its players. The league had lost seven men since the antitrust hearing before Judge Landis concluded, causing Gilmore to declare, "I am greatly surprised that organized baseball should have induced our players to break their contracts while our suit is pending in the United States Court." "We have not taken a player since the hearing or before who was under a contract with them," he continued. "I am going to Indianapolis tomorrow to consult our attorneys and see what, if any, steps can be taken. If the Federal Court decision is in our favor we shall of course bring up these offenses in a supplementary complaint, but it is doubtful anything can be done in advance of the decision."[10]

As Gilmore had anticipated, the league ultimately announced that it had decided not to take any action against the defecting players, opting instead to wait for a ruling from Judge Landis. However, even though the start of the season was rapidly approaching, no decision from Landis was in sight. In fact, some were beginning to suspect that a decision would not be forthcoming anytime soon, with the *Sporting News* predicting that "we will all have long white beards before we see or hear the text of that tremendous verdict."[11]

As the weeks continued to pass without a decision, the Federals once again began to explore a possible settlement with organized baseball. In late April 1915, the press reported that officials from the Federal League had met with major league representatives in Chicago to discuss a potential peace agreement.[12] Although the Federals were open to settling with the American and National Leagues, they refused to accede to a global peace agreement preventing them from continuing to raid the minor leagues with impunity. As a result, and contrary to some initial published reports, no peace agreement was reached.[13]

One subsequent press account stated that the meeting had arisen at the encouragement of Judge Landis, who reportedly had decided that he had jurisdiction over the Federals' suit but preferred to have the matter settled amicably to avoid inflicting any damage on the game. Based on the contemporaneous correspondence between organized baseball's attorneys, however, there is no indication that Landis was in any way involved in arranging the settlement meeting. In fact, the *Sporting News* would later report that the Federal League had spread the rumor of the judge's involvement with the hope it would motivate organized baseball to settle.[14]

As the calendar turned to May, and with no settlement or decision appearing imminent, the St. Louis Federals once again tried to resolve the still-pending case against Armando Marsans. Marsans remained subject to an injunction preventing him from playing for the Feds, and was reportedly growing increasingly restless, allegedly threatening to return to the major leagues if the Federals were not able to get him back on the field in short order.[15] Privately, organized baseball debated what to do if Marsans did in fact offer to return to Cincinnati. On the one hand, National League president John Tener worried that if Cincinnati permitted the player to return, it would allow the Federal League to allege that the team had wrongfully interfered with him. This, Tener feared, could have a deleterious effect in the Chicago antitrust suit, given his understanding that "no action was to be taken either by organized ball or the Federal League in the Marsan's [*sic*] case and certain others, until the decision of Judge Landis had been handed down."[16] Conversely, others cautioned that if Cincinnati refused to accept Marsans then the injunction would likely be dissolved, given that one of the conditions for its continuance was that the team remain ready and willing to employ the player.[17]

Ultimately, these worries were for naught, as the St. Louis Federals took several steps over the next few months to assuage Marsans. First, to show the player that his lawsuit was progressing, the club deposed several officials from the Cincinnati Reds and St. Louis Cardinals on May 3, 1915. In particular, much of the questioning focused on media reports that Cincinnati had attempted to trade Marsans to the Cardinals. This evidence was presumably intended to show that the Reds viewed Marsans as replaceable, contrary to an assertion in its lawsuit, and therefore that an injunction was no longer warranted. Several of the witnesses admitted that a tentative deal had been reached between the clubs, pending both Judge Landis's decision as well as Marsans's willingness to return to organized baseball.[18] They insisted that the trade was never finalized, though. The National Commission's attorney Ellis Kinkead later trivialized this line of questioning, stating, "I do not regard the testimony as very material."[19] Nevertheless, it did at least arguably help undermine Cincinnati's contention that Marsans was an irreplaceable player whose defection inflicted a significant injury on the team.

Then in mid-June, the Federals formally petitioned Judge Landis to lift the St. Louis court's preliminary injunction against Marsans. Specifically, they argued that Cincinnati was unable to honor Marsans's prior contract—as required under the injunction—because the National Commission's own rules stated that any player repudiating his contract must be placed on the disqualified-to-play list. Moreover, St. Louis contended, Marsans was being significantly harmed by the injunction, forced to sit idly while his skills degraded.[20] Consequently, the team urged the court to dissolve the injunction.

Although Landis indicated that he preferred to hear the matter in private, believing there was nothing "to be gained by either side in having any newspaper notoriety made of the matter," organized baseball insisted that any motion to modify the injunction be made in open court.[21] As a result, Landis held a public hearing on June 28, 1915, during which he declined to dissolve the injunction against Marsans. The judge did indicate that a decision resolving the January antitrust hearing would be forthcoming soon, however, explaining that he had delayed his opinion for the benefit of the game.[22]

Landis's pronouncement seemed to indicate that he had concluded that he possessed jurisdiction over the matter, but feared that by ruling in favor of the Federal League he would significantly harm the national pastime. Indeed, the Federals seized on this announcement, interpreting it as a sign the league would prevail in the case, considering there would presumably be no need to withhold a decision in favor of organized baseball. The *Sporting News* had a different take, though, opining that even if the Federal League won the case and Landis voided all player contracts, it would still do little to help the rival circuit given that most players would hurry back to the major leagues anyway in light of the Federals' apparent weakened financial condition.[23]

Despite Landis's promise that he would issue a decision shortly, several more weeks passed without a ruling. Organized baseball received several informal reports from the judge through its local Chicago counsel during this time, the first suggesting that an opinion would be released before Landis's vacation in mid-August, and the second saying that he would rule around September 1.[24] Once again, however, both deadlines came and went without a decision.

Increasingly frustrated, the Federal League announced in early August that it would no longer patiently wait for a decision in the Chicago suit, but would instead proceed as if the case had never been filed. Jim Gilmore justified the decision by stating, "As there is no telling when Judge Landis will make known his decision, we are forced to go after players now so as not to be left in a hole."[25] Consequently, the Federals once again stepped up their pursuit of players under contract with organized baseball, primarily focusing on those in the upper levels of the minor leagues, with some modest success.

The St. Louis Federals also grew tired of waiting for Judge Landis to rule, and decided to file a motion on August 10 asking the federal district court in St. Louis to dissolve the injunction against Marsans. When Cincinnati initiated the suit in 1914, local Judge David P. Dyer was out of town for several weeks, necessitating that Judge Sanborn from the Eighth Circuit Court of Appeals rule in his place. With Dyer now back, the Federals decided to try to present their case to a potentially more receptive audience. In fact, National Commission chairman August Herrmann received word shortly after St. Louis' latest motion was filed that "[a]ll of the officials of the Federal League are [Judge Dyer's] friends and political friends also and are very well connected."[26]

The St. Louis team relied on several arguments during the subsequent hearing. First, it reiterated the argument it had made to Judge Landis in June, asserting that even if Marsans agreed to return to Cincinnati he would be ineligible to play under the National Commission rule disqualifying any player who repudiated his contract for three years. Thus, the team contended, Cincinnati was unable to uphold its end of Marsans's contract, and as a result the injunction should be dissolved.[27]

More significantly, however, St. Louis also asserted a new argument, namely that Judge Sanborn had overlooked an important limitation in Marsans's contract with Cincinnati when issuing the injunction. Specifically, even though the contract stated in several places that it covered the 1914, 1915, and 1916 seasons, the provision in the agreement in which Marsans had agreed not to perform for any other team—that is, the negative covenant on which the injunction was premised—only specified a term covering the 1914 season. Accordingly, the club argued, the injunction should have expired at the end of the previous season.

The Federals had first discovered this potential loophole in April, asking Cincinnati at the time to voluntarily agree to dissolve the injunction for the 1915 and 1916 seasons. Not surprisingly, the Reds refused, contending that when read in its entirety, the agreement clearly bound Marsans for three seasons.[28] It is not clear why St. Louis did not raise this issue in its earlier motion before Judge Landis.

In response, Cincinnati's attorneys argued that it would be improper to overturn the preliminary injunction after both Judge Sanborn and Landis had already approved it. Judge Dyer took issue with the suggestion that Landis had any power over the present proceedings, and eventually ended the hearing by suggesting that all that remained was for him to interpret the contract.[29] Cincinnati's lawyer, Ellis Kinkead, took this announcement as a sign that the judge was looking for a reason to dissolve the injunction, given that Judge Sanborn had previously interpreted the contract himself. The attorney was also disheartened when Dyer told him after the hearing that he doubted whether it was fair to continue to prevent Marsans from playing.[30]

As Kinkead had anticipated, Judge Dyer dissolved the injunction several days later on August 19, 1915.[31] In his opinion, the judge agreed with St. Louis' argument that the negative covenant in Marsans's contract only applied for 1914. He held that the handwritten date in the provision clearly limited it to a single season, noting that there was plenty of space to write in all three years if that was what the parties had intended. Dyer further concluded that because the contractual provision was clear on its face, there was no reason to refer to the other sections of the agreement when interpreting it.[32] As a result, Marsans was once again allowed to play for the St. Louis Federals. He would struggle to overcome his year's hiatus, however, hitting only .177 over the team's final thirty-six games.

Although Kinkead believed that Judge Dyer's decision was incorrect, he nevertheless took the ruling in stride, noting that the opinion would have a limited impact given that it was premised entirely upon a typographical error unique to Marsans's contract. All the same, he vowed to immediately appeal the decision. Kinkead also recommended that major league teams be more careful when executing multiyear contracts in the future, counseling them to make sure that each year covered by the agreement was written into every relevant clause in the contract.[33]

By the end of the 1915 season, the media concluded that no decision from Judge Landis was imminent, and that no end to the baseball war was in sight. The Federal League began to prepare for 1916 by publicizing its plans to invade New York City by building a $1.75 million stadium in

Manhattan. Jim Gilmore would later claim that this announcement was part of an elaborate bluff to bring organized baseball to the negotiating table. Other commentators have questioned the veracity of these claims, though, contending that at least initially the league appeared to sincerely intend to place a team in New York.[34]

Bluff or not, the continued viability of the Federal League took a major blow in October when Robert Ward, owner of the Brooklyn Federals and one of the league's primary financial benefactors, died unexpectedly of pneumonia.[35] The loss of a moneyed investor like Ward—who was helping underwrite several of the Federal League's other franchises—was a particularly crushing blow given that a number of the circuit's teams had struggled mightily throughout 1915. Notably, both the Buffalo and Kansas City franchises were on the brink of bankruptcy by season's end, while several other teams in the league had been forced to lower their ticket prices to ten cents—well below the twenty-five-cent minimum price charged by the major leagues—to attract fans.

As a result, the Federals began to more desperately pursue a settlement with organized baseball. The league had sporadically continued its informal discussions with various representatives of the major leagues following the April meeting in Chicago. In early August, Harry Sinclair arranged to meet August Herrmann in Columbus, Ohio, to discuss a potential peace agreement.[36] Then in October 1915, a delegation of Federal League representatives held an informal peace conference with the National Commission in Philadelphia during the World Series. During a meeting at the Bellevue-Strafford Hotel, the Federals revived an earlier proposal to expand the American and National Leagues to ten teams each, suggesting that the Federal League franchises in Brooklyn, Pittsburgh, Baltimore, and either Buffalo or Kansas City be absorbed into the leagues. They also asked that Charles Weeghman and Harry Sinclair be allowed to buy existing major league teams. Although organized baseball was prepared to allow the two Federal League owners to purchase big league clubs, they considered the expansion proposal a nonstarter, preferring to maintain eight teams in each major league. The two sides nevertheless continued to engage in exploratory talks over the next few weeks.[37]

Subsequent newspaper reports regarding the October negotiations caught the attention of George Pepper—organized baseball's lawyer in the suit before Judge Landis—who wrote to National League president John Tener warning him that a settlement with the Federals could itself potentially violate antitrust law. Specifically, Pepper feared that any peace agreement resulting in the rival circuit either being merged into organized baseball, or eliminated entirely, would give rise to a claim that the major leagues had illegally monopolized the industry under the Sherman Act. The attorney advised Tener that "if the suit were to be withdrawn or some form of consent decree obtained from the court, this might be laid hold of by an aggrieved outsider as further evidence of the power of the combination and be used to make fresh trouble for organized baseball, either in the courts or in the Attorney General's Department."[38] Consequently, Pepper urged the major leagues to refrain from entering a settlement until Judge Landis had issued a ruling in their favor.

Organized baseball's other counsel, John Galvin and Ellis Kinkead, concurred with Pepper's advice, prophetically warning that it was also possible that "a stockholder of a Federal League club who might claim to have suffered loss" as a result of the settlement could himself bring a new challenge under the antitrust laws. The two attorneys suggested that if a resolution appeared to be in reach, the major leagues should first go to Judge Landis and request that he issue a ruling before finalizing the peace agreement.[39]

Despite its legal counsels' warning of the potential dangers of settling with the Federals, the National League continued to actively pursue peace throughout November and early December. During a December 13 meeting in New York City, the presidents of all eight National League clubs placed a call to Jim Gilmore—who was also in the city at the time conferring with Harry Sinclair—and asked if he was willing to "come over and fix this thing up."[40] Gilmore and Sinclair eventually agreed to meet with the National League officials that afternoon, and by the end of the evening had worked out a tentative peace agreement. Under the terms of the proposed deal:

1. The Federal League would cease to exist;
2. Sinclair or his assignee (understood to be Charles Weeghman) would be allowed to purchase the Chicago Cubs from Charles Taft, with the National League contributing $50,000 of the purchase price;
3. The National League would pay the estate of former Brooklyn Federals owner Robert Ward $10,000 per year for the next twenty years, so long as the American League would agree to do the same, for a total payment of $400,000;
4. The National League would pay the Pittsburgh Federals $25,000, again assuming the American League would agree to do likewise;
5. All players in the Federal League would be eligible to return to organized baseball, but the Federals would remain liable under any players' contracts that were not sold back to major league teams; and
6. The two sides would agree to dismiss the antitrust lawsuit before Judge Landis in Chicago.

Although not a part of the tentative agreement, it was also understood that Philip Ball, one of the wealthy backers of the St. Louis Federals, would be given an option to purchase the St. Louis Browns of the American League.[41] Ball and American League president Ban Johnson had surprisingly become friends during the course of the Federal League challenge, and Johnson now desired to add the millionaire to his ownership group. The parties would later supplement the agreement to also explicitly provide that all other pending litigation would be dismissed as part of the settlement.[42]

Toward the end of the meeting with the National League, Gilmore asked that the Baltimore Federals be given $200,000 in the settlement, a request that was laughed down by the senior circuit's officials. Gilmore later explained to Sinclair that he thought he should start the negotiations with a high offer for Baltimore, but assumed that the team would ultimately be satisfied with receiving an International League franchise.[43] As a result, though, the tentative agreement did not include any provisions for Baltimore, Buffalo, or Kansas City, the latter two of which were of lesser concern given their insolvency and likely imminent forfeiture back to the league. Nevertheless, on the whole Gilmore and Sinclair were able to cut an exceedingly generous deal, given that the National League had agreed to contribute nearly a half-million dollars to a league hovering on the brink of dissolution, especially in light of the realization that it was increasingly apparent that Judge Landis had no intention of issuing a ruling against organized baseball in the Federals' antitrust suit.

Even though the Federal League leadership and National League owners were amenable to the terms of the proposed agreement, they still needed to obtain the consent of the American League to finalize the deal. The National League immediately dispatched Pittsburgh owner Barney Dreyfuss to Chicago, where the American League club presidents were themselves conferencing. Dreyfuss explained the terms of the proposed settlement to the group, imploring them to approve the agreement. As he later recalled, "Peace is better than war, and I told the American League magnates so. We reached terms with the Federal League which are agreeable to both them and the National League and our proposition met the approval of the American League. Our close relations with the American League made it desirable that complete accord exist on the question, and it looks as if we had reached that." Ban Johnson confirmed his league's endorsement of the deal, announcing to the press that "[t]he end of the baseball war is in sight. The plans for peace submitted by Mr. Dreyfuss were agreeable to the American League . . . and we shall appoint a committee to go over the details."[44] As Johnson's statement indicated, a party of six American League owners quickly left for New York to iron out the final settlement terms with the Federal and National Leagues.

Meanwhile, Jim Gilmore contacted the BaltFeds' management and asked them to immediately come up to New York for an important league meeting. With the league's executives in attendance at the Biltmore Hotel on the morning of December 17, Gilmore confirmed that he had entered a settlement with organized baseball and that as a result the league would be disbanding.[45] The Baltimore representatives were understandably furious, especially when they learned that no provisions had been made for their franchise in the settlement agreement. Although the participants would later dispute exactly what occurred during the rest of the meeting, a committee of Gilmore, Sinclair, and Weeghman was ultimately appointed to meet later that evening with representatives from the major leagues to finalize the peace plans.[46] Carroll Rasin, Baltimore's club president, also accompanied the three to the meeting.

Representatives of the three leagues, along with several minor league officials, met later that evening at the Waldorf-Astoria Hotel. Early in the meeting, Gilmore assured the assembled parties that the group of himself, Harry Sinclair, Charles Weeghman, and Rasin had full authority to act on behalf of the entire Federal League.[47] Notably, Rasin never disputed this assertion, a fact that would become significant in subsequent litigation. The parties then began walking through the tentative agreement reached between the Federal and National Leagues several days earlier, approving the first several provisions of the deal without objection.

By the time the conference reached the topic of the Federal League's assumption of liability for its remaining player contracts, however, Harry Sinclair interrupted the proceedings to announce that the Federals were not necessarily prepared to accept this provision in its entirety. Instead, he explained that he and Gilmore had negotiated the proposed agreement on the understanding it would serve merely as the framework for the settlement, with the final details left to be worked out during the current meeting. For instance, he noted, the proposed agreement did not include any provisions relating to the Federal League's Baltimore, Buffalo, or Kansas City franchises.[48]

This announcement generated quite a bit of consternation among organized baseball's officials, especially the American League owners who had traveled from Chicago on the understanding that they would simply be ratifying the agreement presented to them by Barney Dreyfuss a couple of days earlier. Jim Gilmore sought to assure the magnates that the Federals still agreed to "the meat of that tentative agreement," but just wanted to fine-tune its wording. Eventually, both sides agreed that the Federals could call an attorney into the room to advise them regarding the terms of the proposed deal.[49] Gilmore sent word to Stuart Janney, the Baltimore Federals' attorney who had accompanied the team's delegation to New York that morning, and was apparently the only Federal League lawyer present in the city.

Upon his arrival at the meeting, Janney—himself a shareholder in the Baltimore franchise—did not address the player contract issue, but instead launched into a discussion of his team's interest in the peace negotiations. Janney's participation in the meeting would later become a central issue in Baltimore's subsequent litigation against organized baseball. The attorney stated that his city wanted a big-league franchise and was willing to purchase an existing team from its owner. He also promised that his clients would provide an attendance guarantee to ensure that the other clubs in the league did not lose any road ticket revenue as a result of transferring a team to the city. August Herrmann eventually interrupted Janney, asking him if he realized that the relocation of a franchise would require the unanimous consent of the other teams in the league. Herrmann then surveyed the National League owners to see if they would approve a change to the league's circuit. After receiving several no votes, Janney dejectedly acknowledged that his proposal seemed to have been rejected.[50]

Herrmann then reminded Janney that the American League might still be willing to allow one of its franchises to move to Baltimore. Knowing that his league would never approve the relocation of a team to the city, but sensing an opportunity to have some fun with the attorney, Chicago White Sox owner Charles Comiskey sarcastically asked how much Baltimore would be willing to pay for his team. Comiskey then suggested that the city really did not want a major league squad at all, but instead simply sought a minor league franchise.[51] Janney denied this, but the Chicagoan continued to bait him: "Baltimore, a minor league city, and not a hell of a good one at that," Comiskey eventually declared.[52]

"That's right," chimed in Brooklyn Dodgers owner Charles Ebbets. "It is one of the worst minor league towns in this country. . . . You have too many colored population to start with. They are a cheap population when it gets down to paying their money at the gate."[53]

At this point, August Herrmann intervened to restore order: "Well, the Baltimore representative is certainly entitled to this hearing, but it must be very evident that a condition of this kind that you seek cannot be brought about. . . ." Sensing that he was fighting a losing battle, Janney asked if some other accommodation for Baltimore might be possible, with the parties eventually agreeing to defer the matter to a committee to be formed at a later date.[54]

The officials then returned their focus to approving the tentative peace agreement. In particular, they discussed the dismissal of the antitrust suit before Judge Landis. The National League's attorney, John Toole, suggested that the suit should be dismissed before an agreement was finalized, so that the leagues did not find themselves "in disfavor with the Court out there," given Judge Landis's "decided notions on what ought to be done." The Federals objected to this proposal, with Janney instead offering that "the most that could be done . . . would be to wire our respective counsel to appear before the Court tomorrow and advise him that there are matters under discussion which may ultimately result in an agreement . . . and suggest it would be proper for him to delay rendering a decision. . . ."[55]

Toole disagreed, arguing that the Federals had nothing to lose at this point by dismissing the suit, noting the apparent absurdity of Charles Weeghman negotiating to purchase a team as part of the settlement while continuing to simultaneously charge that the club belonged to an organization that was "a criminal conspiracy." The Federals ultimately put their foot down, however, with Harry Sinclair asserting that dismissing the suit before a settlement had been finalized amounted to asking the rival league to sign a blank check. Consequently, the parties agreed to have their attorneys ask Judge Landis whether he would object to a settlement of the action, and planned to resume the deliberations a few days later in Cincinnati.[56]

Despite the lack of a definitive agreement, both sides appeared confident that they would eventually reach a suitable deal. Ban Johnson announced to the press that peace was assured, while Jim Gilmore predicted that "you will hear that a satisfactory agreement has been signed between the Federal League and Organized Ball" in the next couple of days.[57]

The parties reconvened at the Sinton Hotel in Cincinnati on December 22, where a sizable crowd gathered outside to catch a glimpse of the baseball magnates. The three members of the National Commission represented organized baseball at the meeting, while Gilmore, Weeghman, and Sinclair appeared on behalf of the Federal League. Although there is no indication what, if anything, the two sides had learned from Judge Landis in the interim, they were quickly able to finalize the peace settlement upon resuming their discussions. The final agreement largely incorporated the terms that had been agreed to by the Federal and National Leagues a few days earlier in New York, with a few modifications. Specifically, Harry Sinclair agreed to accept liability for the remaining player contracts belonging to the Federal League's Kansas City, Buffalo, and Newark franchises, while the circuit's other teams would assume responsibility for their own remaining contracts (the Chicago and St. Louis Federals would ultimately be permitted to amalgamate their players with the rosters of the major league teams their owners were acquiring in the settlement). In exchange, the two major leagues each agreed to pay Sinclair $10,000 per year for the next ten years, a total payoff of $200,000.[58]

Although the leagues were able to resolve the matter of the Federals' remaining player contracts, the Baltimore situation proved more vexing. The two sides initially discussed granting the BaltFeds' shareholders a franchise in the International League, but the minor league's president Ed Barrow quickly vetoed that plan.[59] Barrow's unwillingness to work with the Feds was understandable given that his circuit had sustained heavy financial losses the previous two years while combating Federal League competition in several of its key cities (including Baltimore, Buffalo, and Newark). As the Cincinnati conference was winding down, Jim Gilmore made one final effort to resolve the situation by calling Baltimore's officials and asking, "Will the Baltimore stockholders take $50,000 in settlement and keep the ball grounds and the ball team?"[60]

"Unquestionably, they will not," replied Janney. "[T]he ball team . . . [and] grounds would be a liability and not an asset."

Gilmore then asked what they wanted, and Janney offered, "If you bring us a proposition of $75,000 and you take the ball team and grounds, then we might consider it." Gilmore said he would confer with the other dealmakers, but quickly called back to report, "There is nothing doing on that. You better take the other [offer]." Janney refused, and instead threatened to oppose the withdrawal of the antitrust suit before Judge Landis or move for an injunction to prevent the peace agreement from going into effect.[61]

Consequently, organized baseball and the Federal League officials again agreed to defer resolution of the Baltimore situation, delegating the issue to a separate committee consisting of the three members of the National Commission, Gilmore, the International League's Barrow, and one representative each from the BaltFeds and BuffFeds—whose shareholders were also holding out hope for some consideration in the final settlement—to be appointed by Gilmore. After the agreement was signed, the magnates welcomed the press into the room, where Herrmann recited the terms of the peace pact. After announcing that "[a]ll Federal League magnates, players and umpires are hereby made eligible for Organized Baseball," he joked that "[w]e would also make the fans eligible, but there weren't any." Jim Gilmore reportedly responded "with a low cry of anguish" before "ordering refreshments for the crowd."[62]

Herrmann also announced that he remained hopeful that a mutually agreeable solution to Baltimore's grievances could be found: "We have done nothing regarding Baltimore and the final outcome may be very advantageous to the Baltimore Federal League owners. That matter is still in the hands of the committee appointed to settle that question. The Baltimore people may get more than they have anticipated."[63]

Several days after the Cincinnati meeting, John Tener wrote to George Pepper explaining the league's decision to enter a settlement despite the attorney having advised against it. Tener defended the action by noting that although Pepper's recommendations were considered and appreciated, the owners ultimately decided they could not afford to wait any longer. "All parties concerned, after waiting patiently for almost a year for Judge Landis to render a decision, have decided that for all they know the decision may never be rendered, and they could not go on indefinitely in the baseball business under present conditions." He closed the letter by noting, "All has been done in good faith and I sincerely hope no grevious [*sic*] error has been made."[64]

The committee to resolve the Baltimore issue was prepared to meet in Cincinnati on January 5, 1916, but never held a formal meeting. Indeed, although the Baltimore delegation was in town, it refused to attend the meeting, instead sending a letter to August Herrmann threatening to hold the National Commission accountable for any damages the franchise sustained as a result of the peace agreement. The team was understandably hesitant to place its fate in the hands of the committee given that a majority of its membership was clearly predisposed to settle the matter with little regard to Baltimore's interests. Nevertheless, the committee announced that it would reconvene two weeks later in New York City.[65]

Before the group could meet again, however, International League president Ed Barrow announced that he was resigning from the committee, having grown fed-up with Baltimore's delay. Barrow declared that he would refuse to engage in any further discussions regarding the resolution of the Federals' concerns, and that his league would not accept any of its former rivals in its ownership ranks.[66] This effectively put an end to any speculation that the Baltimore would be given a franchise in the minor league.

As the weeks continued to pass and no prospects for a settlement appeared on the horizon, the Baltimore shareholders voted unanimously on January 27 to raise $50,000 to continue pursuing an antitrust lawsuit against the major leagues. The club believed it had a strong chance to secure a damages verdict under the Clayton Act, which in turn would be tripled under the law.[67] The *Sporting News* trivialized the announcement, declaring, "The Baltimore people are not helping their case any by threatening dire things in court unless they get what they want." The paper went on to argue that "[i]f the whole Federal League, with its boasted financial backing and its high-priced legal talent, could not get a Federal court decision that would disrupt the foundations of baseball as a national institution, it is not likely that one set of disgruntled adventurers in a discredited city can succeed. And even should they do the worst they threaten, they probably would find that they had accomplished little." It further speculated that the team was simply seeking a settlement sufficient to allow its shareholders to pay off an earlier $50,000 loan they had incurred following the 1915 season.[68] Had this been the case, however, then the team would presumably have accepted Gilmore's final offer in late December.

Some within organized baseball were similarly skeptical of Baltimore's ability to derail the peace process at this late date, though, reportedly believing instead that the team's litigation threats were merely a "monumental bluff." For instance, Ban Johnson stated that he was "in no way interested in what the Baltimore club does," while new Chicago Cubs owner Charles Weeghman added, "I suppose the real trouble is that they want a major league franchise. I understand there isn't a chance for them to get it."[69]

At the same time Baltimore officials were raising the funds necessary to pursue antitrust litigation, one of the team's shareholders was attempting to persuade the federal government to launch its own investigation of the peace agreement under the Sherman Act. In particular, club stockholder Henry Strohmeyer persuaded Baltimore Congressman John Linthicum to contact the U.S. attorney general to inquire about whether the settlement was illegal. The Justice Department responded several days later, issuing a statement "that the transaction does not appear to constitute any ground for action." Nevertheless, Linthicum vowed to pursue a possible congressional inquiry on behalf of Baltimore, an investigation that never materialized.[70]

The longer the Baltimore stalemate dragged on, the more anxious organized baseball became to have the antitrust suit before Judge Landis dismissed. Ban Johnson eventually forced the issue, threatening to refuse to execute any more provisions of the peace agreement until the suit was withdrawn. Johnson's posturing finally persuaded the Federals that the time had come to dismiss the suit. Attorneys representing both the Federal League and organized baseball appeared before Landis on Friday, February 4, 1916—more than a year after the initial hearing—formally notifying the court that the case had been tentatively settled, and requesting that it be dismissed. The Federals' attorney was forced to admit, however, that the "Baltimore club objects to this dismissal." As a result, Landis scheduled a hearing for the following Monday, February 7, at which time he ordered Baltimore's attorneys to appear to explain why the team believed the case should not be withdrawn.[71]

As requested, Baltimore attorney Stuart Janney appeared on Monday and explained to Judge Landis that his clients believed the "destruction of the

Federal League is in a sense the very consummation of the conspiracy alleged in the original [complaint]." Janney acknowledged, though, that the present suit was not the appropriate means to challenge the settlement, given that the case had originally been brought to enjoin organized baseball's harassment of the now-defunct Federal League.[72] Thus, he declared, Baltimore would not object to the dismissal of the suit so long as it was allowed to file a new antitrust lawsuit against the major leagues at a later date, an announcement that reportedly sent a "buzz of excitement" through the courtroom.[73] Landis agreed to dismiss the case "without prejudice," enabling the team to pursue its own antitrust litigation in the future.

Judge Landis then offered a few words explaining his nearly thirteen-month delay in rendering a decision in the case:

> The motion for a preliminary injunction was presented to this Court about a year ago, a little over a year ago. The whole structure of organized baseball was thrown into litigation. . . . There was a very full argument of everything involved and a very simple proposition tendered to the Court for the Court's decision. However, from the Court's own knowledge . . . resulting from thirty years of acquaintance with the subject matter of your litigation, before most of you gentlemen who were in that litigation knew anything about any such thing as baseball, convinces [*sic*] the Court that an appropriate order on this application for a temporary injunction reaching to the extent that that order would have to reach . . . would have been if not destructive, vitally injurious to the subject matter of the litigation. . . .
>
> [A]nd so the question which I had to decide in addition to the legal questions submitted by that application, was whether or not I would forthwith enter an order that would . . . therefore necessarily injur[e] the rights of both the litigants, an order in view of the character of which neither litigant could leave the Court a victor. . . . [A]nd I decided, after taking counsel with my own judgment as I had to limit myself to counsel, I decided that this Court had a right, if not a right a discretion, to postpone the announcement of any such order, and that is the reason that the entry of that order was postponed.

Landis closed the proceeding by assuring the audience that "there wasn't the slightest evidence presented to this Court from which the most suspicious person could draw even the shadow of a notion impugning the good faith of [baseball] as a game or any individual ball player's activity as a player."[74]

Following the hearing, Janney announced that August Herrmann had virtually assured him Baltimore's remaining issues would be smoothed over. "I hope this will be speedily accomplished," Janney stated. "The Baltimore Club has an ample remedy at law for any damages which it may sustain and could also proceed under the Clayton act if it does not receive equitable treatment."[75] Indeed, the fact that Judge Landis's pronouncement seemed to indicate he believed the Federals had presented a legitimate case under federal antitrust law surely emboldened Baltimore's belief that it could prevail in a later suit.

The *Sporting News* had a different take, however, arguing that Landis's declaration was a moral victory for the major leagues that would be difficult for future opponents of organized baseball to overcome. The paper reasoned that Landis's decision to delay his ruling in the case would persuade future courts to show similar caution when applying antitrust law to the nation's pastime, to ensure that they did not harm the game.[76]

Meanwhile, although some have subsequently criticized Landis for sitting on the case for more than a year, effectively ensuring the Federal League's demise, this criticism is not entirely fair.[77] During the hearing in January 1915, the Federals limited their immediate request for relief to an injunction prohibiting organized baseball from doing two things: (i) interfering with its players, such as by initiating or continuing to prosecute any court actions, and (ii) denigrating the league in the press by questioning its financial condition or referring to it and its players with derogatory terms like "contract jumper" or "outlaw." Though the major leagues did persuade several Federal League players to return to organized ball prior to the start of the season, overall organized baseball did not significantly interfere with the Federals in 1915. Notably, no new litigation was initiated by the major leagues against the Federal League or its players following the hearing before Judge Landis. While it is of course possible that the league would have received a boost from a favorable ruling in the case, overall the Federals effectively received much of the relief they had sought from organized baseball's deference to the pending judicial proceeding. Indeed, the confluence of a national economic recession in the mid-1910s and the onset of World War I greatly undermined the financial viability of the Federal League, irrespective of any favorable court ruling it might have received. Thus, the ultimate impact of Landis's refusal to rule has probably been overstated.

For his part, August Herrmann took issue with the final portion of Judge Landis's statement. He feared that Landis's declaration that the players had not been impugned in any way by the lawsuit could be interpreted as a sign that they had done nothing wrong by jumping their contracts. He also worried about Baltimore's unresolved grievance, urging Ban Johnson that "[i]n my judgment, we should take some action with reference to this matter and try to straighten out the Baltimore situation, if we can, in order to prevent further litigation."[78]

As Herrmann soon discovered, however, reaching a resolution with Baltimore would prove quite difficult.

6

An Aborted Trial

February 1916 to June 1917

In the weeks following the dismissal of the Federal League's antitrust suit, organized baseball worked behind the scenes to resolve its budding dispute with the Baltimore Federals. The efforts to assuage the team were primarily focused on working out an arrangement between the BaltFeds and their counterparts from Baltimore. Specifically, the major leagues hoped that they could persuade Jack Dunn, owner of the city's International League team, to purchase the BaltFeds' stadium, thereby securing some settlement proceeds for the rival franchise.

A week after Judge Landis dismissed the suit in Chicago, National Commission chairman August Herrmann wrote to American League president Ban Johnson reporting that Dunn was willing to assume the Federals' lease on the park for its remaining eight years at $5,000 per season. Herrmann believed that if Dunn would slightly increase his offer, then the special committee formed to settle the Baltimore situation could adopt the proposition as its suggested resolution of the matter.[1] The National Commission was simultaneously receiving encouragement along these lines from the BaltFeds' attorneys, who wrote to Herrmann in mid-February encouraging the International League to purchase the stadium. Although the lawyers maintained that this would not completely satisfy their clients, they did suggest it would help mitigate the damages that they continued to hold "[t]he National Commission responsible for."[2]

As a result, Dunn and the BaltFeds would continue to negotiate over the next several weeks, to no avail. Ban Johnson reported to Herrmann on February 28 that the International League club had made several different offers to purchase the stadium, all of which were "received in a most discourteous manner." Johnson reiterated his assessment that "[p]ersonally, I have always been prepared to pass on the Baltimore situation." Nevertheless, Herrmann continued to insist, "I do wish this Baltimore matter could be fixed up in some way."[3]

At the same time that organized baseball was dealing with Baltimore, it was also trying to resolve its own outstanding legal fees from the Federal League's antitrust suit. The National League's counsel in the case, George Pepper, submitted a bill to John Tener shortly after Judge Landis dismissed the suit, requesting payment of an additional $5,000 bonus he had been promised if the league received a "favorable decision" in the case (on top of the $5,667.66 he had already received for services rendered). The National League's president objected to the request, arguing that Landis never issued an opinion in the case, and in fact had "indicated that no decision would have [ever] been made."[4]

Nevertheless, Pepper saw no reason why he should not be fully compensated when the National League itself voluntarily settled the case before the court had issued a decision. "This case called for prompt service of a special sort, at the busiest time of the year, and at a distant point. All other business was laid aside and an effort made to put at your disposal the best service that counsel could render." As a result, he asserted, "the sum of $10,000 is, in my judgment, reasonable professional compensation." Pepper closed by politely threatening to sue the league if it did not pay him as agreed: "I should be reluctant to have to press for the collection of a professional charge."[5]

While the National League and its counsel were debating fees, Jack Dunn was making what he intended to be his final offer to the BaltFeds in late February. He agreed to pay the team $20,000 for its stadium and equipment, as well as assume the remaining eight years on the underlying real estate lease. The team failed to accept the offer by Dunn's imposed deadline, however, and as a result he began to move forward with plans to build a new stadium on a different site.[6] Through the negotiations, though, organized baseball learned that the directors of the Baltimore club were apparently divided about whether to accept the purchase offer or instead pursue litigation against the major leagues. In fact, the team's attorney, Stuart Janney, reportedly confessed to Dunn that he was "about ready to drop the whole business" because "he was getting sick of the way his crowd was acting."[7]

Despite his earlier pledge not to work with the Federals, International League president Ed Barrow nevertheless implored Dunn to make one final offer to the Baltimore ownership group in hopes of resolving the team's complaints once and for all.[8] Dunn reluctantly agreed, increasing his offer to $25,000 along with the assumption of the lease. The BaltFeds accepted the offer on March 3, 1916, during a meeting of the franchise's shareholders.[9]

Upon receiving word of the agreement, the press speculated that the transaction effectively resolved Baltimore's claim against organized baseball.[10] August Herrmann hoped to take advantage of the deal by proposing that the special committee tasked with resolving Baltimore's grievances endorse Dunn's purchase as the final settlement of the team's interests. The National Commission's chairman continued to fear "that unless the Committee take some action in this matter that organized baseball may be involved in some damages suit later on."[11] The BaltFeds' attorneys quickly disabused Herrmann of the notion that they were satisfied with the transaction, however, sending a letter to the chairman explaining that the $25,000 purchase price for the stadium "represents a great loss, but we were obligated to take it as there was only one market available." "You will, of course, understand that the Federal Base Ball Club of Baltimore, Inc. holds you and the members of the National Commission and the constituent members of the Leagues represented by you responsible for all loss sustained," the attorneys warned.[12]

Consequently, with the threat of litigation persisting, Herrmann suggested that the National Commission suspend any payments to the other former Federal League teams under the peace agreement until the Baltimore situation was resolved. He argued that it might "be unwise for us to settle with the Pittsburg [*sic*], Brooklyn and Newark Federal League Clubs until we have satisfactory assurance that there will be no litigation along the lines indicated in this communication."[13] Indeed, by withholding payments to the other Federal League magnates, the major leagues would increase the pressure on their former rivals to resolve Baltimore's grievances internally.

As the weeks continued to pass without a resolution, the *Sporting News* ridiculed Baltimore for continually threatening to sue without ever following through: "We plead with the Baltimore Feds to get busy—file that suit and end this terrible suspense." Several days later, however, the *Baltimore Sun* reported that the team would in fact soon be launching an antitrust suit against the major leagues, once its attorney of choice, William Glasgow, returned from a vacation in Bermuda.[14]

Indeed, the BaltFeds gave the *Sporting News* what it asked for on March 29, 1916, filing a federal antitrust suit against organized baseball in the United States District Court in Philadelphia, Pennsylvania. Its complaint named the National League, the American League, and their sixteen member teams as defendants, along with Herrmann, Johnson, Tener, and three of the Federal League's former magnates: Jim Gilmore, Charles Weeghman, and Harry Sinclair. The team clearly relied heavily upon the complaint the Federal League filed in Chicago, even going so far as to repeat some of the same mistakes the earlier document had contained when identifying the major league teams' formal corporate names. After describing the

American and National Leagues generally, Baltimore's complaint discussed the two league offices' sources of revenue, including their contracts with equipment manufacturers and their allotted share of each team's ticket sales. Obviously aware of the central role that the interstate commerce issue had played in the Chicago suit, the team alleged that these activities rendered the "business of giving exhibitions of baseball for profit in and among the various States of the United States . . . essentially and fundamentally commerce among the several States." The complaint then parroted the language of Sections 1 and 2 of the Sherman Act, accusing the defendants of both entering "into a contract . . . combination . . . or conspiracy . . . in restraint of trade," and having "monopolized or attempted to monopolize" the industry.[15]

From there, Baltimore continued to build its case that federal antitrust law applied to professional baseball by explaining that the business required the transportation of both players and umpires across state lines to stage exhibitions between teams from different cities. In particular, the club alleged that organized baseball increased its profits by pitting teams from various states and regions against one another, contending that "intercity, interstate and intersection competition is the very essence of the business of baseball." As the Federal League had done before, the complaint then accused the National Commission of maintaining control over the nation's supply of professional players through its blacklisting and reservation practices, claiming that the stated purposes of the National Agreement "are, for the most part, pretenses, shams, subterfuges and disguises." It also repeated the allegations from the earlier action in Chicago, charging that organized baseball had conspired to destroy the Federal League by calling it financially irresponsible and threatening to blacklist its players.[16]

Baltimore's complaint then turned to new accusations, discussing the suit filed with Judge Landis and asserting that the National Commission had, "through cash contributions and by persuasion or intimidation," caused each of the Federal League's other seven teams to agree to withdraw the suit and no longer compete with the major leagues. It walked through the various settlement provisions granted to its former colleagues, accusing Gilmore, Sinclair, and Weeghman of agreeing to join organized baseball's conspiracy in exchange for "pecuniary and other advantages." The club explained that the collapse of its league had effectively driven it out of professional baseball, noting that a franchise must belong to an organization of at least five other teams to provide consistent competition. By destroying the rival circuit, it argued, organized baseball and the former Federal League executives had illegally conspired to eliminate competition in the baseball industry, in violation of both federal and state antitrust law.[17] Thus, the BaltFeds were asserting the very type of claim that the major leagues' attorneys had feared prior to the execution of the peace agreement.

However, rather than seek an injunction dissolving the National Agreement and National Commission—as the earlier Federal League suit had requested—Baltimore only sought monetary damages in compensation for its loss. Specifically, the team alleged that it had been harmed by a total of $300,000, a sum it contended should then be trebled—in accordance with a provision in the Clayton Act—bringing its entire request for relief to $900,000.[18] Although Baltimore did not itself seek an injunction in the case, the press nevertheless speculated that the federal government might try to obtain one by launching a formal investigation of the baseball monopoly should the team prevail in the suit.[19]

Organized baseball's leadership responded confidently to the suit. August Herrmann declared that it "had been expected for a long time. Personally I do not believe the Baltimore people have a leg to stand on in the courts."[20] John Tener also denied liability, arguing that "[i]t was our understanding that the Federal League was acting for all its component clubs and had proper authority so to act in everything that was done toward a settlement of all conditions. In effecting an adjustment of baseball conditions we are satisfied we did nothing inconsistent with the Sherman anti-trust law or the Clayton act. Therefore, we fail to see where we are liable as set forth in the suit of the Baltimore Federal League Club."[21]

New Chicago Cubs owner Charles Weeghman—a defendant in the suit—similarly dismissed the claims, contending that "[a]t the time of the dissolution of the Federal League, President James A. Gilmore, Harry Sinclair of New York and I were authorized by the six Federal clubs in good standing to settle the affairs of the league. We thought we did settle them in the best way possible, and, until this suit action [*sic*] was made public I thought everybody was satisfied. . . . President Carol Raisen [*sic*] of the Baltimore Club was one of the club leaders who authorized us three to go ahead and settle the affairs of the league." Weeghman then added, "I am sure President Gilmore, Mr. Sinclair and I did all in our power for all the clubs and men concerned in the peace settlement."[22]

The reliably partisan *Sporting News* also dismissed the BaltFeds' chances in the case: "the Baltimoreans, all legal authorities seem to agree, have nothing to back up their claims whatsoever." The publication acknowledged that "[a]s a matter of simple justice, they probably were as much entitled to such payments as were those who shared in the holdup, but they were not sharp enough to get their bit then, and there is small hope for them to get it now through a lawsuit." It further accused the team of hypocrisy: "Having turned up its nose at filthy lucre once it has the nerve to ask it now. To be consistent it should stick to its first demands and ask the court to provide it with a franchise in one of the major leagues."[23]

In the same issue, the *Sporting News* also ran a column by noted baseball columnist and Federal League critic Joe Vila, who declared, "Baltimore, always a minor league city, is the victim of false pride and absurd claims." Vila suggested that organized baseball could defend itself by arguing that the team's hands were unclean because it had repudiated all of its remaining player contracts after the Federal League folded (an allegation that would later prove untrue).[24] Though the major leagues would ultimately allude to Baltimore's own unethical conduct during the proceedings, they would not formally assert the unclean hands defense in the trial because the argument only applied in cases seeking an injunction, not a damages suit like that filed by Baltimore.

The initiation of Baltimore's lawsuit quickly motivated organized baseball to take several related actions. First, now once again requiring his services, the National League agreed to pay George Pepper the entire $5,000 bonus he had demanded for the favorable resolution of the antitrust suit before Judge Landis. It then retained him to lead its defense against Baltimore.[25]

Then, adopting August Herrmann's earlier suggestion, organized baseball informed the other former Federal League owners that it would suspend any further payments under the peace agreement until the new lawsuit was resolved. The major leagues reasoned that both sides had agreed that each of their members would be bound by the pact, and until the Federals could show that all of their teams would abide by the settlement, organized baseball was not obligated to uphold its end of the agreement. "It is apparent that the Federal League has not carried out the obligations it took in the peace agreement," John Tener explained. "The National and American Leagues naturally decline to pay for something that they have not received. Until the Federal League keeps its promises and secures from its constituent clubs an acceptance of the peace agreement, no payment will be made under the agreement."[26] Although the Federals complained that the decision was unfair, the major leagues' attorneys remained confident that the former rivals would not sue to enforce the peace agreement, believing they would instead "make efforts at adjustment before hazarding a law suit."[27]

Unlike most of the earlier litigation between the Federal League and organized baseball, there was no need for the court to hold an immediate hearing to consider whether to grant preliminary relief since Baltimore did not request an injunction. Instead, the suit proceeded on a much slower timetable than the earlier legal skirmishes, with Baltimore spending much of the summer of 1916 serving the official court summons upon the twenty-four defendants in the case. The team presumably chose to file suit in Philadelphia because it was the closest city with teams in both the American and National Leagues, enabling the BaltFeds to serve each major league team with process when it visited town.[28]

The team nevertheless found it difficult to serve several of the defendants. First, the three former Federal League magnates named in the case—Jim Gilmore, Charles Weeghman, and Harry Sinclair—each attempted to evade service by ceasing to travel through Pennsylvania for business, rerouting any trips to New York City through other states. The tactic proved effective, as none of the three were ever served with process in the case.[29]

Meanwhile, two of the major league team defendants formally contested Baltimore's manner of service in Philadelphia. Both the St. Louis Browns and the Washington Senators petitioned the court to set aside the plaintiff's attempted service, arguing that the court documents had not been presented to an agent legally authorized to accept service on each respective team's behalf. They also denied that they were transacting any business in the state, thus contending that they were not subject to the Pennsylvania court's jurisdiction.[30] It is not clear why these were the only two teams to challenge the service of process. Baltimore responded to the petitions by asking the court to issue new summons for both clubs to be served in their home states, pursuant to a provision in the Clayton Act. St. Louis again objected to this subsequent service attempt, reiterating its argument that it was not subject to the Pennsylvania court's jurisdiction because it did not transact sufficient business in the state.[31] Unfortunately, the record does not reflect how the court resolved the dispute.

Rather than contest service, the majority of the defendants instead willingly submitted themselves to the court's jurisdiction by filing answers—styled "Affidavits in Defense"—to Baltimore's complaint. These responses were filed intermittently over the rest of 1916 and early 1917, after each defendant was formally served with process in the lawsuit.[32] In the answers, the defendants denied that they were engaged in interstate commerce—once again characterizing any transportation of players or umpires as "incidental"—or that they had dominated and controlled the supply of professional players. Rather, they insisted, they simply signed players to voluntary and lawful contracts. The defendants further denied that the National Agreement was intended to restrict competition in the industry, instead asserting that it was formed out of necessity to centralize the management of the game and increase the public's confidence in the sport. Relatedly, they contended, their rules and regulations were "reasonable . . . for the holding of successful public exhibitions of the national game." As a result, the defendants denied that they had violated the law, either by conspiring in restraint of trade or by monopolizing the professional baseball industry.[33]

Although organized baseball had originally vowed that it would not settle the lawsuit—instead reportedly desiring to have the antitrust issue decided once and for all—by November 1916 the major leagues appeared more amenable to resolving the case out of court. A series of press reports announced that the two leagues had come to the conclusion that they needed to settle Baltimore's suit, but disagreed about how to do so. The American League was apparently floating a plan in which Baltimore would be offered a spot in a new, third major league to be established from existing International League and American Association minor league squads. The National League reportedly did not believe the BaltFeds would agree to such a scheme, and instead pushed the American League to shift its notoriously unprofitable Washington franchise to Baltimore, a proposition that the junior circuit rejected.[34]

There were several possible motivations for organized baseball's new, apparent amenability to settlement. First, by November several of the Federal League's former owners had grown increasingly frustrated that their settlement proceeds were being held up because of Baltimore's suit, threatening to initiate their own legal action to force payment under the peace agreement. The *Sporting News* reported that these same magnates were in fact discussing a possible revival of the Federal League.[35]

In addition to the pressure being applied by the restless former Federal Leaguers, organized baseball now also reportedly believed that Baltimore's suit presented a serious threat. As *St. Louis Globe-Democrat* columnist John Sheridan recounted, despite August "Herrmann's bold talk . . . the suit of the Baltimore Federal League club to recover damages . . . is giving the powers of [the major league] organizations no end of worry." "Had Judge Landis been obliged to give a decision it is understood that the fabric of Organized Baseball would have been torn to pieces," he explained.[36] Indeed, as George Pepper warned John Tener early in the most recent proceedings, not only would Baltimore be able to assert the same contentions presented in the Federals' earlier case, but the team's complaint also asserted new conspiracy claims arising out of the peace agreement that "differ[ed] entirely from the action brought at Chicago; hence [requiring] preparation . . . along entirely different lines."[37]

Even the *Sporting News* was forced to concede that "there are several points in which the plaintiff Baltimoreans are better fortified . . . than were the complainants in the old suit of the Feds." In addition to being able to take advantage of all of the arguments that were previously asserted during the Chicago antitrust suit, the paper believed the team would also benefit greatly from its new conspiracy claim. Gilmore, Weeghman, and Sinclair "will be compelled to face court in defense of the very principles which they opposed," it predicted. "They will have to defend the institutions which they sought to destroy." "Imagine the glee of a well-trained lawyer turned loose against this trio, especially Charles Weeghman, who has entered Organized Baseball, which he helped to fight in the Landis suit against this same body!" Consequently, the paper cautioned, the BaltFeds' suit presented "just as great a menace to the peace and permanence of baseball as it is at present conducted . . . as there was in the one before Judge Landis," warning that "Organized Baseball has no right to take this case lightly or be overconfident."[38]

Despite the major leagues' reported anxiety over the case, it does not appear that they seriously pursued a settlement with Baltimore at the time. Instead, as the calendar turned to 1917, both sides continued their preparations for trial. The suit was originally scheduled to begin on February 13, and then later on April 12, only to be postponed by agreement of counsel each time.[39]

Because both sides would be presenting live testimony from their witnesses in court, they were not required to submit formal affidavits as had been the norm in the earlier, expedited Federal League litigations in which the courts had generally relied only on written testimony because of time constraints. Instead, the parties worked to procure the evidence they would need for trial. In March, Baltimore sent out a series of eighteen subpoenas requesting that the defendants produce various documents or asking the court to compel certain witnesses to appear to testify at the trial. For example, the team demanded that the defendants bring to court copies of the initial, tentative peace agreement and final signed settlement with the Federal League, as well as both major leagues' contracts with Western Union and their official equipment manufacturers. Baltimore also sought to compel the attendance of legendary Philadelphia manager Cornelius McGillicuddy—better known as Connie Mack—and reporter Joe Vila from the *New York Evening Sun* as potential witnesses in the trial. Similarly, the defendants filed their own subpoena requesting that Jim Gilmore be compelled to attend the hearing to testify as a witness, and asking that he bring a number of Federal League documents with him to court.[40]

At the same time both sides were making their final preparations for trial, they were also dealing with changes to their legal teams. Originally, the American League had hired renowned Philadelphia attorney John G. Johnson, perhaps the leading Supreme Court litigator of his time, to represent it, while the National League had once again engaged George Pepper and his colleague Samuel Clement. However, the seventy-seven-year-old Johnson died on April 14, 1917, after a brief illness. As a result, the American League was forced to replace Johnson with his law partner, Frank P. Prichard, another prominent Philadelphia attorney.[41]

Meanwhile, Baltimore had retained the aforementioned William Glasgow Jr., considered at the time to be one of the nation's leading authorities on the Sherman Act. Although the noted "trust-buster" continued to sign court filings on behalf of the plaintiff up until the morning the trial began, for unexplained reasons it became impossible for him to argue the case himself.[42] As a result, the BaltFeds' attorney and shareholder, Stuart Janney—a forty-three-year-old graduate of the University of Maryland Law School—was forced to try the case to the jury, with Glasgow's associate Chester Farr assisting him in the representation. Janney was ill prepared to handle the demands of Baltimore's case on such short notice, but nevertheless elected not to seek another continuance of the trial.[43]

The day before the trial was scheduled to begin, the National Commission held one final meeting with its attorneys to prepare the defense of their case. After the meeting, National League counsel Samuel Clement shot down any remaining rumors that the major leagues would settle the case: "Our defense is complete, and it will be a fight to the finish."[44] Indeed, the *Sporting News* was now reporting that the previous winter's rumors that the American League would relocate its Washington franchise to Baltimore had in fact originated from the BaltFeds as a bluff.[45]

The trial in *Federal Baseball Club of Baltimore, Inc. v. National League of Professional Baseball Clubs* began promptly at 10 A.M. on Monday, June 11, 1917. A number of baseball dignitaries were in attendance for the start of the proceedings, including not only the three members of the National Commission, but also the owners of the Boston Braves, Brooklyn Dodgers, Philadelphia Athletics, and Philadelphia Phillies, all of whom reportedly "listened intently to ever[y] word of testimony and arguement [*sic*]."[46] Federal district court Judge Oliver B. Dickinson presided over the trial. The fifty-nine-year-old jurist had been appointed to the federal bench three years earlier by President Woodrow Wilson. With no known connections to baseball, Judge Dickinson was not expected to be as familiar with, or as deferential to, the national pastime as Judge Landis had been in the earlier Federal League suit.[47] Indeed, on several occasions throughout the trial, the judge asked the attorneys to provide a further explanation of some feature of the sport, owing to the fact that he was learning many of the details for the first time.

The proceedings began with each side's counsel presenting their opening statements to the jury. Although the statements unfortunately were not transcribed, from contemporaneous press reports we know that Stuart

Baltimore Federals shareholder and attorney Stuart Janney stepped in at the last minute to serve as the team's primary counsel during its trial in Philadelphia (Photo courtesy of Stuart S. Janney III)

Janney spoke on behalf of Baltimore, while George Pepper represented the defendants. Janney provided a lengthy preview of the plaintiff's case, tracing the history of professional baseball from 1873 through the formation of the Federal League and its ultimate demise in 1915. In particular, he alleged the BaltFeds were completely unaware of the Federal League's negotiations with organized baseball until after the peace agreement was consummated,

Judge Oliver B. Dickinson presided over Baltimore's antitrust suit in Philadelphia (First published in *History of the Delaware County National Bank: With Biographical Notes of Its Officers*)

and contended that the major leagues' monopoly and reserve clause had forced Baltimore to pay advance salaries totaling $30,000 to entice players to sign with the team. Janney also addressed the issue of whether professional baseball was interstate commerce, and thus subject to the Sherman Act, focusing on the frequent travel between states by organized baseball's more than ten thousand players. Moreover, he noted, every major league team was required to maintain a scoreboard providing live updates from other games across the country, illustrating the importance of interstate competition to the business. Given these facts, Janney pledged that the plaintiff would prove that organized baseball had engaged in "a clear case of restraint of trade" in violation of federal antitrust law.[48]

Meanwhile, Pepper introduced the defense's case by contending that baseball was not a commercial business and thus was not subject to federal antitrust law. The attorney further insisted that organized baseball never intended to monopolize the industry, but instead entered the peace agreement with the Federals merely to restore public confidence in the game. He also tried to paint Baltimore's case as being disingenuous, noting that the franchise tried to acquire a major league team well before it decided to charge organized baseball with being an illegal monopoly. Finally, he defended the reserve clause by arguing that it was more than fair to players, asserting that players always agreed to the provision under their own free will.[49]

Following the opening statements, Stuart Janney began the presentation of Baltimore's case by calling L. Edwin Goldman—one of the franchise's original incorporators and a member of its board of directors—to the stand as the trial's first witness.[50] The decision to have Goldman testify highlighted an awkward aspect of the plaintiff's case: like Janney, Goldman was also serving as counsel to the team in the trial, meaning that two of Baltimore's attorneys were themselves key witnesses to the events at issue in the suit (Janney had participated in the peace conference at the Waldorf-Astoria in December 1915). In this sense, it may have been more practical for the team to have allowed Glasgow's associate Chester Farr to try the case himself, thereby avoiding any apparent conflict of interest on the part of its attorney-witnesses.

In any event, Goldman's testimony initially focused on the formation of the BaltFeds, as well as the general structure and operation of professional baseball. He explained that the club had approximately seven hundred shareholders coming "from every walk in life," and had employed twenty-five players for both the 1914 and 1915 seasons. He also discussed the construction of the team's stadium, noting that the franchise had signed a ten-year lease for the grounds upon which the park was built, and then incurred significant expense to excavate a hill, level the land, install drainage, and build stands.[51]

Moving on to the operation of the professional baseball industry in general, Goldman explained that a franchise must belong to a league of other, similarly situated teams who provide it with the consistent competition necessary to maintain fan interest. In particular, he emphasized the significance of pairing teams from different cities, states, and regions against one another in competition: "it is the city rivalry . . . that is the stimulus that brings the public to the parks." Goldman further noted that, at the time, the major leagues promoted "intersectional" rivalries by compiling and publicizing the results of games involving each league's eastern block of teams against its western franchises.[52]

Turning his attention to the organization of professional baseball, Goldman testified that the industry was controlled by "what was popularly known as Organized Base Ball," a conglomeration employing practically every professional player in the country. Not only did this control allow organized baseball to eliminate any competition between its teams for players, but he further explained that it also provided a barrier to the Federal League's entry into the field, because players were hesitant to leave the major leagues for fear that they would be blacklisted and never allowed to return.[53]

Finally, Janney questioned Goldman about the current status of the Baltimore franchise. Rather than launch into a discussion of how organized baseball had destroyed the Federal League, Goldman instead replied only that the circuit "was disrupted" in January 1916, and as a result Baltimore was unable to continue playing baseball because each of its league rivals had gone out of business. He then explained that the team was thus forced to sell its stadium in an attempt to recoup a portion of its investment.[54]

Frank Prichard handled the cross-examination of Goldman on behalf of the defendants, focusing his interrogation on two primary points: (i) the ability of rival organizations to enter professional baseball, and (ii) Baltimore's own inequitable conduct. On the first point, Prichard forced the witness to acknowledge that the American League had been able to elevate itself to major league status in 1901, and that no law existed preventing "anybody else from forming a Major League." However, when Prichard later asked Goldman what prevented Baltimore from starting its own new league that day, the witness nimbly replied, "the kind of competition that destroyed the one we were just in."[55]

From there, the defense counsel turned his attention to discrediting Baltimore's business practices. While noting that the Federal League had itself maintained a ten-year reserve clause, Prichard questioned the witness about the organization's explicit disregard of organized baseball's reserve provision. The attorney specifically asked Goldman about Baltimore's signing of players like Otto Knabe, John Quinn, and Bill Bailey, each of whom Prichard asserted had repudiated a contractual obligation to organized baseball to sign with the Federals.[56] Though these allegations did not directly undermine Baltimore's case, organized baseball's counsel nevertheless undoubtedly hoped they would sour the jury's impression of the plaintiff's ethics.

Prichard finished his cross-examination by focusing on Baltimore's own role in the settlement of the Federal League war. He suggested that the team had been involved in several peace conferences with the major leagues, an allegation that Goldman staunchly denied. Rather, the witness maintained, the team had not become aware of the settlement negotiations until receiving a telegram from Jim Gilmore on December 15 or 16, 1915. Goldman then insisted that his team only attempted to purchase a major league franchise once it became apparent that the Federal League's fate had been sealed. Following a brief redirect by Janney, during which Goldman confirmed that Baltimore had never consented to having a special committee resolve its grievances under the peace agreement, and a short re-cross-examination, the witness was excused.[57]

Janney's next witness was David Fultz, a former professional player who was then serving as president of the Baseball Players' Fraternity, an early attempt to unionize professional players. Fultz testified that the major leagues faced no real competition at the time his organization was founded in 1912, and that under organized baseball's reserve clause, a player dissatisfied with a contractual offer had no option but to either re-sign with his existing club or else retire. Fultz said that throughout his entire professional career he had only seen two major league contracts that did not include a reserve clause: his own in 1901, and that of Max Carey, the Pittsburgh Pirates' Hall of Fame outfielder, in 1916.[58]

Before Janney could finish his examination of the witness, however, Judge Dickinson interrupted to adjourn the proceedings for the evening.[59] The *Philadelphia Inquirer* complained that the adjournment came "[j]ust when both sides were developing a batting rally and the game was becoming interesting," while the *Christian Science Monitor* summed up the start of the trial by stating, "Judging from the first day's session, the Federal League $900,000 suit against organized baseball is going to be a great legal battle." Indeed, the *Inquirer* noted, both sides' attorneys had large piles of documents with them in court, indicating "that the firing of the big guns is being held back" until later in the suit.[60]

Day two of the trial began with Fultz returning to the witness stand. Janney intended to pick up where he had left off the day before by discussing the necessity of transporting players across state lines, but Judge Dickinson quickly interrupted to inform him that there was no need to rehash the testimony Goldman had provided the day before. Instead, the plaintiff's attorney questioned Fultz about whether anyone from the National Commission had ever asked him to expel a Federal League player from his fraternity's membership. After an extended objection by the defense counsel regarding the relevancy of the incident, which Judge Dickinson overruled, the labor organizer testified that he had automatically suspended the Federals' players under the fraternity's own bylaws. The answer appeared to take Janney by surprise, as he quickly sought to confirm that he had understood Fultz correctly. The witness explained that his fraternity only represented players in certain leagues, so once a player left for the "non-protected" Federal League, his membership in the organization was temporarily suspended.[61]

Janney then asked Fultz again whether anyone from the National Commission had ever requested that he expel players defecting to the Federal League from the fraternity, with the witness confirming that August Herrmann had once made such a demand. Fultz said he refused to comply, however, choosing to remain neutral in the war between the Federals and organized baseball. Fultz's testimony concluded with an abbreviated cross-examination and redirect focused primarily on the importance of the reserve clause in maintaining competitive balance in professional baseball.[62]

The next witness Janney called to the stand was sportswriter Joseph Vila, the notorious Federal League critic who had written a column in the *Sporting News* the year before lambasting Baltimore's suit. Vila's testimony primarily centered on several articles he had written in 1914 and 1915 quoting American League president Ban Johnson. Vila confirmed that Johnson had effectively stated during a 1914 interview that the Federal League was a "joke," and that he would fight the rival league until it was "counted out." The author refused to confirm a quote appearing in a column he had written in 1915, however, admitting that he would often "put things in [those columns] and quote somebody without ever talking to them."[63] For his part, Johnson appeared to approve of the quotations attributed to him in the articles, reportedly making "little effort to suppress his smile" as they were read to the jury.[64]

The final witness of the trial's second day was well-known former major league player and manager Edward Hanlon, a BaltFeds shareholder and member of the team's board of directors. Janney began by asking Hanlon about his extensive career in professional baseball. In particular, the attorney emphasized the witness's expertise in appraising the value of professional baseball teams, as Hanlon had been consulted or personally involved in six different franchise sales. Before Janney could continue, however, Judge Dickinson interrupted to announce that, owing to a pre-existing appointment, he would have to adjourn court early for the day, pushing the rest

Baltimore Federals shareholder Edward "Ned" Hanlon played a central role on the witness stand during the team's suit against organized baseball (Library of Congress, Prints & Photographs Division, LC-DIG-ggbain-17672)

of Hanlon's testimony back until the following morning.[65] The attorneys reportedly used the rest of the afternoon to "thrash out some legal points at issue" in the case among themselves, with the hope of "saving much time that would otherwise be taken up in argument in the court room."[66]

Having established Hanlon's expertise in assessing the value of professional baseball franchises the day before, Janney began Wednesday's session by asking the former major leaguer to place a value on the BaltFeds franchise. Hanlon estimated that the team was worth approximately $205,000 prior to the destruction of the Federal League, given the investments it had made in its stadium, the size of Baltimore's population, and the roster the team had assembled. He later contended that the franchise would have been worth at least $100,000 more had it not been forced to overcome organized baseball's blacklisting policy, which he said required the team to pay excessively high salaries to persuade players to sign.[67]

Janney finished his questioning by asking the witness what had happened to the team's assets after the Federal League collapsed. Hanlon testified that without anyone left to compete against, the franchise's value was completely destroyed. Because the team no longer had any use for its stadium, and the park was fit for no other purpose than playing baseball, the franchise was forced to sell the facility to the only other professional team in town for $25,000. Hanlon also explained that the franchise's remaining player contracts quickly went from being assets to liabilities, because the team was still obligated to pay the players despite no longer having any use for them.[68]

George Pepper conducted the defense's cross-examination of Hanlon. He primarily focused his efforts on undermining the credibility of the witness's valuation of the Baltimore franchise, forcing Hanlon to disclose that not only was he still a stockholder in the club, but that he also owned the land upon which the team had built its stadium. "So . . . when you are asked to place a value on the land and the lease, you are going to be asked to value something that belongs to yourself, is it not so?" Pepper asked. "Yes, sir," the witness replied.[69]

The next witness Janney called was National Commission chairman August Herrmann, who the *Philadelphia Inquirer* described as "a ready witness" easily able to answer "all questions fully and some times at greater length than required."[70] The plaintiff's counsel used the magnate's testimony to emphasize the monopolistic nature of the National Agreement and organized baseball. He began by having the witness acknowledge that the agreement bound practically every professional team in the country. Although Herrmann attempted to argue that there were countless semiprofessional teams operating outside the agreement, he was forced to concede that these squads did not actually compete with organized baseball. The chairman would also later admit that the National League's constitution fixed the minimum ticket prices each of its eight franchises must charge their patrons.[71]

Janney then turned his attention to baseball's interstate elements. He elicited testimony from Herrmann regarding the transportation of players and equipment from state to state, all of which was paid for by the major league teams. He also asked the witness to discuss the major leagues' contracts with Western Union, providing for live game updates to be transmitted nationwide.[72]

Finally, Janney questioned Herrmann about the reserve clause. The witness acknowledged that any player contract not containing the provision had to be specially approved by the National Commission. Although Herrmann insisted that players were nevertheless free to sign contracts without a reserve clause, he conceded that most teams would be unwilling to sign a player to such an agreement, thus admitting that players effectively had to agree to the provision. The chairman also estimated that major league teams spent approximately $400,000 per year purchasing players' contracts from the minor leagues.[73]

During a short cross-examination, Pepper tried to minimize the impact of some of Herrmann's concessions. First, he had the witness discuss the origins of the National Agreement to explain the conditions that necessitated the formation of the pact, with Herrmann recounting that "the conditions were very bad. There was conflict between the American League and the National League, there was rowdyism on the ball field, and discipline could not be maintained." The executive also clarified that the National Commission cared a great deal about the interests of the ballplayer, identifying several protections it had created for players under the sport's governing regulations, and pointing out that salaries had consistently risen since the National Agreement was formed. Finally, Herrmann asserted that nearly everyone in organized baseball was satisfied with the agreement, noting with pride that aside from the Federal League, organized baseball had not been involved in any litigation in the fourteen years since the accord was formed.[74]

On the fourth day of the trial, Janney called Otto Simonson, the Baltimore architect who had designed and supervised the construction of the plaintiff's stadium, to the stand. Janney hoped to have the witness testify regarding the value of the ballpark, but the court sustained an objection by Pepper on the grounds that the architect was not qualified to appraise the structure's postconstruction resale value, but instead could merely discuss its construction costs. As a result, Simonson provided a few trivial details regarding the design of the park before being dismissed.[75]

Janney then recalled Edwin Goldman to the stand to question him about the franchise's damages. Goldman reported that Baltimore remained liable for nearly $47,000 in player contracts it had entered for the 1916 and 1917 seasons. He further testified that although the team had notified each of its players that their services were no longer needed shortly after the Federal League collapsed, it had never disclaimed its liability under the contracts. Finally, Janney asked Goldman to briefly discuss the peace agreement entered between the Federal League and organized baseball. The witness once again avoided any detailed discussion of the negotiations that led to the settlement, instead simply confirming the basic terms of the agreement.[76]

Following Goldman's testimony, Janney abruptly announced that the plaintiff was resting its case.[77] The *Christian Science Monitor* would later state that Baltimore's decision to close its case appeared to have been made "suddenly," while the *Philadelphia Inquirer* reported that the decision "was something of a surprise."[78] Indeed, Baltimore had provided little evidence that organized baseball had actively conspired to damage or destroy the Federal League. The most relevant testimony the plaintiff presented regarding the actual conspiracy itself was Goldman's recitation of the peace agreement's terms, hardly a compelling illustration of the nefarious plot Baltimore had alleged in its complaint.

After the plaintiff rested, the defense called its first witness, National League president John Tener, who the *Sporting News* would later compliment as having "made an excellent witness."[79] Tener discussed the structure of the minor league system, trumpeting the opportunities available to players to advance their careers within organized baseball. He also testified about the National League's various sources of income, admitting that it received $20,000 per year from Spalding for the right to produce the league's official baseball, but denying that the league office received any money from its contract with Western Union (the proceeds of which he claimed were distributed to its eight teams).[80]

Tener then addressed the New York peace conference of December 17, 1915. He started by noting that both Janney and Carroll Rasin attended the meeting on behalf of the Baltimore club. During this discussion, George Pepper acknowledged, "We are a little embarrassed, because the natural course would be to put Mr. Janney on the stand, which we cannot do because he is counsel in the case." Pepper would go on to emphasize Tener's testimony regarding Baltimore's attempts to acquire a major league team during the meeting, arguing that it undermined the plaintiff's present claim that organized baseball was an illegal monopoly. Judge Dickinson questioned the relevance of this testimony, though, suggesting that there was nothing wrong with the franchise "endeavoring to make any substitute arrangement that [it] could" once the demise of its league was assured.[81]

During a brief cross-examination, Baltimore's counsel Chester Farr asked Tener whether any notes existed from the December 17 peace conference, apparently unaware that a stenographer had been present at the meeting. Pepper offered him a copy of the transcript, with Farr responding that he would need to take some time to read through the meeting minutes that evening, and requesting the right to recall Tener later in the proceedings for further cross-examination.[82] It is hard to imagine an attorney being caught so unaware today, given the modern legal system's extensive pretrial discovery process. But under the procedural rules in place in 1917, parties were able to spring potentially explosive evidence like this on the other side in the midst of a trial.

Following Tener's testimony, the defense once again called August Herrmann to the stand. Herrmann began by asserting that rather than raiding the rosters of organized baseball for talent, the Federal League could have instead built a minor league system of its own to develop players. In fact, he noted, the league had attempted to do just that during its final season, affiliating with New England's Colonial League in 1915. During a brief exchange between counsel, Chester Farr acknowledged that he had never heard of the Colonial League before, with the American League's attorney Frank Prichard interjecting, "There is a great deal in your case that you have not heard of, and you will learn some more as you go along. There may be something more you will learn before we get through," perhaps referring to the contents of the peace meeting transcript Farr had just received.[83]

Prichard then asked Herrmann how much he believed the Baltimore club had been worth at the time of the peace agreement. "In my opinion it was not worth a dollar," the executive testified. "I think it had less value than any franchise in the Federal League at that time." He would later explain the basis for his appraisal, stating that he did not believe the team's attendance figures could support the exorbitant salaries it had committed to pay, especially in light of Baltimore's general reputation as a "failure" of a baseball town.[84]

After denying that he had ever asked Fultz to have the Players' Fraternity expel the Federal League's players, Herrmann then addressed the events leading up to the signing of the peace agreement between organized baseball and the rival organization. He said he met with Baltimore's representative prior to the official settlement conference on December 17, at which time they allegedly told him the Federals had authorized a committee of four to represent them at the peace meeting that evening. He then testified that Jim Gilmore repeatedly stated during the meeting that his league's representatives had been authorized to act on behalf of the entire organization. Herrmann also noted that Baltimore refused to attend a meeting of the special committee formed to resolve its grievances a few weeks later in Cincinnati, even though its representatives were in town at the time.[85]

On cross-examination, Farr attacked Herrmann's assertion that the Baltimore club was worthless at the time the Federal League disbanded, asking whether the fact that it was able to sell its park for $25,000 changed his valuation. The magnate said that it did not, because he knew the Federal League was on its last legs at the time, significantly reducing the franchise's value. Farr rejected this explanation, noting that organized baseball paid the Federals more than $400,000 in the settlement, behavior that was hardly consistent with a belief that the league was about to collapse. After a few moments' hesitation, Herrmann nevertheless insisted that the peace agreement was entered to re-establish the public's confidence in the game, but Farr pushed back. "You were not giving money away, were you, to corpses?" he asked, to which Herrmann conceded, "We were not giving it away, no, sir." Before Farr could continue his interrogation, however, Judge Dickinson noted that the adjournment hour had passed, suspending the proceedings until the following morning.[86]

Friday's session began with Stuart Janney making a surprising announcement: "After a full consideration of this case last night by counsel for the Plaintiff, circumstances have arisen which make us desire to discontinue it. I desire to ask leave of the Court, therefore, [to] formally file a motion of discontinuance. I would say that there has been no settlement of the case."[87]

A year later, Janney would explain that after reviewing the transcript of the peace conference at the Waldorf-Astoria, he became convinced that "it was impossible [for him] to try the suit as counsel" because "the defense was based upon circumstances in which [he] personally had taken part."[88] However, at the time of the dismissal in 1917, Janney released a public statement explaining that "[t]he development of the case convinced counsel for the plaintiffs that the representatives of organized baseball had not entered into a conspiracy to destroy the plaintiffs' business. As this was the basis of the plaintiffs' suit, we felt that in fairness to all parties we should ask that the case be discontinued." Janney would later insist that this initial conclusion "was an obvious error."[89]

Indeed, although the stenographic record certainly weakened the plaintiff's case—given that it confirmed both Rasin and Janney had attended the settlement conference and failed to object when Jim Gilmore purported to have full authority to settle the league's affairs—it was not necessarily fatal to Baltimore's suit. As an initial matter, the attorneys potentially could have argued that the actions of the two executives did not legally bind the Baltimore franchise itself, insofar as neither man had ever been formally authorized to represent the team in such a negotiation. More fundamentally, though, the team's complaint also alleged that the National Agreement itself violated antitrust law, and therefore the club could have maintained that it had been harmed by organized baseball's general practices—such as the reserve clause—well before the formation of the peace agreement.

Baltimore's trial counsel, however, had not effectively proven this latter aspect of its case during its abbreviated presentation of evidence, offering relatively little testimony regarding the damaging effects of organized baseball's system under the National Agreement. Consequently, the BaltFeds' attorneys may have sensed that—in light of the stenographic record—their chances of prevailing in the suit were slim, and simply decided to cut their losses before a final judgment was rendered, thereby preserving their right to bring another lawsuit in the future. Had the case resulted in a jury verdict in favor of the major leagues, Baltimore would have been unable to sue organized baseball again for its involvement in the Federal League's demise.

Meanwhile, the dismissal of the suit reportedly was "totally unexpected on the part of the defense." In court, Pepper responded to Janney's announcement by stating that the defense would not object to the dismissal, reiterating that no "suggestion of settlement" had been made. He also expressed his "very great gratification at the [plaintiff's] decision." Both sides' attorneys then thanked each other, as well as Judge Dickinson, for the congenial nature with which the case had been tried. Dickinson concurred, "commending counsel in this case for the manner in which you have conducted it. . . ."[90]

Not surprisingly, the major leagues were overjoyed by the dismissal. "We feel immensely delighted at the result," August Herrmann announced. "It proves that we are operating fairly, and that organized baseball comes out of court with clean hands." Similarly, John Tener declared: "The outcome of this suit is a vindication of the integrity of baseball, and I feel much gratified. Monetary settlement of this affair was impossible, to have paid one cent to the Baltimore club would have been a tacit confession that organized baseball was guilty of the charges made, and for that reason we were prepared to make a fight to the finish. . . ." Meanwhile, Ban Johnson claimed that he was "not at all surprised at the result. There was never any conspiracy by organized baseball, no underhand work, nor was any harm done any one."[91]

The *Sporting News* also took great pleasure in the outcome of the suit, stating, "It has been a long period of turmoil, but at last it is over." "With the forfeiting of the legal game here last week by the Baltimore Federals," the paper continued, "the way has been paved for the men who have the destiny of the national pastime in their keeping to go about their business untrammeled by thoughts of submarine attacks from rivals. . . ."[92] It also proclaimed that the dismissal vindicated Ban Johnson, who had insisted on litigating the case rather than settling with the plaintiff. "The last has been heard, therefore, of Baltimore in opposition to Organized Baseball, and the last has been heard of its threats," the periodical declared.[93]

The *Sporting News* would soon discover, however, that Baltimore did not intend to go away as quietly as the paper believed.

7

Baltimore Goes to Trial, Again

June 1917 to April 1919

Despite the press reports heralding the end of all Federal League–related litigation, the major leagues quickly learned that they had not heard the last of the Baltimore Federals. Indeed, the very same day that the team terminated its lawsuit in Philadelphia, Baltimore's counsel sent a letter to organized baseball's attorneys, George Pepper and Frank Prichard, notifying them that the plaintiff continued to believe that the peace agreement was signed "in prejudice of [its] rights," and demanding that no settlement payments be made to the other former Federal League clubs "until the rights of the Federal Baseball Club of Baltimore . . . have been properly adjusted." "Should payments be made," the letter warned, Baltimore would "hold all the parties thereto to their full legal responsibility for any such acts."[1]

The letter was prompted by a conversation that Baltimore's counsel, Stuart Janney, had had with Pepper and Prichard shortly before notifying the court of his decision to dismiss the Philadelphia case. After Janney informed his opposing counsel that he was withdrawing the suit, Pepper mentioned that he anticipated the other former Federal League teams would begin pushing for their promised settlement payments under the peace agreement. Therefore, Pepper suggested, Baltimore should notify his clients if it objected to the major leagues abiding by the settlement terms.

Pepper in fact believed that Baltimore had a potential legal claim to a portion of the settlement proceeds. In a letter he wrote summarizing the events of the Philadelphia trial, Pepper said that "[t]he facts brought out at trial [had] disclose[d] a rather curious situation." Specifically, he believed that former Federal League executives Jim Gilmore, Charles Weeghman, and Harry Sinclair had owed the league's shareholders—including the BaltFeds—a fiduciary duty requiring them to place the interests of each of the organization's teams ahead of their own personal self-interests. By agreeing to a settlement that did not provide any relief to Baltimore, the three executives arguably breached this fiduciary duty to the club. Thus, Pepper thought, the BaltFeds might be able to prevail in a lawsuit against the three men personally. He remained convinced, however, that Baltimore could not successfully sue organized baseball because the stenographic notes of the December 1915 settlement conference revealed that the major leagues had proceeded in good faith on the understanding that the Federal League executives had full authority to act for the entire league.[2]

Although the initial press reports suggested that Baltimore would follow Pepper's suggested course of action and file a lawsuit against its former Federal League colleagues,[3] the team quickly decided to continue to pursue its potential legal remedies against organized baseball instead. In early July 1917, the team's counsel notified baseball's attorneys that it intended "to re-institute proceedings under the Sherman Act" against the major leagues.[4] The announcement spurred another round of settlement talks between organized baseball and Baltimore, with the parties meeting several times in late July and early August. Most notably, several Baltimore executives and their legal counsel met with the three members of the National Commission at the Waldorf-Astoria in New York on August 6, 1917. Though there is no record of the potential settlement terms discussed at the meeting, National League president John Tener reportedly announced after the conference that he believed the parties "would soon come to a satisfactory adjustment" of the dispute.[5]

Nevertheless, by the end of August no settlement had been reached. As a result, Baltimore's attorneys once again sent a letter to the major leagues warning that the team would soon be refiling its suit, and inquiring "whether it is worth while to talk settlement before any further step is taken."[6] This time, however, organized baseball declined to pursue further negotiations. National Commission chairman August Herrmann had become dubious of the BaltFeds' litigation threats, arguing to John Tener "that the Baltimore people are simply bluffing. They are referring to a settlement before another suit is brought. I do not believe that they are entitled to a dollar. If another suit is instituted it will have to be defended by us along the same lines that we defended the last suit."[7]

Contrary to Herrmann's intuition, though, Baltimore followed through with its threat by formally filing suit against organized baseball on September 20, 1917, in Washington, D.C. It is not clear why the team elected to bring its new suit in Washington. The club may have ruled out refiling the case in Philadelphia to avoid any potential prejudice resulting from the voluntary dismissal of its earlier suit. Meanwhile, as George Pepper noted, Baltimore could not "successfully proceed in [the] Maryland District [court] because none of the defendants can be found within [the state] for purposes of service."[8] As a result, the team's attorneys may have simply decided to bring the new suit in the nearest major league city.

The case was filed in Washington's federal district court—known at the time as the Supreme Court of the District of Columbia—and once again named both the American and National Leagues, their sixteen teams, the three members of the National Commission, and Gilmore, Weeghman, and Sinclair as defendants.[9] The complaint—formally titled a "Declaration" pursuant to local practice—was nearly identical to the one Baltimore filed the year before in Philadelphia, with two main exceptions.

First, the team formally separated its case into two separate antitrust claims, one alleging that organized baseball had illegally monopolized—or attempted to monopolize—the baseball industry following the formation of the National Agreement in 1903, and the other focusing on the major leagues' conspiracy to destroy the Federal League, ultimately culminating in the peace agreement of 1915.[10] The only other significant change that the team made to its pleading was to eliminate an allegation in the Philadelphia complaint claiming that each of the Federal League teams but Baltimore had authorized the committee of Gilmore, Sinclair, and Weeghman to negotiate with the major leagues at the Waldorf-Astoria in December 1915. Instead, the new declaration merely contended that the league's other teams had "agreed to discontinue the business of professional baseball."[11] This change would enable the plaintiff's counsel to deny that a committee had ever been formally authorized to negotiate on behalf of the Federal League, which in turn would help to downplay the fact that Carroll Rasin and Stuart Janney had failed to lodge any objection during the Waldorf-Astoria settlement meeting.

Otherwise, Baltimore's declaration duplicated the allegations from the Philadelphia suit nearly verbatim. The team repeated its earlier contention that organized baseball had monopolized the industry through both its domination of the market for professional players via the reserve clause and blacklist, as well as by guaranteeing both major and minor league teams exclusive control over their territories. The declaration also once more stressed that baseball was engaged in interstate commerce, again emphasizing both the travel by players and umpires across state lines, along with the importance the major leagues placed on inter-city and inter-regional competition between teams. As before, Baltimore asserted that organized baseball's activities violated not only federal antitrust law but also the common law of monopoly and conspiracy, and again requested $300,000 in damages.[12]

Although both Stuart Janney and Edwin Goldman were once more listed among the attorneys of record for Baltimore on its declaration, the team did not repeat its earlier mistake by letting witnesses to some of the key events serve as its primary trial counsel. Instead, the BaltFeds retained two new lawyers to try the suit. The first was William L. Marbury, a University of Maryland Law School graduate who was widely considered Baltimore's pre-eminent trial attorney. The fifty-nine-year-old lawyer had honed his craft serving as a United States district attorney in Maryland under the appointment of President Grover Cleveland, before later gaining national prominence in private practice by arguing a number of high-profile cases throughout the country. Marbury's legal acumen was so well regarded that President Woodrow Wilson reportedly approached him about a potential nomination to the United States Supreme Court, only to have the attorney turn the position down to continue practicing law.[13]

In addition to Marbury, the BaltFeds also engaged prominent Washington, D.C., attorney Charles A. Douglas for the case. The decision to retain Douglas was somewhat surprising given that the fifty-five-year-old's law practice was then heavily focused on international legal issues in Latin America. In fact, Douglas was serving at the time as the American consul for the recently recognized Mexican government headed by revolutionary general Venustiano Carranza. Nevertheless, the Georgetown University Law School graduate gave Baltimore's trial team the voice of a respected member of the local bar.[14] Together, Marbury and Douglas would present a much more formidable case than Janney had been able to muster on short notice in Philadelphia.

Shortly after filing the lawsuit, Baltimore's new counsel issued a statement to the press explaining their action: "In its essential features the [Washington] suit is the same as the one dismissed in Philadelphia in June. There are now two counts in the declaration instead of one. The first charges the peace agreement as the cause of the disruption of the Federal League; the second, that the monopolistic nature of the combination of organized baseball made it impossible for the Federals to compete. . . ." The statement also justified the club's decision to dismiss its prior suit: "The case in Philadelphia was dismissed because a peculiar condition arose. It suddenly became necessary for the leading counsel for the Baltimore stockholders also to become one of the important witnesses. While this condition may not have seriously jeopardized the Baltimoreans' case it undoubtedly would have led to much confusion on the part of the jury. For that reason the counsel for the Baltimore stockholders asked that the case be dismissed, inasmuch as they knew it could be reinstituted on the same or new grounds at any future time."[15]

Renowned Baltimore attorney William L. Marbury represented his city's Federal League team at trial in Washington, D.C. (Collection of the Maryland State Archives, Special Collections, William L. Marbury Sr., MSA SC 5590-02-0063)

One striking difference between the new lawsuit and Baltimore's earlier case was the comparative lack of media attention it generated. Whereas the initiation of the prior lawsuit had resulted in significant press coverage, the new case garnered only a brief mention in the nation's major newspapers. Even the baseball-centric *Sporting News* relegated the story to a short blurb at the bottom of page two of its next issue.[16] The lack of press coverage reflected the National Commission's own muted reaction to the new suit. Uncharacteristically, only a single member of the commission released a statement regarding the filing of the case, with August Herrmann bluntly telling reporters, "Of course we will defend the suit. That's about all that can be said at this time. I was very much surprised to see that the case had come up again."[17]

The major leagues' nonchalant attitude toward the suit was also apparent in their hiring of legal counsel for the case. While the National League once again opted to retain George Pepper and his colleague Samuel Clement, American League president Ban Johnson decided to let Benjamin Minor—president of the league's Washington franchise and a local D.C. attorney—handle the case on behalf of his organization. Not only did Minor lack Pepper's credentials as a proven, nationally recognized trial attorney, but he was also himself a witness to the events at the Waldorf-Astoria in December 1915, potentially raising the same concerns Stuart Janney's representation of Baltimore had triggered in Philadelphia. Nevertheless, Johnson had "grow[n] weary of these tremendous fees which are paid attorneys," and therefore preferred to let Minor handle the case for an estimated cost of less than $2,500.[18] Meanwhile, Pepper was hesitant to split the defense of the case with co-counsel in light of "the unpleasant developments which have attended the former litigation" in Philadelphia. It is not clear what specific problem he was alluding to during the earlier trial, but even John Tener would later implore Ban Johnson to let Pepper "take command" of the defense, "recalling our experience at Philadelphia."[19]

Pepper was also understandably concerned about taking the case considering that the National Commission had once again not yet paid him for his work in the Philadelphia trial. This delay caused Pepper to exclaim, "I do not recall, during a professional experience of some thirty years, any such discourteous treatment as had been accorded me by the National Commission." Although Pepper was ultimately paid in February 1918 for his services in the prior suit, the specific terms of his representation in the new case would remain unresolved until only about a month before trial.[20]

Despite its seeming lack of concern over Baltimore's new suit, organized baseball did nevertheless consider the possibility of settling the case in the weeks after it was filed, with John Tener having reportedly been given full negotiating power to deal with the BaltFeds.[21] Privately, however, some members of the National Commission continued to doubt the sincerity of Baltimore's intentions to follow through with the suit. "It has been my opinion all along that the Baltimore Feds' only purpose in filing the suit had been under the idea that Organized Baseball must make a settlement with them out of court," August Herrmann wrote to Ban Johnson in November 1917. "I believe the time has come when we should get to the finish with a case of this kind and ascertain positively whether we are violating the Sherman Law or not. Unless this is done we will have trouble right along, as soon as an adjustment is made with one party another one will 'popup.' Therefore, I reply 'Lets go to the mat with them.'"[22]

Indeed, organized baseball received several back-channel reports in late 1917 suggesting that Baltimore had no desire to actually try the case in Washington. First, Ban Johnson learned from an acquaintance of a Baltimore shareholder in November that the team did not expect to win the new lawsuit, but merely hoped to compel a settlement from the major leagues. Similarly, one of organized baseball's attorneys informed August Herrmann in December that he had been told confidentially that Baltimore was hoping to settle the case for at least $135,000.[23] These reports further confirmed Herrmann's skepticism of Baltimore's true intentions in the litigation. As a result, organized baseball does not appear to have seriously pursued a settlement of the case.

Part of the reason that the National Commission may not have initially taken Baltimore's new lawsuit more seriously was that its attention was divided at the time between several other pressing concerns. First, as Pepper had anticipated, the other former Federal League owners were growing increasingly restless because the major leagues had not yet resumed their payments under the 1915 peace agreement. Organized baseball's attorneys preferred to continue withholding payment until Baltimore's new suit was resolved, fearing that any performance under the agreement could weaken their position under antitrust law by providing additional evidence that the major leagues had attempted to fortify their monopoly. Nevertheless, the National Commission desired to "make a settlement in this matter at once," with August Herrmann fearing that the commission would have to defend itself in court against "a suit brought to recover moneys due under what is known as the 'Peace Compact'." As a result, baseball's attorneys encouraged their clients to at least demand that the former Federal League officials indemnify the major leagues for any court costs, attorneys fees, or damages resulting from Baltimore's new lawsuit before making any payments under the peace agreement.[24]

Organized baseball thus entered negotiations with Harry Sinclair and an attorney representing Brooklyn Federals owner Robert Ward's estate to work out a suitable arrangement. The parties ultimately finalized the agreement in February 1918, with the former Federal Leaguers providing a bond covering some part of the major leagues' potential liability in the pending Baltimore suit. It is unclear whether Sinclair and the Ward estate agreed to assume all liability, or only a portion of it, in the final agreement. However, an early draft of the contract provided that the former rivals would only have to reimburse the major leagues for any damages resulting from a claim that the peace agreement "was made without the consent and in violation or fraud of" Baltimore's rights.[25] This relatively narrow provision thus would not have protected the major leagues against Baltimore's broader antitrust claims targeting the overall operation of the National Agreement and organized baseball's conspiracy to destroy the Federal League. Although the press speculated that the agreement between the Federals and the major leagues was a sign that Baltimore would soon withdraw its suit, baseball officials insisted that that was not the case, stating that they were not optimistic that the dispute with the BaltFeds could be amicably resolved.[26]

Perhaps more significantly, though, the National Commission was also distracted by the increasingly frequent internal attacks it faced in 1917 and 1918 following a series of controversial rulings. The troubles began in 1915, when a dispute arose between the National League's Pittsburgh Pirates and the St. Louis Browns of the American League over the rights to talented prospect—and eventual Hall of Fame first baseman—George Sisler. Pittsburgh insisted that it owned the rights to Sisler under a contract he signed in 1911, while St. Louis contended that the agreement was void because Sisler was only seventeen at the time it was executed, believing instead that its later contract with the player was controlling. The dispute eventually made its way to the National Commission, where league presidents Ban Johnson and John Tener split their votes along party lines. This forced August Herrmann to cast the deciding ballot. Based on legal advice conclusively stating that Sisler's initial contract was invalid, Herrmann elected to dismiss Pittsburgh's complaint in 1916, awarding Sisler to St. Louis. The decision outraged Pittsburgh owner Barney Dreyfuss, who vowed to unseat Herrmann from the National Commission. Dreyfuss would work to undermine Herrmann's support among National League owners over the next several years, eventually leading to calls for a neutral chairman to head the commission. In fact, several major league owners reportedly went so far as to approach former United States President William Howard Taft in November 1918 about the position, but he disavowed interest.[27]

Although the National Commission survived the Sisler dispute intact, the fault lines that it had opened would be ruptured several years later. In June

1918, both the American League's Philadelphia Athletics and the Boston Braves of the National League contended that they held the rights to pitcher Scott Perry following his return to organized baseball from an independent, outlaw team. After another split vote by the National Commission, Perry was awarded to Boston. However, unlike in the Sisler case, the American League did not abide by the commission's ruling, with Philadelphia manager Connie Mack instead filing a lawsuit to enjoin Perry from pitching for Boston. This understandably angered the National League, whose teams had accepted the Sisler ruling despite their disagreement with it.[28]

Consequently, the already strained relations between the two league presidents worsened—Ban Johnson still resented the National League for capitulating too quickly to the Federals in 1915—as John Tener refused to sit on the commission until Philadelphia's lawsuit was dismissed and Perry was free to pitch for Boston. Tener even encouraged his league's owners to boycott that year's World Series, but they refused. As a result, Tener announced he was resigning the league's presidency in August 1918. Longtime National League secretary John Heydler was then appointed the organization's new president, thereby joining Johnson and Herrmann on the National Commission.[29]

Fortunately for organized baseball, the trial schedule in Baltimore's new suit accommodated the distraction. As the American League's counsel Benjamin Minor had noted shortly after the suit was filed in 1917, owing to the congestion of the Washington court's docket, the trial would not be heard until March 1919. Thus, following the entry of the defendants' respective pleas in the case in November 1917—which contained only a brief, general denial of Baltimore's allegations—the case sat for more than a year without progressing.[30]

Once the calendar turned to 1919, however, organized baseball was eventually forced to begin preparing its defense in earnest. At the urging of Benjamin Minor, August Herrmann wrote a letter to Ban Johnson and John Heydler in January 1919, imploring his colleagues to begin taking the case more seriously: "In my judgment this suit is very important and should be looked after carefully, because we must have in mind that we are trying it in their own territory where a jury may be more favorable to local interests. . . ." Johnson, however, remained overly confident, contending that "[t]he Baltimore Federal suit, to me personally looks like a joke affair, and I am confident it will be swept out of the Washington courts in a jiffey [*sic*]."[31]

In the meantime, the National League sought to finalize its arrangement with George Pepper to handle its defense of the case. Undoubtedly recognizing he had the upper hand in the negotiations given the late date, Pepper informed the league that he would only take the case if he represented all the defendants—including the American League—as lead trial counsel. He also demanded a $5,000 retainer paid in advance, with an additional $15,000 due if the defendants prevailed in the trial anytime during its first week. If the trial went longer, he cautioned, his fee would increase. To show that he was not bluffing, Pepper added, "As I am very busy and very tired I am most reluctant to go to Washington and try a long and difficult case. . . . If, therefore, my terms are not acceptable to both Leagues, I shall be glad to be relieved of professional responsibility."[32]

With just a few weeks left before the scheduled start of the trial, August Herrmann recognized that it "would be very unfortunate indeed if we were to lose Mr. Pepper's services in the coming trial at Washington." As a result, organized baseball had no choice but to accept the attorney's demands. Even Ban Johnson reluctantly agreed to allow Pepper to serve as lead trial counsel in the case, relegating Benjamin Minor, his preferred lawyer, to a supporting role.[33]

In addition to his salary demands, Pepper also requested that all major league club owners attend the trial, which he considered to be "more serious and much more formidable than the law suit" in Philadelphia. In particular, whereas the previous suit had focused primarily on an alleged conspiracy between organized baseball and the Federal League, he anticipated that the new trial would take a "broader scope . . . under the Anti-Trust Law, and is therefore more serious." Johnson, however, remained unconvinced: "I will notify the American League club members that Lawyer Pepper has advised the presence of all club-owners at the trial. This to my mind is a needless expense of time and money, but I do not want my opinion to run contrary to Mr. Pepper's wishes."[34]

As the trial approached, both the plaintiff and the defendants once again worked to collect the evidence they would present to the jury. In early March 1919, the parties exchanged requests asking that numerous documents be made available for inspection at trial, including copies of each league's respective contract with its official baseball manufacturer, as well as various player contracts and league meeting minutes. Then, later in the month, Baltimore convened a meeting of its shareholders to not only provide an update on the status of the litigation, but also to identify which of the stockholders would appear as witnesses during the trial.[35]

Meanwhile, organized baseball worked to secure the assistance of several former Federal League executives in its defense. Although Gilmore, Sinclair, and Weeghman were named as defendants in the suit, they had once again managed to evade service and therefore were not subject to the court's jurisdiction in the case. Nevertheless, the major leagues hoped to persuade

Gilmore and Sinclair to cooperate, explaining that the case was not only "considered most vital and important to all baseball interests," but also that "[a]n unfavorable finding in this suit . . . would publicly brand [the two men] as parties to an illegal conspiracy." In particular, organized baseball's attorneys wanted to secure testimony from the two regarding "the financial condition of the Federal League and each of its constituent members at the time of the peace agreement and for sometime prior thereto," evidence that they hoped would weaken the plaintiff's damages claim.[36]

While Sinclair "was opposed to appearing at" the trial, Gilmore was more than happy to testify on behalf of the defendants. He even offered to bring a copy of the minutes from the Federal League meeting where he, Sinclair, and Weeghman had allegedly been authorized to negotiate a settlement with organized baseball, noting that several other former league executives present at the meeting might also be willing to testify. Gilmore was unwilling to produce the original meeting minutes book, however, fearing that it "would open up to the plaintiff some new avenue of attack."[37] What that attack might have been is, unfortunately, not explained in the correspondence.

With the trial rapidly approaching, the national media finally began to pay attention to the case. Declaring that "[i]t has been so long since that suit was started and so long has it laid dormant that most of us have about forgotten the basis of it," the *Sporting News* reported that organized baseball's attorneys "profess to see no trouble ahead in disposing of the suit . . . and say [it] may even be thrown out of court without a trial." Although it was eager "to see what sort of an [attempt] could be made at proving Organized Baseball a trust," the paper nevertheless concluded that "if any 12 men can be found to agree that the Baltimore Feds were out a lot of coin because of a settlement that left them without a league to operate in—well, we'll agree it is time to abolish the trial by jury system and let verdicts be reached by the star boardor [*sic*] in an insane asylum." It also predicted that the suit would provide the baseball magnates in attendance with an opportunity to complete "several player trades pending, a side issue that will be of more interest to the public probably than the proceedings in court."[38] Meanwhile, the *Washington Post* reported that the suit was expected to be an extended legal battle, with independent experts split as to the trial's likely outcome. Nevertheless, the Baltimore Federals were reportedly "pretty chipper over their prospects" and confident they would win the case.[39]

Although the trial had originally been scheduled to begin on March 10, and then March 24, it was ultimately delayed until March 25, 1919, owing to several other pending matters before the court. Justice Wendell Phillips Stafford would eventually preside over the case. A former justice on the

Justice Wendell P. Stafford presided over Baltimore's trial in Washington, D.C. (Library of Congress, Prints & Photographs Division, LC-H25-105830-G, photograph by Harris & Ewing)

Supreme Court of Vermont, Stafford was appointed to the federal bench in 1904 by President Theodore Roosevelt. The highly respected Stafford was considered to be one of the most learned judges on the Washington court.[40]

The trial opened on March 25 with a number of baseball luminaries in attendance, including all three members of the National Commission as well as representatives of at least five different major league teams. Following the selection of the (all-male) jury, William Marbury presented a two-hour-long opening statement on behalf of Baltimore. Marbury began by warning the jurors that they were likely in for a lengthy trial, but one that he hoped would be "not altogether uninteresting." He then assured the jury that the plaintiff had no desire to steal Washington's franchise or to hurt the national pastime in any way. Quite to the contrary, he praised baseball as developing the finest qualities in the nation's youth, crediting the sport with having "made the American soldier almost invincible upon the [World War I] battlefields of Europe last year."[41]

The Baltimore attorney then explained the legal basis for the lawsuit, describing the Sherman Act to the jury. In particular, he emphasized the antimonopoly provisions contained in Section 2 of the act, promising the jurors that he would prove that organized baseball was "the most complete, the most perfect, and the most ruthless monopoly that the American people ever had an opportunity to see." From there, Marbury launched into an extended discussion of the history of organized baseball dating back to 1894. During his exposition, the attorney talked about the formation of the National Agreement in 1903, and the ways in which it constrained professional players through both the reserve clause and blacklist. He asserted that this control over the players enabled organized baseball to monopolize the industry.[42]

Marbury went on to describe the formation of the Federal League, praising its founders' intentions of bringing major league ball to some of the large cities neglected by organized baseball. He noted that the Baltimore shareholders had invested upward of $240,000 in their franchise, and documented how the team had been forced to pay exorbitant salaries to players to persuade them to disregard the reserve clause and risk being blacklisted by the major leagues. He also discussed the peace agreement of December 1915, emphasizing that Baltimore had never been notified of the pending settlement until a tentative deal had already been reached. Although he acknowledged that Baltimore's attorney Stuart Janney was present at the settlement conference and had inquired about obtaining a major league team for his city during the peace proceedings, Marbury stressed that the lawyer had never been authorized by the plaintiff corporation to negotiate on the team's behalf. Nevertheless, he justified Janney's actions by comparing him to "a man whose ship is being sunk by a pirate, and who tries to get on the pirate's ship rather than drown," arguing that "it does not lie in the mouth of the pirate to reproach him for doing it."[43]

Finally, Marbury addressed some of organized baseball's anticipated defenses in the case. He stressed to the jury that even if the National Agreement had introduced some positive benefits to the game, the beneficial nature of a trust was no defense to the charge of illegal monopolization under the Sherman Act. He also assured Justice Stafford that Baltimore would prove baseball was in fact engaged in interstate commerce, and thus subject to federal antitrust law.[44]

Following Marbury's introduction of the case, George Pepper announced that the defendants would defer their opening statement until after the plaintiff had presented its evidence. As a result, Marbury called his first witness to the stand, his co-counsel and one of the directors of the Baltimore corporation, L. Edwin Goldman.[45]

As in the Philadelphia trial, Goldman's testimony was used to provide relevant background information to the jury, including a discussion of the formation of the Federal League, the history of organized baseball, and the general operation of the professional baseball industry.[46] Even though this testimony covered much the same ground as in the prior trial, Marbury's questioning of the witness was more orderly and thorough than Janney's had been in the earlier case. From the start, then, it was evident that the plaintiff would present a much more effective case than it had in Philadelphia.

Goldman's direct testimony carried over into the trial's second day, when he explained both the reserve clause and ten-day release provisions to the jury, discussing how they allowed the major leagues to dominate the player market and thus monopolize the professional baseball industry. In particular, Goldman recited several examples of the ways in which players were abused by organized baseball under the two provisions. He also told the jury that the BaltFeds had had "a great deal" of difficulty convincing players to sign with the team because of the major leagues' policies. As he recounted: "We had to take old ball players. We had to give them a long-term contract. In a great many instances, practically in most instances, we had to eliminate the ten-day clause from their contracts. We had to pay them very substantial sums on account of the salary that we contracted to pay them." He also briefly mentioned the peace agreement of 1915 and its resulting "disruption" of the Federal League, before explaining that the club was subsequently forced to sell its stadium for only $25,000, a loss of more than $55,000 from what it had originally cost to build.[47]

Once Marbury had completed his direct examination of Goldman, Pepper launched into a cross-examination of the witness. The attorney challenged Goldman's characterization of the National Agreement, contending that it had remedied a number of the problematic conditions that had overrun the game prior to its enactment in 1903 (such as rampant contract jumping and rowdyism). Pepper also attacked the notion that organized baseball had monopolized the player market, asserting that the demand for major league–caliber players in fact far exceeded the supply. He further forced the witness to concede that the Federal League had included a reserve clause in its own player contracts, and that such provisions generally helped preserve competitive balance by preventing richer teams from acquiring all the best players.[48]

Before Pepper could complete his cross-examination, however, Marbury interrupted the interrogation to request that the plaintiff quickly be permitted to present the testimony of an out-of-town witness before the court adjourned for the evening. With no objection from opposing counsel, Marbury called Otto Knabe to the stand. Knabe—Baltimore's player-manager during its two-year existence—testified regarding his experience trying to recruit ballplayers to the Federal League. In particular, he explained that players were hesitant to sign with the Federals because they "felt that if they left [the] major league[s] . . . they would have a lot of trouble getting back into organized baseball. That was the reason they gave me."[49]

Day three of the proceedings once again began with Goldman on the stand as the defense resumed its cross-examination from the day before. This time Pepper questioned the witness about Baltimore's involvement in the Federal League's settlement talks with organized baseball. The witness acknowledged that Carroll Rasin was officially serving in the capacity of Baltimore club president, and that Stuart Janney was formally the team's legal counsel and a member of its board of directors, when the two attended the peace conference at the Waldorf-Astoria in December 1915. Goldman insisted, however, that no one from the club had any firsthand knowledge of the settlement negotiations prior to Rasin being summoned to New York by Jim Gilmore, and that Baltimore had never agreed to be bound by the resulting peace agreement.[50]

Following a brief redirect and re-cross-examination, Goldman was excused. Charles Douglas then formally presented to the jury the terms of the Federal League's settlement with organized baseball, reciting both the tentative agreement reached on December 13, 1915, along with the final agreement of December 22, 1915, in their entirety.[51]

Once that was completed, Marbury called former professional player James "Runt" Walsh as his next witness. Walsh discussed his decision to sign with the BaltFeds prior to the 1914 season, after his prior contract with the Philadelphia Phillies had been assigned to a minor league franchise in Montreal. He explained that he had demanded a three-year contract from the Federals, and insisted that the ten-day release provision be struck from his agreement, because he believed that he would be unable to return to organized baseball after signing with the rival league. The witness also mentioned Montreal team president Sam Lichtenhein's attempts to persuade him to breach his contract with Baltimore, including the letter Lichtenhein sent in February 1914 threatening that Walsh would be blacklisted for three years if he suited up for the Federals.[52]

Walsh then described the way he had been treated by organized baseball following the demise of the Federal League. He said that he was assigned to a minor league franchise in Memphis for the 1916 season, and that during the following off-season the team tendered him a contract worth $1,800 less than he had made the year before. As a result, he decided to quit playing baseball to work for a steel company instead. Marbury deftly used this incident to highlight the unfairness of the reserve clause to the jury:

> Q. Why did you not go with some other club than the Memphis club?
> A. I could not do that without their consent.
> Q. Why could you not? Did you have any contract to stay there forever?
> A. No, sir.
> Q. Why was it necessary to get the consent of the Memphis club before you could go and negotiate for employment with some other club?
> A. I was reserved by that club for the following year.[53]

After Walsh completed his testimony, Marbury called another professional player, George Maisel, as his next witness. The plaintiff's attorney used this testimony to focus the jury's attention on the manner in which organized baseball could shuffle players across the country without their input or consent. Maisel recalled that he had started his career in Baltimore in 1912, before being assigned to a club in Harrisburg, Pennsylvania. From there, he was drafted by St. Louis, reassigned to Baltimore, and then sent to Scranton, Pennsylvania, before being sold to Detroit. Detroit then shipped him to Montreal, who ultimately released him to San Francisco. Following a successful season in the Pacific Coast League, Maisel was then reclaimed by Detroit, only to be sold to Portland, Oregon, upon his return from active military duty.[54]

Marbury's next witness, John Priest, recounted how he had similarly bounced around between the major and minor leagues for years before ultimately receiving a salary offer so low that he was forced to leave the game to work in the Baltimore shipyards. Undoubtedly recognizing that he could do little to rebut these accounts, George Pepper only conducted an extremely abbreviated and largely fruitless cross-examination of the three former players on behalf of the defense.[55]

New National League president John Heydler would later highlight this testimony as being particular damaging to organized baseball: "The evidence which, in my opinion, has so far made the most unfavorable impression on the Court is that of Players 'Runt' Walsh, Prieste [*sic*] and George Maisel, who showed how for a period of years they were shunted around from Club to Club, or from coast to coast, as in Maisel's case. A typical letter from Mr. Lichtenhein of Montreal to one of his players who had signed with the Federal League was also a bad spot in evidence."[56] Indeed, by focusing on the plight of professional players in organized baseball—as the Federal League's counsel had skillfully done before Judge Landis in Chicago—rather than simply emphasizing the impact the peace agreement had had on Baltimore, the plaintiff was able to illustrate the broader harmful effects of the major leagues' monopoly, in the process presenting a more compelling case to the jury than its former counsel had mustered in Philadelphia.

Marbury closed that afternoon's session of the trial by presenting the testimony of two witnesses from the earlier suit in Philadelphia. The parties' counsel had agreed that the prior testimony of then–Players' Fraternity head David Fultz and *New York Sun* and *Sporting News* reporter Joe Vila would be read in its entirety to the jury.[57] Thus, the jurors heard Fultz's allegations that August Herrmann had asked him to kick Federal League players out of his organization in 1914, along with Vila's discussion of the statements Ban Johnson had made to him in March 1914 regarding Johnson's intentions to fight the Federals to the end.[58]

On Friday, March 28—the fourth day of the trial—Marbury called a series of seven BaltFeds shareholders to testify on behalf of the plaintiff. These men each provided brief testimony regarding the popularity of the team and the strong demand for major league baseball in Baltimore in 1914.[59] The only one of the seven who testified for more than a few minutes was the day's second witness, the BaltFeds' president Carroll Rasin, who confirmed that he had no knowledge of the tentative peace agreement prior to receiving a telegram from Jim Gilmore asking him to immediately come up to New York City in December 1915. He also told the jury that neither the club's board of directors nor its shareholders had ever authorized anyone to negotiate with organized baseball on behalf of the franchise.[60] Marbury hoped that this information would mitigate any damage done by Rasin and Janney's attendance at the Waldorf-Astoria peace conference, believing that for the plaintiff corporation to be legally bound by the men's actions, it must have formally authorized them to act on its behalf.

Despite the narrow focus of Marbury's direct examination of Rasin, Pepper cross-examined the witness at length about his participation in the peace process. He began by asking the club president whether the Federals had held a league meeting on December 17, prior to the meeting with the officials from organized baseball at the Waldorf-Astoria later that evening. Rasin acknowledged that there had been a conference between representatives from several of the Federal League's teams, but refused to characterize it as a formal meeting of the league's board of managers. Pepper pressed the point, however, announcing, "I have here what purports to be the minutes of a meeting of the Board of Managers of the Federal League of Professional Baseball Clubs, duly convened and held at the Biltmore Hotel in the city of New York on Friday, the 17th day of December, 1915. I want to ask you, whether on reflection, you are not inclined to think that it was rather more of a meeting than you first indicated."[61]

"No, sir," Rasin confidently replied, "it was no meeting." He went on to state that it was "laughable" that anyone had recorded minutes from the conference, which he described as "a fist fight." He further explained that the discussion had quickly devolved into a heated argument with "a lot of ugly words passed" between the Baltimore contingent and Harry Sinclair once the team was informed that no provisions had been made for it in the tentative peace agreement. Rasin also insisted that Baltimore had consistently refused to agree to participate in the settlement, denying that he had proposed formally authorizing a committee to negotiate with organized baseball on behalf of the Federal League that evening. Rather, he contended, Gilmore, Weeghman, and Sinclair had appointed themselves to negotiate with the major league officials, with Rasin ultimately having to force his way into the peace conference at the Waldorf-Astoria after his colleagues had failed to invite him to the meeting.[62]

Rasin also admitted that he and Baltimore's Edward Hanlon had briefly met with August Herrmann on the afternoon of December 17, following the Federal League's conference but before the official peace meeting that evening. He conceded that the men had inquired about whether Baltimore might be able to obtain a major league franchise, but insisted that at all times they were asking on behalf of the city of Baltimore itself, rather than as representatives of the BaltFeds corporation.[63]

Following the completion of Friday's testimony, Justice Stafford released the jury for the weekend, but before doing so warned them to avoid any discussion of the case in the interim. Recognizing the high-profile nature of the suit, he cautioned, "I do not suppose anybody would intentionally try to say anything to you to influence you in any way—I have no reason to think so—but in a case of public interest like this unless you are a little on your guard you might overhear things. Take pains not to engage in any talk about the case, or any discussion of it."[64]

After the close of the first week of the trial, John Heydler sent an update on the status of the case to all of the National League's club presidents. In the letter, he acknowledged that "[t]he Baltimore Federals are presenting a stronger front and building up a more formidable case than in the 1917 trial at Philadelphia," noting in particular that Marbury was "rated as the leading Maryland attorney." "It goes without saying that our side is being handled in the same highly capable manner by Mr. Pepper as in former hearings," he reported, predicting that the major leagues' defense would "be most complete and thorough. It is likely therefore, that the hearing will continue all of next week and possibly the week following." Heydler closed by once again stressing the importance of having as many of the league's owners in attendance at the trial as possible: "In my judgment all Club Presidents who attended the joint Peace Meeting at the Waldorf December 17, 1915, should be present at trial in the coming week. Their evidence may be called for and needed."[65]

Meanwhile, the *Sporting News* summed up the first few sessions of the proceedings by noting, "There is . . . evidence and there are facts alleged, etc. It is all very confusing, but not so very interesting when the players who are willing to be slaves are demanding our attention by appearing in the early box scores." "All we can hope for," the paper concluded, "is that it soon will be over and finally disposed of. . . ."[66]

The second week of the trial began with Marbury calling another series of witnesses to the stand. This time he questioned seven former members of the BaltFeds' board of directors, each of whom briefly testified that neither the team's directors nor its shareholders had ever authorized Rasin, Janney, or anyone else to negotiate with organized baseball on the corporation's behalf.[67]

In addition, Marbury also called two more former professional players, Harry Mowrey and Clarence Russell, to the stand. Mowrey testified regarding the pressure applied to him by Pittsburgh owner Barney Dreyfuss and then–National League president John Tener in 1914 once they discovered he was negotiating with the Federals. In particular, he told the jury that Tener warned him that "he did not expect the Federal League to last 24 hours." Mowrey explained that he eventually re-signed with Pittsburgh after the BaltFeds refused to deposit his entire three-year salary up front in a bank, a condition he insisted upon because of the perceived instability of the league. He also noted that for the same reason, he had demanded at least $1,500 more in salary from the Federals than he had ever made in organized baseball.[68]

Meanwhile, Russell's testimony focused on his suspension from organized baseball after he agreed to play for a semiprofessional club in exchange for a larger salary than his prior minor league team had offered. He also recounted how he had been forced to hold out at one point during salary negotiations with the Philadelphia Athletics over an additional $300 in salary—after the team had purchased his contract for $12,000—and explained that he eventually decided to leave professional baseball several years later when he realized he could make more money working for a local steel company than his minor league club was willing to pay him.[69]

Only Edward Hanlon, the Baltimore shareholder and former major league player and manager who had appeared for the plaintiff in Philadelphia, testified for more than a few minutes that Monday. Despite speaking for more than three hours, Hanlon reportedly "held the interest of the jury during the whole time he was on the stand." In particular, along with confirming that the BaltFeds had never authorized anyone to negotiate with organized baseball on the club's behalf, Hanlon once again focused his testimony on the franchise's value. After discussing his lengthy experience appraising major league franchises, Hanlon repeated his prior testimony estimating the value of the Baltimore team at $205,000. He explained that as of December 1915 the club's stadium was worth $100,000, while its player contracts were valued at $30,000, and the franchise's membership in the Federal League was worth an additional $75,000. The witness further alleged that the franchise would have been worth at least $75,000 more had it not been for organized baseball's reserve clause, which increased the price the team was forced to pay its players. Hanlon concluded his direct testimony by stating that he remained confident the team would have ultimately been profitable had it not been for the interference of the major leagues.[70]

On cross-examination, Pepper challenged the witness's valuation of the team by noting that there had been no prior sale of a Federal League franchise upon which to base his estimate. He also questioned Hanlon about the necessity of the reserve clause, with the witness maintaining that it was an unnecessary provision. Instead, Hanlon contended, teams could achieve the same benefit by signing their players to long-term contracts without imposing the onerous restrictions of the reserve clause. Nevertheless, he was forced to concede that the provision did increase a franchise's value by providing it with a consistent stream of talent.[71]

Finally, Pepper tried to use Hanlon's experience to rebut some of the testimony Baltimore had presented to the jury establishing the harmful effects of organized baseball's monopoly. Specifically, he asked the witness a series of questions about the salaries Hanlon had earned during the various stops in his playing career, noting that the player's pay had consistently increased throughout the years despite his alleged lack of bargaining power under the reserve clause.[72]

On Tuesday April 1, Charles Douglas began the sixth day of the trial by presenting a series of documents to the jury. In particular, he formally introduced the American and National Leagues' respective contracts with their baseball manufacturers, along with the National League's contract with Western Union providing for the distribution of its scores via telegraph.[73] This evidence helped support the plaintiff's contention that organized baseball was engaged in interstate commerce, insofar as each of the three contracts involved activities that were generally considered at the time to be commerce among the states.

Douglas then recited a number of decisions rendered by the National Commission in appeals brought by players under the reserve clause. Not only did these rulings once again illustrate the inherent unfairness of organized baseball's player restraints, but they also helped demonstrate its monopoly over the market for professional players by showing that the commission ultimately controlled the fate of the men involved. In addition, Douglas read an opinion resolving a dispute between two competing minor leagues over the right to place a team in Rock Island, Illinois.[74] This case highlighted organized baseball's division of exclusive territorial rights among its teams, another potential antitrust violation preventing clubs from directly competing with one another within the same city.

Once these documents were presented to the jury, the plaintiff's counsel announced that they wished to have the previously transcribed deposition testimony of Stuart Janney read into evidence. Janney had been called to active military service in France shortly after the dismissal of Baltimore's suit in Philadelphia, and therefore was unavailable to testify in person at the Washington trial. In his deposition, Janney discussed at length his involvement in the peace negotiations between the Federal League and organized baseball. He explained that he had first learned of the settlement upon meeting with Gilmore in New York on December 17, confirming that Baltimore's representatives had objected to the proposed agreement at that time. He further recounted that upon being summoned to the meeting at the Waldorf-Astoria later that evening, Carroll Rasin "met me at the door and stated he wanted me to ask them—or the situation was such, that if I asked them for a franchise for Baltimore it would be awarded . . . or that he thought there was a good chance of their doing so," a proposal that was nevertheless "received with ridicule."[75]

Although he insisted that he never told the assembled officials that he was authorized to represent the BaltFeds at the Waldorf-Astoria meeting, Janney admitted that his official capacity at the conference was unclear:

> I don't know myself. I was there personally interested in having what I considered major league baseball in Baltimore. I was also of counsel for the Baltimore Federal League Club, and I wanted to get a settlement offered to make good the

> situation for the Federal League club, which I could bring back to the Baltimore League Club and present to the corporation. I also wanted to get for the citizens of Baltimore the character and style of baseball, in competition with cities that it would be a matter of pride for them to compete with. It was under those circumstances that I went there urging the claim of Baltimore.

Janney also recalled his subsequent telephone negotiations with Gilmore several days later, stating that he had refused a $50,000 settlement offer on behalf of the franchise, but suggested that the team's shareholders would consider accepting $75,000 so long as the major leagues assumed all liability for Baltimore's stadium lease and remaining player contracts.[76]

Before the reading of Janney's deposition transcript could be completed, however, Marbury interrupted to once again allow an out-of-town witness to testify before the court adjourned for the evening. Specifically, the plaintiff called Robert Morrow, an accountant who had conducted an audit of the Baltimore franchise's books in 1917, to the stand. Morrow testified that the team had lost $35,000 in 1914 and $34,000 in 1915. He also noted that its shareholders still remained liable for more than $29,000 in contractual obligations to players for the unplayed 1916 and 1917 seasons, along with $42,000 in other outstanding debt. On cross-examination, he further testified that the team had spent a total of $71,000 on player salaries in 1915, a fact that the defendants would try to exploit later in the case.[77]

Wednesday's proceedings began with the resumption of the reading of Stuart Janney's deposition testimony. Janney acknowledged that he had traveled to Cincinnati in early January 1916 to attend the scheduled meeting of the committee established to resolve Baltimore's claims under the peace agreement, but said that he ultimately told Gilmore that the club would not agree to have its interests submitted to the committee for binding resolution. He described the former Federal League president as being "a little acrimonious" during the conversation, and said that Gilmore "told me that we were making a mistake. I retaliated by informing him that I thought he had made a very grave mistake in making the settlement that he had made in New York without informing us, that he had violated our rights and been recalcitrant to his duty as [league] president, and had made himself subject to serious charge."[78]

Janney also confirmed that the BaltFeds received several letters from Gilmore in November 1915 that had led it to believe the league would stage a 1916 season. Specifically, on November 1, Gilmore wrote to the team requesting that it provide him with "a statement of the approximate cost to operate [Baltimore's] club during the next season" so that he could get "an idea of how much cheaper you think you can operate in 1916 than you could in 1915." Then on November 30, Gilmore forwarded a report he had received about a promising young prospect in Pennsylvania, encouraging Carroll Rasin to investigate.[79] Together, these communications helped substantiate Baltimore's claim that it had been proceeding with its preparations for 1916 without any idea that a potential settlement was looming.

The deposition included a cross-examination of Janney conducted by Pepper's colleague Samuel Clement. The attorney repeatedly pushed Janney to admit that he had requested a major league team for the BaltFeds during the Waldorf-Astoria peace conference—a request that the defense believed undermined the plaintiff's allegation that organized baseball was an illegal monopoly—but the witness refused to go further than admitting that he "was there in a dual capacity, you might say. We were all Baltimoreans, and we were owners or directors of the Federal Baseball Club of Baltimore." Any attempt to acquire a major league franchise, he insisted, was made on behalf of the city of Baltimore and not the Federal League club, although he acknowledged that if he had obtained a team, then that may have satisfied the shareholders. Later, he would once again confirm that he had never been authorized to seek a franchise on behalf of the BaltFeds, nor had he been authorized to negotiate with Gilmore over the phone in the days following the New York peace conference. Instead, he stated that during the latter conversation his request for $75,000 was simply a guess as to what his client's stockholders would accept, and that any agreement he reached with Gilmore would have had to have been approved later by the team's board of directors.[80]

Clement also grilled Janney about his decision to voluntarily dismiss the Philadelphia lawsuit. The witness admitted that after reviewing the transcript of the December 17, 1915, peace conference he informed organized baseball's counsel the next morning that he would be asking the court to discontinue the case. During the redirect portion of the deposition, Janney explained that although he may not have clearly expressed himself to opposing counsel at the time, he had come to believe that it would be "impossible to try the suit as counsel" given that "the defense was based upon circumstances in which I personally had taken part." He further testified that he later clarified his reasoning to Frank Prichard, the American League's counsel in the case. Clement would challenge this explanation during the re-cross-examination, noting that Janney did not mention his personal involvement to the court when dismissing the case, and insisting that one of Baltimore's other attorneys could have taken over the case. Janney disagreed, maintaining that it would have been "very inconvenient and ill-advised to" switch lead counsel in the midst of the trial.[81]

Once the recitation of Janney's deposition transcript was completed, Marbury announced that the plaintiff was resting its case. The *Sporting News* contended that by the time Baltimore had finished presenting its evidence, "it needed rest. This gave them nearly two weeks in court, and the general opinion seemed to be that they had not made much of a case."[82] In reality, though, Baltimore's counsel had presented a much more thorough and effective case on behalf of the franchise than Janney had offered in Philadelphia, illustrating not only the extent of organized baseball's monopoly, but also the harmful effects that the monopoly had had on both the Federal League and professional players at large.

Consequently, George Pepper faced the challenge of presenting a persuasive rebuttal in defense of the major leagues.

8

The Defense and Verdict
April 1919

"Gentlemen of the jury, it is bad enough to have to sit for hours and listen to witnesses," George Pepper began his opening statement, "but you are really to be commiserated where it comes to the point where you have to listen to the talk of lawyers." "Our friends [the plaintiff's counsel] have been at the bat quite a long time," he continued, "it has been a long inning, but I do not think many players have crossed the plate. I do not know just how the time has been consumed."[1]

Turning to the substantive merits of the case, organized baseball's attorney emphasized to the jury the seriousness of Sherman Act cases, contending that any verdict in favor of Baltimore would imply that the defendants had committed a criminal act. He also attempted to minimize the impact of the plaintiff's evidence highlighting the mistreatment of professional players by noting, "This is not a suit by a player claiming that he has been damaged, and if you were of the opinion that various players had received a raw deal from organized baseball, that would not be a ground for finding a verdict for the plaintiff."[2]

Pepper then told the jurors that he would be presenting a seven-pronged defense on behalf of his clients, several of which involved questions of law for Justice Stafford to decide, and the rest questions of fact for the jury's deliberation. First, he said, the defense would argue that baseball was not interstate commerce, and thus did not fall within the scope of federal anti-trust law. Second, even if the court concluded that professional baseball was interstate commerce, he would nevertheless contend that Congress would not have wanted the Sherman Act to apply to competitive sport. Third, he would assert that organized baseball never intended to monopolize the market for professional players, but instead only signed the players it needed to fill out its rosters.[3]

Next, Pepper said, he would argue that organized baseball had entered the 1915 peace negotiations with the Federals in good faith, believing that the league's representatives were authorized to negotiate on behalf of the entire organization. In particular, Pepper insisted that Baltimore's team president, Carroll Rasin, should not have been allowed "to sit silent" during the settlement conference, in the process "giv[ing] us the impression that he likes what is going on, and then afterwards go out into the street and scream that he has been raped and injuriously dealt with against his will." Similarly, he contended, because Baltimore's attorney Stuart Janney had sought a major league franchise for the BaltFeds during the peace meeting, the team's suit should be dismissed because the club had sought to join what it now alleged is an illegal organization.[4]

Sixth, baseball's attorney offered to prove that organized baseball was not responsible for the Federal League's demise, and instead promised to show that the league was already doomed to fail at the time the peace agreement was executed because of the massive financial losses it had sustained. In this context, Pepper explained, the Federal League had in fact tricked organized baseball into believing that the rival circuit intended to invade New York City in 1916, pulling off "one of the greatest bluffs that has ever been known in this country." Finally, he said, the defense would assert that even if organized baseball was to blame for the Federal League's collapse, the Baltimore franchise was effectively worthless at the time the league dissolved, meaning that the defendants did not owe the plaintiff any damages.[5]

Pepper would have to wait until the following day, Thursday, April 3, to begin presenting his case, at which time he called former Federal League president Jim Gilmore as his first witness. Gilmore's testimony would ultimately consume a full day of the trial. He began by describing his organization's financial condition in 1915, stating that by June the league was losing so much money that he and several of the other executives had come to the conclusion that continuing beyond the end of the season was a "hopeless task." He noted that both the Kansas City and Buffalo franchises were effectively bankrupt, and that the Federals did not believe they could attract the new investors necessary to resuscitate either team. At the same time, however, the league owners refused to carry on in 1916 with just a six-team circuit.[6] Consequently, Gilmore said he had determined that the league had no choice left but to pursue a settlement with organized baseball.

In hopes of obtaining some additional leverage in any settlement negotiations, Gilmore testified that he decided "to put over one gigantic bluff" on the major leagues. He explained that he formulated a plan in which the Federals would claim they intended to build a massive, 55,000-seat stadium in Manhattan for the 1916 season. In addition to publicizing that his league had leased two square blocks of real estate for the project, he also had an architect prepare renderings of the planned park. "We then had photographs taken, and pictures taken, of it, and published . . . over the country and we had one beautiful painting made and put in a window at 43rd and Broadway, which caused considerable comment, and the result was, I think, that everybody in the country thought that we were really going to invade New York City." To keep his true intentions secret, Gilmore only shared the real purpose of his scheme with three other people in the Federal League: Harry Sinclair, Robert Ward, and Pittsburgh Federals vice president Corry Comstock, the architect who designed the stadium renderings.[7]

From there, Pepper questioned the witness about the Federals' subsequent peace negotiations with organized baseball. Gilmore recounted how he had initially rebuffed the National League's request to hold a peace conference in December 1915, before he and Sinclair eventually agreed to meet. He then discussed his subsequent negotiations with the National League club presidents, noting in particular that he had asked for $200,000 for Baltimore during the initial talks, only to find that the other side "all laughed at me."[8]

Once the tentative agreement with the National League was finalized, the witness explained that he assembled a meeting of the Federal League's board of managers in New York to discuss and approve the deal. In contrast to Carroll Rasin's earlier sworn testimony—in which Rasin had scoffed at the notion that any record was kept of the meeting—Gilmore said that he had transcribed the minutes himself, alleging that Rasin had proposed granting a three-man committee full authority to negotiate a final peace agreement with organized baseball. Although Rasin was not a member of the negotiating committee, Gilmore said, he was nevertheless invited to attend the meeting with the major league magnates later that evening, further contradicting Rasin's prior testimony.[9]

Pepper then sought to offer the transcript of the Waldorf-Astoria peace conference into evidence, drawing a strenuous objection from Baltimore's counsel William Marbury. Pepper argued that the minutes showed Gilmore had affirmed several times throughout the meeting that he had full authority to negotiate with organized baseball. He contended that this evidence was relevant to show that his clients had acted in good faith when proceeding with the negotiations, and did not wrongly conspire to destroy the Federal League. In response, Marbury asserted that the question of good faith was irrelevant under the Sherman Act, and that unless the defense could prove that the Baltimore corporation had itself formally authorized its representatives to act on its behalf, then the defendants were liable regardless of the purity of their intentions. Justice Stafford conceded that "the legal situation presented is a somewhat perplexing one," but decided that it was better to allow the relevant portions of the transcript—but not the complete record—into evidence for the time being. However, he reserved his final decision as to the relevancy of organized baseball's intent for later in the trial. As a result, the jury heard several passages from the transcript in which Rasin failed to object when Gilmore claimed to have full authority to negotiate on behalf of the Federal League.[10]

Pepper then moved on to ask Gilmore about the subsequent conference held in Cincinnati on December 22, 1915, during which the terms of the peace agreement were finalized. The witness testified that he called Baltimore's representatives during the meeting and offered them $75,000, but that the club declined the settlement offer. This directly contradicted Stuart Janney's earlier testimony claiming that Gilmore refused to offer Baltimore more than $50,000, and had rejected the club's $75,000 counteroffer. Finally, Gilmore gave the jury his appraisal of the value of the Baltimore franchise, stating that he did not believe anyone would have been willing to buy the team at any price in the fall of 1915, given that it was clear at that point that the Federal League would not be able to continue another season.[11]

Charles Douglas handled the cross-examination of Gilmore for the plaintiff, launching into what the press described as a "vigorous" interrogation "carried on in a ruthless fashion."[12] Douglas sought to establish the impact that organized baseball's reserve clause, blacklisting, and defamatory statements had on the fledgling Federal League. Gilmore consistently denied that these practices had had any effect on his organization, claiming in particular that the major leagues' reserve clause "did not bother me at all," and that he could not complain about the way organized baseball had treated the Federals. In fact, Gilmore maintained, he knew relatively little about the operation of the reserve clause or the National Agreement at the time he was running the Federal League, stating that he relied heavily on the advice of his lawyers when it came to such matters. He further insisted that the failure of his circuit had nothing to do with organized baseball's activities.[13]

These questionable assertions by Gilmore opened the door for Douglas to impeach his credibility before the jury. Douglas introduced a copy of the Federal League's complaint from the antitrust case heard by Judge Landis in Chicago, noting that Gilmore had sworn to the veracity of all the allegations in the pleading. He then proceeded to recite various passages from the document, each of which directly contradicted the witness's current assertion that organized baseball's interference had had little effect on the Federal League. For instance, he highlighted the Federals' earlier allegation that the major

Charles Douglas grilled Jim Gilmore during his cross-examination on behalf of Baltimore (Library of Congress, Prints & Photographs Division, LC-H25-106046-G, photograph by Harris & Ewing)

leagues' blacklisting and defamatory statements were inflicting "substantial and irreparable injury" on the rival league. Gilmore repeatedly blamed any discrepancies between his current testimony and the earlier pleading on the passage of time, contending that he had not thought about these events for years. Douglas, however, offered the jury a different explanation: Gilmore was either lying then or lying now.[14]

The plaintiff's counsel eventually moved on to question Gilmore about a letter he sent to Carroll Rasin on October 13, 1915, in which the witness expressed confidence in the BaltFeds' financial viability and encouraged the team to continue to sign players for 1916. Gilmore admitted that he had failed to disclose the truth regarding his New York City bluff to Baltimore, but argued that it was necessary to maintain its secrecy to ensure the plan's success. He also stated that he had believed at the time that Baltimore would ultimately be able to recoup any subsequent investments it made in its team as part of any settlement agreement. Douglas used these concessions to further undermine Gilmore's credibility, noting that the witness admitted he had been all too willing to lie to a number of people to pull off his alleged bluff.[15]

Douglas finished his cross-examination by challenging Gilmore's authority to enter into the initial, tentative peace agreement with the National League on December 13, 1915. He noted that the negotiations had not been preapproved by the Federal League's board of managers, and contended that nothing in the organization's bylaws "gave [Gilmore] the extraordinary power . . . of closing the doors . . . [and] ending the life of the Federal League, without ever consulting with the directors or stockholders of these constituent clubs who had all this money invested in their local organization." The witness nevertheless insisted that he had little choice but to negotiate a settlement given the league's financial condition, and maintained that his actions were "absolutely square, open and above board."[16]

The *Baltimore Sun* reported that Douglas's interrogation of Gilmore "was so interesting and important that Justice Stafford, who usually adjourns court promptly at 3 o'clock, held it in session for almost an hour overtime in order that the cross-examination of Mr. Gilmore might not be interrupted." In particular, the paper characterized Douglas's use of the Federal League's complaint in the Chicago action as being especially "damaging," noting that "if those who are to follow him for the defense make no better showing than Mr. Gilmore Organized Baseball might as well throw up its hands in this lawsuit. Almost every fact and circumstance cited by Mr. Gilmore in his all-day appearance before the jury was turned against his cause during the galling cross-examination." Indeed, the *Sun* reported, "[f]or the first time since the trial began the exceedingly able Mr. Pepper seemed perturbed" during Douglas's cross-examination.[17]

The defense continued the presentation of its case the following morning by calling two more former Federal League executives to the stand. The first was William B. Ward, the son of former Brooklyn Federals owner Robert Ward. The younger Ward explained that he had become the club's president following his father's death in October 1915, and attended the

Federal League's meeting in New York on December 17, 1915, on the team's behalf. He confirmed Gilmore's testimony from the day before, stating that Carroll Rasin had proposed that the Federals form a three-man committee with full authority to finalize the peace negotiations with organized baseball on behalf of the entire league.[18]

Similarly, the second witness of the day, Pittsburgh Federals vice president Corry Comstock, also verified that he had attended the league meeting in question—in place of the team's normal representative, its president Edward Gwinner—and that Rasin had made the motion to create a negotiating committee with full authority to settle with the major leagues. In addition, he reiterated Gilmore's testimony that the plan to build a stadium in Manhattan was a bluff, and that only he, Gilmore, Robert Ward, and Sinclair had been privy to the true nature of the plan.[19]

Douglas attempted to undermine the credibility of both witnesses' accounts during cross-examination, arguing that it was hard to believe that Baltimore's representatives would have strenuously objected to the tentative agreement earlier in the day, only to then move to form a committee with full authority to finalize the settlement, especially when the committee did not include anyone from the BaltFeds. Both witnesses stood by their account, however, leaving the jury with two competing claims as to whether Rasin had in fact suggested the formation of the committee.[20] Indeed, given that both sides had some potential motivation to spin the events in their favor—with Baltimore seeking to bolster its legal claims, and the former Federal League executives perhaps hoping to defuse any potential personal liability arising from a breach of the fiduciary duty they owed to the team—it is hard to determine who was telling the truth.

Douglas also used his cross-examination of the witnesses to argue that the Federal League meeting had not been properly convened under the circuit's bylaws, noting that William Ward served as the representative of the defunct Buffalo franchise despite never having been authorized to do so by the team's shareholders. He also contested the propriety of Comstock appearing at the meeting as a substitute representative of the Pittsburgh franchise, arguing that corporate law forbade a company director from sending a surrogate to a board meeting.[21]

Following the testimony of the two former Federal League executives, the rest of the day's court session was consumed by the direct examination of National Commission chairman August Herrmann. The *Baltimore Sun* praised Herrmann's performance on the stand, describing him as being "perfectly at ease before the jury. He knew exactly what he was talking about at all times, and of course made a more or less favorable impression upon the jury." Pepper began the testimony by poking fun at the various allegations of nefarious conduct that had been levied against organized baseball throughout the trial, asking Herrmann, "Will you turn around a little bit and face the jury? I want to let them see what a pirate looks like." He then asked the witness to discuss the creation of the National Agreement, and in particular the troublesome conditions that had precipitated its formation, such as rampant contract jumping and rowdyism. Herrmann also described the history of the reserve clause, along with the operation of organized baseball's draft and waiver systems. He contended that these latter mechanisms were developed to maximize the opportunities for players to advance in their careers, preventing teams from controlling more players than they needed. He further argued that the system provided essential revenue to the minor leagues, with major league teams paying the lower-ranked circuits nearly $2.5 million for players between 1911 and 1916.[22]

Herrmann then disputed the plaintiff's allegation that organized baseball maintained a blacklist, insisting that it merely placed players on an "ineligible list" after they signed with an outlaw league. He testified that the players were largely satisfied with organized baseball's system, noting that disputes under the National Agreement had very rarely resulted in litigation. Indeed, Herrmann said, teams recognized the need to pay players satisfactory salaries to assure that the club received their maximum effort on the field.[23]

From there, Pepper asked the witness about the circumstances that led to the formation of the peace agreement with the Federals. Herrmann discussed his preliminary settlement discussions with various Federal League representatives in 1914 and 1915, before recounting that the National League finally reached a tentative agreement with its rivals in December 1915. From there, he explained that he had met with representatives of the BaltFeds on the afternoon of December 17—ahead of that evening's formal conference at the Waldorf-Astoria—and said that the team's officials told him the Federal League had formally authorized a committee to negotiate with organized baseball on its behalf. He also testified that Baltimore's representatives asked him about the possibility of acquiring an existing major league team, and had specifically mentioned both the Washington Senators and St. Louis Cardinals as potential targets. Baltimore's counsel would later fiercely deny that the Washington team was ever discussed, contending that Herrmann had only mentioned the franchise in the hopes of enraging the local jury. Indeed, the *Baltimore Sun* subsequently reported that "the whole atmosphere of the trial was surcharged with a degree of alarm over what might happen to Washington if Baltimore should win this case. There was a feeling . . . that a victory for Baltimore might wreck Organized Ball entirely or else might in the end result in Washington losing her major league franchise."[24]

Herrmann went on to testify that Gilmore repeatedly maintained that he had full power to act on behalf of the league during the Waldorf-Astoria peace conference, and that he (Herrmann) had first learned that Baltimore was displeased with the settlement terms in January 1916, when its representatives refused to meet in Cincinnati with the committee formed to resolve its claims under the peace agreement. Perhaps more significantly, he affirmed that at no time did organized baseball ever intend to harm the BaltFeds. To the contrary, he insisted that the major leagues entered the settlement with the hope that it would re-establish the public's confidence in the game, and that organized baseball had wanted to help Baltimore as much as possible under the circumstances.[25]

Finally, repeating his earlier testimony from the Philadelphia trial, Herrmann asserted that as of the fall of 1915, he believed the Baltimore franchise "was not worth a single dollar," given its lack of quality players and membership in a league consisting of teams with insufficient attendance to support major league–caliber ball. Specifically, he noted that Baltimore had lost approximately $100,000 in two years, despite boasting payrolls $20,000 to $25,000 less than that of the average major league team.[26]

Following a weekend intermission, William Marbury began his cross-examination of Herrmann on Monday morning, April 7, the tenth day of the trial. The attorney started by attacking Herrmann's contention that organized baseball did not engage in blacklisting, forcing the witness to concede that the majority of the Federal League's players were placed on the ineligible list. The witness maintained that there was a distinction, though, stating that a blacklist referred to "somebody you did not want to take back in your employment," while any player on the ineligible list could file "an application for reinstatement, which would be granted at once." He insisted that the National Commission had uniformly granted players reinstatement in the past.[27]

Marbury then challenged Herrmann's assertion that organized baseball had no desire to destroy the Federal League when it entered into the peace agreement. Although the witness claimed he believed at the time that the rival league was already as good as dead, and that he merely wished to re-establish peaceful conditions in the game by entering the settlement, Marbury argued that the major leagues would not have agreed to pay the Federals $729,000—a sum that included both the settlement payments and the subsequent amount paid by major league teams to acquire the Federal League's players—if the rival circuit's fate was already sealed. The attorney also noted that the peace agreement itself expressly stated that the settlement proceeds paid to Pittsburgh and Brooklyn were conditioned on each team either assigning its stadium to organized baseball, or ensuring that it would never again be used for baseball, evidence that showed the major leagues wanted to eliminate potential competition.[28]

Finally, the plaintiff's counsel attempted to undermine Herrmann's contention that the Baltimore franchise was effectively worthless in December 1915 owing in part to its lack of quality players. "Do you know how far their failure to get good players was due to the fact that none were to be had unless they could be purchased . . . from organized baseball?" he asked. Herrmann responded that the team could have obtained quality players if it was willing to pay them enough, but Marbury countered that "the difficulty which they had in getting players was due to the enforcement of the reservation clause of organized ball." He ultimately forced the witness to admit that the fear of being placed on the ineligible list could have affected some players' willingness to enlist with the new league.[29]

The next witness called by the defense was legendary Philadelphia Athletics manager Cornelius McGillicuddy. Pepper began by asking, tongue in cheek, "It is a fact, is it not, that this ruthless monopoly has restricted your name to Connie Mack?" Turning to more serious matters, the manager's testimony primarily served to rebut that offered earlier in the plaintiff's case by former professional player Clarence Russell, who had claimed that he was forced to hold out to get the Athletics to raise their salary offer. Mack explained that his original offer to Russell of $2,100 was higher than he would normally give an inexperienced player, but that he nevertheless ultimately agreed to pay him an additional $300 for the season. Mack went on to note that he paid the pitcher the entire $2,400 even though Russell hurt himself by throwing too hard too soon in spring training, and thus only appeared in three games that season.[30]

On cross-examination, Marbury grilled Mack about the effect of the reserve clause, arguing that players had no choice but to accept the salary offered by the team that controlled their rights. "If you have a right to keep [a player] on the reservation list for an indefinite time until he does agree, what is the difference between him and a man who is a peon or a slave?" the attorney asked.[31] "Oh, pshaw!" Mack responded, "I don't like to think that you think a ball player is a slave." "That is what you are making of him, according to my understanding of the law," Marbury retorted. Ultimately, Mack conceded that players have little choice but to accept the best offer their team is willing to make.[32]

Following an intermission for lunch, Pepper began his direct examination of American League president Ban Johnson. As with Herrmann, Pepper asked Johnson to discuss the formation of the National Agreement in 1903, and in particular to describe the unstable conditions it was intended to correct. The witness then went on to defend organized baseball, declaring it "an open book. I do not believe there is a business in the world conducted as openly as baseball." Moreover, some form of organization and a reserve rule were "absolutely necessary," he believed, to provide the stability required to ensure that the public enjoyed a high level of play. Pepper then asked Johnson if professional baseball could continue to exist if the current system was found to be illegal under the Sherman Act, but Justice Stafford refused to allow the question, possibly hinting at his disposition by stating that the question essentially asked if organized baseball could survive "[w]ithout controlling the market and keeping out competition."[33]

Instead, Pepper moved on to discuss the circumstances leading up to the peace agreement with the Federal League. Johnson insisted that by the close of the 1915 season he was convinced the Federals were "beaten to a frazzle," but nevertheless agreed to participate in the peace negotiations because he feared the league still had just enough life left to "kick up a lot of nasty trouble." He said he hoped the settlement agreement would improve the conditions in the game and "wipe out the guerilla warfare," acknowledging that he "wanted to brush [the Federal League] from the stage." Johnson confirmed that the Federals' representatives repeatedly stated they had the authority to negotiate throughout the peace conference at the Waldorf-Astoria, while noting that no one ever objected to these assertions at the meeting. He also expressed his belief that Rasin and Janney were both satisfied with everything that occurred that night, before deciding to change their course several days later.[34]

Charles Douglas used his cross-examination of the witness to establish the theme that organized baseball had consistently sought to eliminate competition throughout its history. Noting that the American and National Leagues vied with each other for players prior to the formation of the National Agreement, he contended that the 1903 agreement was itself in fact intended to destroy competition. Although Johnson refused to characterize contract jumping as "competition," he acknowledged that the 1903 agreement was intended to curtail the practice. He also admitted that the two leagues generally ceased to compete with each other following the execution of the agreement.[35]

Later, Douglas challenged Johnson's assertion that organized baseball did not enter the 1915 settlement for the purpose of eliminating competition from the Federal League. The attorney once again noted that the peace agreement granted the Pittsburgh Feds $50,000 in exchange for the destruction of its stadium, a concession that Johnson attributed to the National League's original negotiations with Gilmore and Sinclair. "I could not see any reason why Pittsburgh should be given $50,000," he explained. "As a matter of fact, I did not want to give a five-cent piece to Pittsburgh."[36] "What you wanted to do was to knock them out?" Douglas asked in response. "Knock them out; that is it," the witness replied.[37]

A few minutes later, Johnson characterized the $400,000 that organized baseball agreed to pay the Ward estate under the agreement as "[a] very good investment," enabling the major leagues to "get rid of a bunch of gorillas." Although the witness would later try to take back his answer, the damage had already been done, as Douglas had effectively and colorfully established that Johnson did in fact wish to drive the Federal League out of business. Johnson then attempted to argue that the peace agreement was merely intended to "re-establish normal conditions in baseball," but Douglas jumped on this statement, noting that to the major leagues "normal conditions" effectively meant "non-competitive conditions."[38]

New National League president John Heydler took the stand the next morning, kicking off the eleventh day of the trial. During a brief direct examination, the witness confirmed that no one from Baltimore ever objected to the peace negotiations during the conference at the Waldorf-Astoria.

John Heydler replaced John Tener as president of the National League in 1918, and testified during Baltimore's trial in Washington, D.C. (Library of Congress, Prints & Photographs Division, LC-DIG-ggbain-15266)

Heydler also noted that there were approximately two thousand fewer professional players under contract with the major and minor leagues in 1919 than there had been in 1913, men whom Pepper characterized as "free agents as far as organized ball is concerned."[39] The attorney believed this fact helped undermine the plaintiff's contention that organized baseball had monopolized the entire market of professional players.

Douglas then extracted a few helpful concessions from Heydler on cross-examination. First, he forced the witness to concede that organized baseball never released a player if it thought he had any value, meaning that the two thousand free agents Heydler referred to a few moments before were all players that the major and minor leagues no longer wanted. Turning to the peace agreement, Heydler then explained that it had been necessary for organized baseball to settle with the Federal League to restore public confidence in the sport, which he contended had been shaken by the "constant player jumping." This explanation led to the following exchange:

> Q. Therefore, you had to get rid of the cause of it.
> A. I would say that.
> Q. Was not the Federal League the cause of it?
> A. Yes, sir.[40]

The plaintiff's counsel would later highlight this testimony as an admission by Heydler that organized baseball did in fact intend to destroy competition when it entered the peace agreement with the Federal League.

Following the completion of Heydler's testimony, Pepper announced that the defense rested its case. Baltimore then presented brief rebuttal testimony by recalling both Edward Hanlon and Carroll Rasin to the stand. Hanlon denied that any of Baltimore's representatives had ever asked August Herrmann about the availability of Washington's franchise, and affirmed that any request for a major league team was made by the men in an individual capacity, rather than as formal representatives of the BaltFeds. Meanwhile, Rasin briefly explained the extent of his knowledge regarding the Federal League's fruitless attempt to reach an agreement with organized baseball in November 1914—mentioned during the direct examination of August Herrmann—under which he said each side would have agreed to respect the other's player contracts.[41]

With both parties' presentation of evidence completed, the case moved on to its next phase, as both the plaintiff and defendants made routine requests for the judge to issue a directed verdict in their favor. In other words, both sides contended that based upon the evidence presented at trial, there were no grounds upon which the jury could plausibly find in favor of the opposition. Justice Stafford agreed to hear arguments on the issue from both sides, with the plaintiff presenting its motion first.[42]

Charles Douglas spoke on behalf of Baltimore, arguing that aside from the issue of the amount of damage inflicted on his client—which he acknowledged was a factual matter to be decided by the jury—none of the other relevant facts had been contradicted by the defense. Specifically, he insisted that it was undisputed that organized baseball had monopolized the industry, with the only defense presented by the major leagues being that mechanisms such as the reserve clause were necessary to maintain professional baseball. Douglas analogized this position to that of cotton farmers in Alabama and Mississippi who had unsuccessfully claimed that a system of peonage was necessary to preserve their industry. He also noted the hypocrisy of the defendants' position, insofar as they had contended on the one hand that the reserve clause had an inconsequential effect on players, but on the other hand was absolutely necessary to sustain professional baseball. "[T]he reservation clause," he thus asserted, "is the black thread that ties together all of the clubs and leagues in organized baseball, from the lowest classification in the minor league to the highest of the major leagues. . . ."[43]

Not only had the evidence clearly established the defendants' intent to monopolize the industry, Baltimore's counsel asserted, but it also unmistakably revealed their desire to drive the Federal League out of business. Although organized baseball's witnesses insisted their intentions were simply to return the sport "to normal conditions" or to "restor[e] public confidence" in the game, Douglas argued that the testimony of all three members of the National Commission revealed that they indisputably hoped to eliminate competition by entering into the peace agreement of 1915. He emphasized the testimony of John Heydler and Ban Johnson in particular, noting that Heydler explicitly admitted on the stand just a few minutes before that they had wanted to "remove the cause" of the contract jumping, which he unabashedly identified as being the Federal League. Similarly, Douglas exclaimed that he had "never expected in my life to meet or see placed in the witness chair in a court room such an incarnation of arrogan[ce], arrogance born of the exercise of unchallenged power," as Johnson, who had openly admitted he wanted to "knock [the Federals] out."[44]

Indeed, the plaintiff's counsel noted, organized baseball had tried to drive its rivals out of business well before the final settlement was consummated, "resort[ing] to newspaper articles and comments for the purpose of destroying the players' confidence in the ability of the Federal League to live." Douglas then characterized the reserve clause as striking "the chief blow that broke [the Federals'] spinal cord," declaring the provision to be "one of the great difficulties that confronted the Federal League." Thus, in light of both the undisputed nature of organized baseball's monopoly, as well as its clear intent to destroy the Federal League, he urged Justice Stafford to issue a verdict in favor of Baltimore on all but the question of damages.[45]

The court then handed the floor over to Pepper to explain his basis for arguing that the defendants were themselves entitled to a directed verdict. After first noting that the U.S. Department of Justice had already considered the peace agreement in 1916 and decided that it did not warrant a federal prosecution, Pepper focused on what he believed "lies at the very foot of this case," namely "[t]he question whether or not baseball played for profit is interstate commerce. . . ." Even if his clients had monopolized the industry, he reminded the judge, Baltimore could not recover under the Sherman Act unless commerce among the states was implicated.[46]

Pepper began by acknowledging that it was well settled that crossing state lines to sell goods constituted interstate commerce, as did the act of transporting individuals between the states. He maintained, however, that playing baseball was more closely analogous to crossing state lines to sell insurance, an activity that the U.S. Supreme Court had ruled was not interstate commerce in the 1869 case of *Paul v. Virginia*. When the "essential feature of the transaction" is the exchange of skill for money in a single state, Pepper asserted, the behavior could not be said to constitute commerce between the states. "It is immaterial whether it is baseball or singing in a concert or cutting off a man's leg. . . . I am not engaged in interstate commerce when I put my skill forth, though I put it forth for money, and he is not engaged in interstate commerce when he receives from me the fruit of the performance of the contract that I have made with him." The attorney argued that this principle was supported by the Clayton Act's declaration that labor did not constitute commerce, reflecting the "fundamental" truth that "the output of the human energy of the citizen . . . is not a subject of commerce."[47]

Next, Pepper addressed what he acknowledged was the one potentially contrary legal precedent the plaintiff could cite, namely the 1914 federal district court decision in *Marienelli v. United Booking Offices*.[48] In *Marienelli,* the court had held that the business of professional booking agents, who brokered contracts between theaters and performers throughout the United States, was interstate commerce subject to the Sherman Act. Baseball's counsel argued that the case of contract brokerage differed markedly from the present litigation, insofar as the booking agent directly profited by bringing together parties from different states in exchange for a commission. In contrast, he argued, the defendants in the present case directly employed the players themselves, and merely happened to arrange for them to perform in different states.[49]

Justice Stafford challenged Pepper's distinction, noting that the American and National Leagues entities themselves could be analogized to booking agents because they scheduled and coordinated games to be played by teams in various states. Pepper maintained that the leagues were distinguishable from the booking agents insofar as the organizations did not earn a commission for their activities, but instead were nonprofit entities. This argument ignored the fact that the evidence at trial had revealed that the league presidents themselves drew significant salaries in exchange for managing their league's affairs, including the drafting of schedules. In any event, the attorney argued, all baseball income was derived from games staged solely in one locality, while the booking agents in *Marienelli* directly profited from inherently interstate activity.[50]

Following the court's adjournment for the evening, Pepper picked up his argument the following morning, on Wednesday, April 9. Having explained why he believed the *Marienelli* case was not pertinent the day before, the attorney instead urged the court to follow two other precedents that he contended were more applicable. First, he cited the case of *Metropolitan Opera Co. v. Hammerstein*[51]—the 1914 New York state trial court opinion he had previously relied on during the hearing before Judge Landis in Chicago—in which the court held that a theater company was not engaged in interstate commerce despite staging operas across a nationwide circuit. The *Hammerstein* court had reasoned that any travel by the theater troop was incidental to the theatrical performances themselves, which did not fall within traditional definitions of "commerce" limiting the term to the manufacture or sale of goods or commodities. This decision, Pepper argued, provided a more apt analogy to the defendants' business than did the contract brokerage at issue in *Marienelli*. In addition, he cited the decision from the *Hal Chase* case in 1914, in which the New York state court had determined that the business of baseball was not interstate commerce (despite ultimately holding that it was an illegal monopoly under state common law).[52]

Next, Pepper asserted that even if Justice Stafford determined that the defendants were engaged in interstate commerce, the court should nevertheless hold that the Sherman Act did not apply to baseball. He explained his reasoning through an analogy to two competing shoe manufacturers. Any agreement between the companies to fix prices or limit output would, of course, be illegal under the Sherman Act, Pepper acknowledged. However, if the same companies worked together to stage competitions to see which factory's employees "could drive the greatest number of rivets in a given time" and sold the public tickets to the exhibitions, then he believed that this latter form of agreement would not be subject to federal antitrust law. Rather, he contended, a case in which the parties must enter agreements in order to compete required a completely different form of regulation. Congress could never have intended that the Sherman Act be applied to a case where "combination is essential," he argued, and "where the evils can be cured, not by dissolving the combination, but by legislating specifically to meet the evils."[53]

To literally apply the Sherman Act to baseball, Pepper continued, would destroy the major leagues, and thus be akin to "LaFontaine's bear," who used a rock to smash a gnat on his friend's face, inadvertently killing his friend in the process. Turning to yet another analogy, he insisted that just as a court would not apply a statute prohibiting the spilling of blood on a public street to a surgeon who performed an emergency operation, Congress never intended to have the antitrust laws applied to competitive sport.[54]

However, even if the court still disagreed, and determined that the Sherman Act was applicable, Pepper nevertheless believed that the plaintiff's own declaration in the case conclusively defeated any allegation that organized baseball had monopolized the industry. In particular, he noted, Baltimore had admitted in its court papers that the Federal League was able to sign three hundred players despite the existence of the reserve clause, an admission that he contended, by definition, showed that the defendants had not monopolized the labor market. Similarly, the plaintiff's declaration also acknowledged that the Federals competed with the major leagues for two years, proving that organized baseball had not monopolized the professional baseball industry generally. Thus, Pepper asserted, Baltimore was left with only an attempted monopolization claim.[55]

He then argued that the team could not prevail on a claim alleging an attempt to monopolize because there was no evidence that the defendants had acted in bad faith. Focusing solely on the 1915 peace agreement—rather than organized baseball's activities during the two-year war with the Federal League—Pepper contended that the testimony provided at trial had proven that the major leagues had relied on a "bona fide belief" that the rival circuit's officials were authorized to enter the settlement negotiations. Because its representatives failed to object at any time during the peace conference at the Waldorf-Astoria, the attorney believed that Baltimore had effectively waived its right to later file suit against the major leagues.[56]

Finally, baseball's counsel asserted, Baltimore had also waived its right to sue the defendants as a result of the letter its lawyers had sent shortly after the dismissal of the Philadelphia trial on June 15, 1917 (discussed at the beginning of Chapter 7). In the letter, the BaltFeds' attorneys had demanded that no payments be made to the other former Federal League teams under the peace agreement "until the rights of the Federal Baseball Club of Baltimore . . . have been properly adjusted." According to Pepper, this letter clearly showed that in lieu of filing a new lawsuit against organized baseball, the team had instead elected to pursue legal action against Gilmore and the other Federal League executives with the hope of obtaining a portion of the proceeds their former colleagues were to receive under the peace agreement. Having expressed the desire to try to reap some benefit from the settlement pact, he alleged, Baltimore could not turn around now and challenge the legality of it in court.[57]

Immediately following the completion of Pepper's argument, Charles Douglas launched into a prolonged rebuttal on behalf of Baltimore. He began by clarifying that the plaintiff did not contend that individual baseball games themselves were acts of interstate commerce, but rather that its contention was premised on the operation of organized baseball's system in its entirety. The attorney noted that the test of whether a particular activity involved interstate commerce hinged at the time on whether its interstate aspects were incidental or necessary to the overall plan. In the present case, the interstate activity was not just essential to the defendants' business, Douglas insisted, but was "woven into the warp and woof of it." Not only were the two major leagues made up of teams from a variety of different states, he explained, but they each coordinated interstate travel by players and umpires, entered into interstate contracts with equipment manufacturers and telegraph service providers, and publicized their games in newspapers nationwide.[58] Consequently, he believed that the interstate features of organized baseball's business were in fact much stronger than those at issue in the *Marienelli* case.

Douglas then discussed the other precedents cited by Pepper, arguing that the *Hammerstein* court had concluded that opera was not interstate commerce because its performances did not necessarily require transportation across state lines, in stark contrast to the major leagues, which inherently depended on interstate travel. Meanwhile, he emphasized the *Chase* court's holding that organized baseball had illegally monopolized the industry in violation of state common law, maintaining that its conclusion regarding interstate commerce had focused only on the status of the games themselves, and not the entire framework of the industry. (Pepper would subsequently point out that this latter characterization was in fact incorrect, as Chase's attorneys had emphasized the entire structure of organized baseball's operations in the case.) In addition to addressing the cases cited by the defense, Baltimore's counsel also highlighted several other decisions in which courts had ruled that a party was engaged in interstate commerce, including *International Textbook Co. v. Pigg,* where the U.S. Supreme Court held that a correspondence course conducted through the mail was commerce between the states.[59]

Moving on from the interstate commerce issue, Douglas argued that there was no basis for Pepper's suggestion that the Sherman Act was never intended to apply to baseball. "What right has counsel to imagine that Congress intended to [give] major league baseball . . . by virtue of an implied exception, a special dispensation" from the law, he asked rhetorically. He also asserted that good faith had never been considered a defense in an antitrust suit, let alone in a case where the defendants admitted "they meant to knock the life out of us." Douglas further noted that even if Justice Stafford agreed that the issue of good faith was relevant to the case, Baltimore's complaint discussed a variety of ways in which organized baseball had attempted to dominate the industry well before entering into the peace agreement.[60] Thus, because the defendants had failed to establish good-faith bases for all of these actions—such as the defamatory statements made to the press about the Federal League—he believed a verdict for the plaintiff was warranted.

Finally, Douglas denied that Baltimore had waived its right to sue organized baseball by virtue of the letter its counsel sent following the dismissal of the Philadelphia suit. He insisted that the franchise simply intended to ensure that the status quo was maintained while it considered its next move, and argued that a waiver of rights must be much more explicit than anything contained in the letter in question.[61]

After Douglas completed his argument, William Marbury rose to add a few additional points to his colleague's rebuttal. Specifically, he emphasized that the plaintiff had not only asserted that organized baseball monopolized the industry by tying up all professional players under the reserve clause, but had also alleged that the major leagues bought up and destroyed all of the Federal League's parks to prevent any potential competitors from using them in the future.

Then, in what would ultimately prove to be one of the most important moments of the entire trial, Marbury placed all of his client's eggs in a single basket, stating that Baltimore was "so profoundly convinced" by its monopolization claims that it would rest its case entirely upon its Sherman Act allegations, thus waiving the common-law claims asserted in its declaration.[62] Though this decision emphasized Baltimore's confidence on the interstate commerce question, it also carried the risk of backfiring if Justice Stafford—or a future appellate court—ruled against the team on the issue.

In a short rebuttal, Pepper accused the plaintiff's counsel of ignoring a critical predicate question, namely "whether the exploitation of personal service for money is commerce." "It does not do any good to emphasize [the interstate aspects of the business] until you have first established that the activity itself is commerce, because if it is not commerce, it cannot be interstate commerce," he insisted. This led to a brief exchange between counsel, with Marbury clarifying that the plaintiff's position was "that the sending of men or property from state to state by rail or otherwise is in itself interstate commerce, and that any business of which sending people in that way . . . constitutes an essential feature, is itself interstate commerce, although other portions of the same business may not be." Pepper disagreed, arguing, "you must start with the proposition that the thing alleged to be interstate commerce is a commercial transaction." "If the people have associated themselves to make money out of an activity which is not in itself commercial, you cannot get it within the Sherman Act," he maintained.[63] This exchange helped highlight the difference between the two parties' positions: Pepper believed the court should focus solely on the underlying activity involved on the playing field, while Marbury contended that the overall structure of the industry was more relevant. Although Marbury's position would surely carry the day today, in 1919 the proper characterization of baseball under the then-existing interstate commerce jurisprudence was a much more difficult and novel question.

Following the completion of the arguments, Justice Stafford abruptly and unexpectedly announced that he was ready to rule. "I suppose it would be more convenient for counsel to know now what course will be taken with regard to the case," he began. The judge then stated that he could not grant the plaintiff's motion for a directed verdict because he believed some important factual issues remained in dispute. Specifically, he explained that even if organized baseball had attempted to monopolize the industry, it was not beyond dispute whether Baltimore had actually been harmed by the defendants' actions, or if the Federal League would have gone out of business anyway irrespective of the major leagues' practices.[64]

Turning to the interstate commerce question, however, Stafford ruled that "organized ball is a phase of interstate commerce. I realize the difficulties of the problem, but on the whole I am inclined to think that it is." Unfortunately, he then declined to "take the time to state at large my reasons for thinking so." Next, the judge said that the issue of whether organized baseball was a monopoly was a question of law for him to decide, given that he did not believe any facts were in dispute on the issue. He once again ruled in favor of Baltimore, concluding that the defendants had "attempt[ed] to create a monopoly," thereby violating the Sherman Act.[65]

"As to this question of good faith," Stafford continued, "I have been a good deal troubled by that . . . [but] on the whole I am inclined to adopt the plaintiff's view of the law . . . and to tell the jury that even if the defendants honestly believed that the officers of the plaintiff club had authority to do what the defendants claim those officers did . . . that that would be no defense." He also rejected the defendants' waiver argument, stating, "I am inclined to think there is nothing which the evidence tends to establish that would amount to a defense in [that] regard."[66]

In sum, Justice Stafford delivered Baltimore a resounding victory, resolving every key question of law in the team's favor. All that remained was for the jury to decide whether the club had actually been harmed by organized baseball's monopoly, and if so, how great its damages had been.

Despite effectively deciding every issue in favor of Baltimore, Stafford nevertheless hinted that he was not entirely convinced by the plaintiff's position: "Where there is very great doubt sometimes I think the Court is justified in deciding a case in one particular way, because by doing so the Court will enable the parties to save themselves a retrial."[67] In other words, the judge recognized that if he ruled in favor of the defense, only to later be overturned on appeal, the parties would have to retry much of their case to a new jury to determine the unsettled issues of fact (such as the extent of Baltimore's damages). Instead, by ruling for the plaintiff on the questions of law, the jury would then be able to resolve the remaining factual disputes, meaning that any erroneous legal ruling could more easily be corrected in favor of the defendants on appeal without the necessity of a retrial.

The *Baltimore Sun* reported that the plaintiff's attorneys were "enthusiastic beyond expression" following Justice Stafford's decision. The paper celebrated the fact that "Organized Baseball has been whipped to a fare-you-well," finding it especially "pleasing to know that Baltimore turned the trick." It praised the work of Charles Douglas in particular, noting that "it is admitted by all interests that he acquitted himself in a masterly fashion." The newspaper anticipated that "the Department of Justice may give consideration to" pursuing a criminal suit against organized baseball under the Sherman Act as a result of the case, and also predicted that Stafford's decision would have a significant impact on professional players, potentially resulting in the elimination of the ten-day release provision and reserve clause.[68]

Meanwhile, the defendants reportedly were "clearly knocked out by the decision."[69] Indeed, John Heydler would later report that Pepper's "disappointment [could not] be measured when the Court decided that our business constituted interstate commerce." He went on to declare that "[t]here never was a greater argument made than that of Mr. Pepper's; and to have that followed by the Court's ruling was bitter disappointment to us all." Nevertheless, organized baseball remained hopeful that it could prevail before the jury, with Heydler observing that "[a] verdict in our behalf on the damage claim would help a whole lot."[70]

The court reconvened two days later on Friday, April 11, with William Marbury presenting the plaintiff's closing argument to the jury. He began by explaining that much of the evidence presented by the defendants over the past few weeks would have to be disregarded because the judge had ruled that organized baseball illegally attempted to monopolize the industry, in violation of the Sherman Act. As a result, Marbury stated, there were only two issues left for the jurors to consider: (i) whether the BaltFeds had been harmed by the defendants' attempts to monopolize, and (ii) if so, how much damage organized baseball's interference had inflicted.[71]

The plaintiff's counsel addressed the second question first, arguing that it was undisputed that the franchise had lost more than $100,000 in two years, with another $30,000 in remaining liability to the players it had signed for the 1916 and 1917 seasons. In addition, he reminded the jury that Baltimore's shareholders had spent more than $82,000 building the team's stadium but were ultimately able to recoup only $25,000 of that investment after its circuit collapsed. Marbury further highlighted Edward Hanlon's testimony estimating that Baltimore's membership in the Federal League itself would have been worth at least $150,000 had it not been for the defendants' wrongful interference. Altogether, he asserted, the team had thus sustained total damages in excess of $300,000.[72]

Having substantiated his client's damages claim, Marbury then returned to the predicate question before the jury, namely whether Baltimore's damages had in fact been caused by organized baseball's attempted monopolization of the industry. He contended that there was no question the losses incurred had resulted from the conduct of the major leagues, noting the series of witnesses who had testified to the strong demand for major league baseball in Baltimore prior to the formation of the Federal League, as well as the team's strong financial backing. Marbury also ruled out the possibility that mismanagement by the club's executives was to blame for its losses, stating that the team could not have found "a more experienced baseball manager than Mr. Hanlon."[73]

Instead, he asserted, the franchise lost money because organized baseball's monopoly prevented it from attracting enough high-quality players. Not only did the defendants threaten to blacklist any player who violated his reserve clause, Marbury reminded the jury, but they also worked to undermine the Federal League's credibility with players and fans by suggesting that its organization could collapse at any moment, as evidenced by the 1914 Ban Johnson interview discussed during the trial. Meanwhile, Baltimore was forced to overpay those few players that it did sign, increasing its losses.[74]

As for the defendants' contention that they had done nothing wrong because the Federal League was effectively finished before the peace agreement was finalized, Marbury made an analogy to a child asking for mercy on account of being an orphan after he had killed both his parents. "The nerve of them, coming here and trying to put a thing like that over on a jury of American men!" he exclaimed. It strained credulity, the attorney continued, for organized baseball to claim that the Federals were finished when it then proceeded to pay nearly "$750,000 for a dead horse." Moreover, he contended, even if the league was effectively finished at the time of the settlement, that only supported the plaintiff's claim that organized baseball had used its monopoly power to harm the organization throughout the course of 1914 and 1915. Accordingly, Marbury closed by asking the jury to render "a verdict to cover the amount of the damage done according to the items that I have given you, which aggregate more than $300,000."[75]

As he had done so often throughout the trial, George Pepper opened his closing argument with a joke. "These are bad days for me," he lamented. Not only had he failed to convince Justice Stafford on the legal issues involved in the case, he explained, but during a debate in Philadelphia the night before, he had also failed to convince an audience "that the constitution of the League of Nations ought to be amended." "So I seem to lose on both propositions, and Mr. Marbury tells me that I have nothing to hope from you men; and my only comfort is Al Jolson, who tells us that this League of Nations is going to fail anyway, because Baltimore is going to insist on getting in it."[76]

More seriously, Pepper told the jurors that he intended to keep his remarks short, because this was not the "kind of case which is going to be very much helped by speech-making from counsel on either side." He went on to speculate that the jury had already decided who was right, and that they either already agreed with his position or else could not be fooled into siding with it. He continued by stating:

> I do not know whether you are going to take a great deal of stock in this talk about the peonage and enslavement of baseball players. Maybe you are. I fancy that you are a good deal like me. When [you] go out here to Washington and see Walter Johnson pitch . . . it may spoil your fun to reflect that [the players] are slaves and peons; I do not know. It does not bother me a bit; and I feel sorry for Mr. Marbury, who, I suppose, would have to go behind the grandstand and

put his lunch at the very thought that American citizens should be kept in such a state of subjection as those fellows are in.[77]

Organized baseball's counsel then encouraged the jury to consider whether the Federal League was a sound enough business proposition in the fall of 1913 that they would have invested their own money in it, and in particular to ask themselves if they truly believed the league's circuit was major league caliber. Quite to the contrary, he suggested, experience had shown that the "public will patronize games up to a certain limit, and beyond that you cannot make anything of it." Pepper also reminded the jury that the league's own president, Jim Gilmore, had admitted on the stand that he knew relatively little about the operation of the baseball industry at the time the Federal League was launched, indicative of the organization's general mismanagement. "[T]he seed of [the Federal League's] death," he contended, had been sowed by the fact it "was an unsound business proposition." As a result, he urged, "you cannot honestly recoup the losses of the Baltimore Club out of the pockets of the defendants."[78]

Pepper went on to assert that rather than believe the Federal League had lots of life left in December 1915, it was more reasonable to assume that the defendants had concluded the organization's death was imminent, but nevertheless that the league could still cause enough trouble to warrant spending $750,000 to restore the public's confidence in the game. Indeed, he argued, Gilmore had testified that he knew the "game was up" by mid-1915. In any event, Pepper insisted that the BaltFeds did not have to pay more to sign players because of the reserve clause, but rather were forced to overpay because the club was negotiating with men who were already satisfied with their terms of employment in better-established leagues.[79]

Finally, the defense counsel challenged Baltimore's damages claim, arguing that the franchise's membership in the Federal League had not been worth anywhere near $150,000 in December 1915 given the team's admitted financial losses, along with the fact that two of its fellow league members were already bankrupt. Consequently, he closed by telling the jury, "I leave the case with you, confident that you will not find a verdict against my clients, unless you are satisfied that we are responsible for the failure of the Federal League enterprise, and for the reasons that I have given I am satisfied that you will never lay that responsibility at our door."[80]

Following the completion of Pepper's argument, Charles Douglas launched into a two-hour rebuttal on Baltimore's behalf, consuming the remainder of the afternoon. Douglas's argument was largely duplicative of Marbury's earlier closing statement, repeating many of the same points his colleague had already impressed on the jury. He placed great emphasis on the testimony of the three members of the National Commission, highlighting in particular Ban Johnson's admission that he was happy to pay $400,000 to get "rid of a bunch of gorillas" and "re-establish normal conditions in baseball" by "knock[ing] [the Federals] out." He also contested the allegation that Baltimore's damages were the result of mismanagement, reminding the jury that the team had more than $300,000 in invested capital, significant popular support in the city, and a large enough population to support a major league–caliber team. The truth of the matter, he asserted, was that organized baseball had "struck the final, fatal blow [to the Federal League] for the specific, express purpose of ending the life of the thing they struck."[81]

Douglas closed Baltimore's case by assuring the jury that "the individuals who stand out representing the plaintiff here, whether laymen or lawyers, are devotees of the great national game of baseball." Nevertheless, he urged that "the body called professional baseball, is suffering from a malady. It is nigh unto death. An operation must be performed if you would save the life of the patient. The law has put the surgeon's knife in your hands. You must have the courage and skill and wisdom to cut deep, gentlemen of the jury, because the dead and rotten tissue has woven itself into and near to the vital organs. You must strike deep enough to the end that the operation shall be a success. If you strike deep enough, you will save the life of the patient."[82] Following the close of Douglas's argument, the court adjourned for the evening, with the jury instructions and deliberations set to begin the next morning.

In its recap of the day's events, the *Baltimore Sun* praised both sides' closing arguments: "No case in recent court history in Washington was more comprehensively argued than was that today. . . . Pepper's address, even while it indicated that the defendants had been staggered by the rulings of the court on Thursday, nevertheless was a fine piece of work. He made an exceedingly impressive presentation and covered his retreat, forced by the court's decision, with as good grace as could possibly have been expected."[83]

The fourteenth and final day of the trial began on the morning of Saturday, April 12. In his instructions to the jury, Justice Stafford explained that he had been forced to decide a greater part of the case than normal, leaving just a few factual disputes for the jurors to resolve. Specifically, he told the jury that although he had decided that organized baseball had attempted to monopolize the industry, the jurors had to decide whether Baltimore had in fact established that it was damaged by the major leagues' activities.[84]

He then proceeded to recite several of the instructions that had been proposed by the plaintiff or defendants. For example, as the plaintiff had requested, Stafford emphasized to the jury that there was no evidence that the BaltFeds had ever joined organized baseball's conspiracy, or had ever authorized anyone to negotiate with the major leagues on the club's behalf. He also explained that any beneficial effects of the defendants' monopoly were immaterial, as was the question of whether organized baseball believed it was negotiating with the Federal League in good faith. Instead, he instructed, the major leagues were responsible for any injury that resulted from their actions.[85]

Turning to the defendants' proposed instructions, the judge confirmed that if organized baseball's actions did not cause Baltimore's damage, then the jury should issue a general verdict in favor of the defense. Similarly, he cautioned, any award of damages must be based on actual, substantiated figures, rather than mere "conjecture or estimate." At the same time, however, he told the jurors that when apportioning any potential damages they could take into account the Federals' awareness of organized baseball's practices at the time they formed the league, a factor that would presumably favor the defendants.[86]

Justice Stafford then offered some additional guidance of his own, suggesting that the jurors should first determine how much Baltimore's franchise was worth absent the defendants' illegal activities, and then decide how much, if any, of its damages could be attributed to organized baseball. Finally, he insisted that the jury base its verdict on reason rather than "passion or prejudice or sympathy or favor," demanding that the jurors avoid any consideration of how those outside the courtroom would view their decision.[87]

After approximately three and a half hours of deliberation, the jury returned at 2:15 P.M. to request additional clarification from the judge regarding one of his instructions. Specifically, the jurors wanted Stafford to repeat the instruction permitting them to consider Baltimore's prior awareness of organized baseball's practices when calculating any potential damages. August Herrmann interpreted the jury's request as a promising signal, later recounting that it led him to conclude that "there would certainly be a mistrial or else a verdict for the defendants."[88]

The jurors then proceeded to deliberate for two more hours before finally returning with their verdict at 4:20 P.M. Contrary to Herrmann's intuition, the foreman of the jury announced that they had found in favor of the plaintiff. He then declared that the jurors had assessed Baltimore's damages to be $80,000, a sum subsequently trebled to $240,000 under the Clayton Act. Meanwhile, Justice Stafford also eventually awarded the club an additional $24,000 for its attorneys' fees, bringing the total judgment to $264,000.[89]

The *Baltimore Sun* would later report that during the deliberations, four jurors had initially wanted to give Baltimore the full $300,000 in damages it had requested (which in turn would have been trebled to $900,000), while four others supported awarding the club $200,000. However, a single juror reportedly insisted that the team was not entitled to any damages at all, and successfully held out until the rest of the jury agreed to lower the award to just $80,000.[90]

Baltimore's counsel nevertheless celebrated the outcome. Shortly, after the verdict was announced, William Marbury declared that "Baltimore's right to major league baseball has been vindicated. A ruthless monopoly which has denied her that right and which had the power and money to strangle the Federal League club has now been found guilty of an unlawful conspiracy to keep our community from enjoying the best there is in this sport." He went on to predict that as a result of the jury's verdict, Baltimore could secure "major league baseball at any time it wishes."[91]

For its part, the National Commission did not issue any immediate reaction to the decision following the close of the proceedings, as several of its members had already left the courthouse to return home by the time the jury issued its verdict. In fact, August Herrmann first learned of the verdict via telegram at a train stop in Cumberland, Maryland, while John Heydler received the news upon his arrival back in New York City that evening.[92]

After regrouping a day later, however, the members of the commission formally responded to the news. Ban Johnson sought to minimize the judgment in his typical style, stating that "[t]he verdict, of course, is a blow to baseball, but we are not particularly distressed, as it was nothing more than we expected under the circumstances. We were bound to appeal, no matter what the amount of damages was." He then took a shot at Baltimore's attorneys, who he claimed were talking like "Lenin and Trotzky" during the trial: "You would have thought we were on trial in Russia. We were charged with all manner of crimes. The attorneys for the plaintiffs referred to me as the 'Czar' of baseball and gave the impression that we were on the threshold of a penitentiary."[93]

Baltimore's attorneys did not hesitate to jab back at Johnson, reminding reporters that "[w]ith reference to Mr. Johnson's statement, it is well to bear in mind statements to newspapers contributed most substantially in the verdict against organized baseball in the present litigation." They also promised that "[w]hatever legal steps hereafter may be taken by organized baseball, we will meet before the proper tribunal, and discuss any questions there; but not elsewhere."[94]

Meanwhile, John Heydler sought to assure the public that "the game will go on as before." "The game is not affected by the decision except in its business aspects," he insisted, "and I believe the public has little interest in those." George Pepper also released a public statement, declaring that the "trial was fair and just, [and] that Judge Stafford was impartial," before promising the press that "[t]hese questions have been started on their way, but final decisions of course, cannot be reached except by appeal. . . . The case will go on first appeal to the Circuit Court of Appeals. It then will be taken to the Supreme Court of the United States unless a reversal is ruled."[95]

Privately, though, Pepper believed that organized baseball had faced an uphill battle from the outset in the case, reminiscing—without any specific explanation—in his memoirs that "[t]he atmosphere of the Washington courtroom was unfriendly to my clients."[96] August Herrmann had a different theory, believing that the jury had been influenced by a story appearing in the *Washington Post* on the morning of the verdict detailing the threatened holdout and suspension of Ray Morgan, a former Washington player who was attempting to negotiate a higher salary from Philadelphia. "[N]o doubt this article was read by a great number of jurors," he later recounted. "Nothing that occurred during the trial through testimony submitted by the Baltimore Federal League Club could have helped their contention any more than this article. I do not suppose that [the author] wrote it intentionally, but the damage was there just the same."[97]

For its part, the *Sporting News* responded to the decision by picking up on Ban Johnson's allusions to communism: "It is not believed that Organized Baseball will be classed as unlawful in the final outcome, but if so, it will be due to the inherent faults of the Sherman law, which . . . should be called a law to kill business and wages and promote Bolshevism." "The Sherman law is calculated to compel corporations to compete when they don't want to," it continued. "It is the same as if a policeman should arrest two men for not fighting."[98] Nevertheless, the paper urged the major leagues not to appeal the decision, fearing that "if Organized Baseball keeps on fiddling with lawyers and listening to their high-priced advice . . . appealing and lawing [*sic*] around, it may get burnt good and plenty, which would serve it right for having anything to do with courts and lawyers as has been pointed out . . . time and time again." "They say the verdict will be appealed . . . to the highest court in the land if necessary," its editorial noted, but "[w]e say, pay the damages assessed and go on and play ball."[99]

Others in the media also placed some of the blame for the trial's outcome on organized baseball's stubbornness. Popular Philadelphia sports columnist Francis Richter believed the major leagues should have taken greater heed of the implicit warning provided by Judge Landis, who had apparently determined that organized baseball ran afoul of the Sherman Act when he decided to sit on the Federal League's earlier suit for a year. "[T]he magnates, evidently not being wise, allowed the very first case that arose, namely the Baltimore Club's damage suit, to go to trial and decision in court." Richter also criticized baseball's attorneys for failing to emphasize to the court the recent withdrawal of the minor leagues from the National Agreement. Indeed, the lower-ranked leagues had split from the agreement in January 1919 following a dispute over its draft provisions, a development that would have helped rebut Baltimore's assertion that the major leagues controlled the entire baseball industry and all professional players. In the end, though, the columnist believed that the "wisest course would [have been] to make some sort of compromise with the Baltimore Club, no matter what the cost."[100]

The shock of the trial's outcome lingered with the National Commission for weeks. Nine days after the verdict, August Herrmann wrote to George Pepper stating that he had "not fully recovered from the Baltimore verdict up to the present time," and noting that he had initially been "thunderstruck" upon learning of the judgment. Similarly, John Heydler wrote to Pepper a few days later, exclaiming, "I am still amazed, after all the logic and force of your argument, that Judge Stafford took it upon himself to hold that professional base ball is interstate commerce."[101] Meanwhile, Ban Johnson privately declared in May that "[t]he court rulings and the jury verdict was, to my mind, the greatest imposition ever imposed on an American institution." Johnson blamed organized baseball's attorneys for the result, telling Herrmann: "I was not at all satisfied with the manner in which our lawyers handled the case. There was lack of 'team work.' The majority of nights I was in Washington I generally retired at half past eight or nine o'clock. I would have been delighted to confer with our lawyers on matters pertaining to the case, and our testimony. This privilege was not granted us. It is my conviction when we start again it must be with a new combination."[102] Johnson was apparently unable to appreciate the role that his own testimony and perceived arrogance had played in the trial's outcome.

Despite the shock of the Washington verdict, organized baseball and its attorneys nevertheless remained hopeful that they would be vindicated on appeal. As Heydler expressed in his letter to Pepper, "I am confident that [the court's ruling] will be reversed on the very next hearing."[103] Heydler's faith would ultimately be rewarded.

9

The Appeal and Final Decision

May 1919 to October 1922

While organized baseball continued to lick its wounds following the verdict in Washington, its attorneys set to work preparing the appeal. The American League's counsel, Benjamin Minor, began to draft a Bill of Exceptions—a required step in the appellate process at the time—in which the defense formally identified all of its grounds for appeal. Owing to several extensions and delays, this process would consume the rest of 1919, with the major leagues eventually finalizing their appeal in February 1920. In total, the defendants identified thirty-five alleged legal errors committed by Justice Stafford during the trial, ranging from various evidentiary rulings—such as the judge's refusal to allow organized baseball to introduce the stenographic minutes from the Waldorf-Astoria peace conference in their entirety—to the court's determination of the interstate commerce issue and its instructions to the jury.[1]

Meanwhile, as Minor worked to perfect the appeal, George Pepper was preparing the brief that organized baseball would present to the Court of Appeals for the District of Columbia.[2] For Pepper, the fight was almost personal. As National League president John Heydler recounted, Pepper was "deeply interested in securing a reversal in the upper court of what he deems more or less a miscarriage of justice." Nevertheless, Heydler reported, Pepper remained "extremely hopeful" regarding the "general prospects of our case on appeal," and "intended to 'make the effort of his life' to win out" in the remaining stages of the lawsuit.[3]

As organized baseball's attorneys worked on the appeal, the press reported that Congress was considering whether to provide some relief to the major leagues. According to an August 1919 report in the *Washington Post,* Congress was contemplating adding baseball to a list of industries that would receive special protection from the antitrust laws in a pending piece of legislation.[4] While such an exemption would have shielded the major leagues from future antitrust challenges, the bill would not have had any direct, retroactive effect on Baltimore's lawsuit. However, no such legislation ultimately passed.

As Congress weighed a potential legislative remedy, a more immediate solution presented itself to the major leagues several months later when the BaltFeds approached organized baseball to discuss a possible settlement of the lawsuit. In November 1919, two of Baltimore's co-counsel in the case, William Rawls and L. Edwin Goldman, visited George Pepper in his Philadelphia office to inquire whether the major leagues would be willing to settle the case out of court. During the meeting, Baltimore's attorneys admitted that the club "was anxious to realize on its recovery," giving Pepper "the impression that they would be willing to scale down the amount of their recovery very considerably." Although Pepper did not completely rule out the possibility of settlement, he nevertheless suggested to his opposing counsel that "a charge of conspiracy under the Sherman Act could not properly be made the subject of compromise."[5]

Privately, however, Pepper informed Heydler that organized baseball's lawyers were split regarding whether to resolve the lawsuit amicably. Though the National League's counsel, Samuel Clement, thought that the case should be settled, Pepper still believed that the defendants "can ultimately prevail" in the appeal, although he conceded that "several of the questions are novel and it may ultimately turn out that my view is mistaken." Should the major leagues decide to negotiate, Pepper suggested a starting point for the discussions: "Looking at the case judicially it seems to me that there is a good deal to be said in favor of regarding the actual [$80,000] verdict of the jury as a reliable estimate by impartial people of what ought to be paid to Baltimore in order to give them a square deal." Moreover, by basing any settlement on the actual damages awarded by the jury, as opposed to the trebled judgment as a whole, Pepper noted that organized baseball could continue to insist that the Sherman Act had not been violated in the case, insofar as it had refused to acknowledge the treble damages award.[6]

Upon receiving word of Baltimore's settlement inquiry, both the American and National Leagues initially appeared amenable to a possible resolution of the dispute. American League president Ban Johnson reported that five of his owners had expressed an inclination to settle the case "if it does not involve too great a sacrifice," while Heydler asked Pepper to "sound out the Baltimore people with a view of securing something definite as to what they [would] consider as a compromise."[7] Nevertheless, Heydler was not particularly optimistic about the chances of a settlement, as he believed "the

Baltimore people want at least $140,000 or $150,000, and my impression is also that unless the amount named is a reasonable one, that the majority of our Club owners would be willing to fight the case out to a finish."[8]

Complying with Heydler's request, Pepper reached out to the BaltFeds' counsel to ascertain their settlement demands, with William Rawls responding that he believed the entire $240,000 judgment reflected the jury's determination of the total amount of damage that had been inflicted on his client. "[T]he verdict was undoubtedly reached with a realization, by the Jury, that the amount of that verdict would be trebled; and was accordingly reduced to $80,000, so that, when trebled, it would cover the amount of the actual investment and loss," he contended. Consequently, Rawls informed Pepper, there was "no chance of closing this matter at any figure arrived at by a supposition that the verdict of $80,000 covered the actual losses of the Baltimore Club." In fact, Baltimore's counsel noted that even before the suit had gone to trial the franchise's board of directors decided that they would not settle the case for anything less than $135,000.[9] With a favorable judgment now in hand, the team's demands would obviously be much higher.

Pepper, in turn, rejected Rawls's interpretation of the jury's verdict, arguing that it is hard to believe "that the jury violated the instructions of the court . . . to the effect that they should find their verdict without reference to the multiplication feature of the [Clayton] Act." Moreover, he warned, any settlement offer premised on the entire treble damages award would be a nonstarter because he "could not advise [his] clients to make an adjustment on the theory that they were settling a charge of criminal conspiracy."[10]

Despite the unpromising tenor of the preliminary settlement discussions, Samuel Clement nevertheless agreed to meet with Rawls and Goldman in mid-December 1919. During the meeting, Baltimore's attorneys offered to settle the case for $225,000, just $50,000 less than the $275,000 organized baseball then owed the club (including the trial court judgment plus attorney's fees and interest accumulated to date). The BaltFeds' counsel justified the offer by arguing that the National League could save nearly $100,000 in taxes by settling the case before the end of the calendar year, suggesting the league could then write the agreement off as a business expense.[11] Although Heydler was willing to present the offer to his owners, he felt "confident they will accept no compromise on such an exorbitant figure." Indeed, the National League owners formally voted to reject the offer ten days later during their annual league meeting, electing to see "the suit . . . carried to its ultimate conclusion."[12] Pepper supported the decision, telling August Herrmann, "I believe that this is quite the right thing and feel sure that we shall come through in the end."[13] There is no indication that the parties ever held any further settlement negotiations.

Besides Baltimore's negotiating position having been bolstered by its favorable jury verdict, there were likely two additional explanations for the team's seemingly exorbitant settlement demands. First, as one National League owner surmised, the financial success of the recently completed 1919 World Series between the Chicago White Sox and Cincinnati Reds may have factored into the plaintiff's request, as "the league treasuries were enriched by the world series and they [Baltimore] figure this [is] the most opportune time to get some money."[14] Even more significantly, however, the *Baltimore American* reported that speculators had purchased stock from a number of the BaltFeds' shareholders after the initial verdict was announced in hopes of profiting when the team ultimately collected upon the judgment. Meanwhile, other shareholders elected to hold onto their shares believing that they would eventually receive a larger return when the judgment was paid.[15] Consequently, a number of the club's current shareholders were inclined to reject any settlement proposal that did not provide a sufficient return on their investment.

With the possibility for settlement fading as the calendar turned to 1920, organized baseball began to focus more intently on preparing its appeal. Given the appellate court's schedule, Benjamin Minor predicted that the matter would not be argued before October.[16] Meanwhile, George Pepper recommended that the major leagues contact former Federal League executives Jim Gilmore, Harry Sinclair, Charles Weeghman, and the heirs of Robert Ward, demanding that they indemnify the major leagues in the event the appeal was unsuccessful. Pepper believed the jury had based its verdict on the Federals' misrepresentations regarding their negotiating authority during the Waldorf-Astoria peace conference, and therefore reasoned that these men should shoulder some of the burden of the judgment.[17] (In reality, any representations by the Federals during the meeting appeared to have little bearing on the decision). Heydler concurred with Pepper, noting that the major leagues still owed both Ward and Sinclair enough under the peace agreement that they could offset the judgment by withholding any future payments should they lose the appeal.[18] Unfortunately, no record exists regarding how, if at all, the former Federal League officials responded to organized baseball's demand.

In mid-June 1920, organized baseball submitted its brief to the Court of Appeals for the District of Columbia. The major leagues' attorneys wanted to ensure that the appellate court appreciated the importance of baseball's various rules and regulations, and therefore "endeavored to fully inform the Court as to every angle of the conduct of professional baseball as a business."[19] Accordingly, they devoted nearly thirty pages of the brief to explaining the formation and operation of the major leagues. In the process, they stressed that competitive sport requires a high degree of organization to regulate teams, game play, and the overall championship competition, as well as to instill discipline in players. The brief also emphasized the importance of the reserve clause, arguing that the provision was absolutely necessary in light of the "disastrous results to the sporting public, to the clubs and to the players, which have always ensued at times when reservations have not been respected, and there has been unrestrained competition for players."[20]

The major leagues' counsel also used this initial background discussion to build support for its legal contention that professional baseball was not interstate commerce, and thus not subject to the Sherman Act. For instance, although Pepper acknowledged that transportation was essential to the business, he nevertheless maintained "it is not the end in view," but "merely the means of getting the players to the point at which the contest is scheduled to take place." In other words, he continued to insist that the transportation was merely incidental to the central feature of the defendants' operations, namely the actual baseball games themselves. Similarly, Pepper analogized the transportation of playing equipment to a surgeon carrying his tools across state lines, activity that he insisted was not interstate commerce.[21]

The brief then described the formation of the Federal League, highlighting the impact that its recruitment of players had had on the two major leagues, and emphasizing instances where players decided to defect midseason to the rival organization. The brief insisted that organized baseball did not fear competition from the Federals in a business sense, but merely wanted to avoid the damaging effect that the loss of these players inflicted on team morale and the major leagues' quality of play. It then recounted the December 1915 settlement negotiations, emphasizing Baltimore team president Carroll Rasin's failure to object during the Waldorf-Astoria meeting, and maintaining that the major leagues had acted in good faith when negotiating the peace agreement, unaware that the BaltFeds objected to the settlement until after it was finalized.[22]

From there, Pepper turned to the legal grounds for the appeal. He focused in particular on four legal errors that organized baseball believed Justice Stafford had committed, each of which it thought warranted a reversal of the trial court judgment. First, the major leagues once again asserted that professional baseball was not subject to the Sherman Act, for several reasons. Most significantly, the brief argued that baseball games did not fall within traditional definitions limiting "commerce" to the exchange of commodities. To the contrary, organized baseball characterized itself as providing little more than "exhibition[s] of athletic skill" by baseball players, from which "on-lookers derive nothing but enjoyment." Thus, because the major leagues did not produce a tangible product, they could not be engaged in commerce.[23]

In making this argument, organized baseball cited several of the same legal precedents it had relied upon during the trial. For instance, Pepper analogized baseball games to the sale of insurance contracts, activity that the Supreme Court had repeatedly held was not interstate commerce even when conducted across state lines. Similarly, he also cited the *Hammerstein* decision holding that local performances of music or drama were not considered interstate commerce. The brief then distinguished the *Marienelli* case discussed during the trial, once more contending that the decision involved only the business of brokering contracts for theatrical performances, and not the actual performances themselves. Finally, Pepper quoted extensively from the opinion in the *Chase* case, emphasizing that the New York state court had held that baseball was not interstate commerce.[24]

Moreover, the major leagues contended, even if they were engaged in commerce, the BaltFeds had failed to prove they had monopolized the industry. Characterizing the trial court as having focused its monopolization findings on the reserve clause and the market for players, the major leagues argued that they never signed players in excess of the number needed, and thus could not be found to have constructed an illegal monopoly. To the contrary, they asserted, Baltimore had in fact been able to hire more than enough players to field its team.[25]

Baseball's attorneys offered two additional reasons why they believed the Sherman Act did not apply to the major leagues. First, they argued that sporting events should remain subject to local, not national, regulation. Rather than provide any legal precedent supporting this assertion, however, their brief merely claimed that if baseball were subject to the Sherman Act, then Congress could go so far as to regulate "all the details of the national game" through "a regulatory body fashioned upon the analogy of the Interstate Commerce Commission," a notion they contended was utterly absurd.[26]

Additionally, the major leagues asserted that Congress never intended to have antitrust law applied to an industry where centralized organization among competitors was necessary to maintain its very existence. In this section of the brief, Pepper noted that even Baltimore admitted that cooperation between teams in a league was essential to professional baseball (for example, teams must agree on a basic set of rules and a playing schedule to stage a season-long competition for the league championship). Just as coordination between the teams in the American or National League was thus necessary, he argued, synchronization between the two major leagues in the form of the National Agreement was similarly essential to stage the annual World Series. Because Congress could never have intended for the Sherman Act to render the World Series illegal, he insisted that federal antitrust law should not be applied to professional baseball absent express instruction from Congress.[27]

Having fully covered the reasons they believed the lower court had erred when holding that professional baseball was subject to the Sherman Act, organized baseball's attorneys next discussed the remaining bases for their appeal. Their second primary argument was that Justice Stafford had erroneously refused to consider whether the major leagues acted in good faith when entering the peace negotiations with the Federal League. Asserting that the American and National League magnates had no way of knowing that Baltimore objected to the settlement, given Carroll Rasin's failure to speak up during the Waldorf-Astoria meeting, baseball's counsel argued that the major leagues could not be found to have engaged in an illicit conspiracy if they sincerely believed that all of the Federal League's teams were willingly negotiating the peace agreement. Indeed, the brief contended, if good faith was irrelevant then anyone could choose to sit by idly while an illegal plan was formulated, only to decide later whether it would be more advantageous to participate in the conspiracy or sue its members for damages. As a result, organized baseball insisted that Baltimore should be bound by Rasin's tacit approval of the settlement, and thus be precluded from filing suit against the major leagues.[28]

Third, the major leagues repeated their assertion that Baltimore had waived its right to sue organized baseball by virtue of the letter its counsel sent following the aborted trial in Philadelphia in June 1917. After quoting the letter in its entirety, the brief argued that the BaltFeds' lawyers had effectively ratified the peace agreement in the communication, thus electing to seek a share of the settlement proceeds rather than pursue further litigation against the major leagues. Baseball's attorneys insisted that Justice Stafford had "entirely misapprehended the significance of this notice," and that when viewed properly, the letter in fact provided an additional basis upon which Baltimore was precluded from filing suit.[29]

Finally, organized baseball contended that the BaltFeds had failed to provide sufficient evidence of the club's alleged damages. Noting that any damage award must be based on fact, and not "a mere guess" or conjecture, baseball's attorneys argued that there was no basis upon which the damages in the case could be assessed because the franchise had never operated absent interference from the major leagues.[30] In other words, they asserted that without some sort of baseline from which to measure, it was impossible to know for sure what impact organized baseball's allegedly illegal activities had had on the rival franchise's profitability. This argument was particularly audacious because it would have effectively permitted any illicit monopoly or conspiracy to avoid paying damages to a rival that entered the field after the illegal activity was already established.

Baltimore responded to organized baseball's legal contentions by filing its own brief several months later, on September 15, 1920. The franchise's written argument was nearly twice as long as that submitted by the major leagues, totaling 181 pages. The BaltFeds' attorneys began by summarizing the key issues in the case, amplifying their rhetoric in the process. For example, they started by explaining that the team had been formed "in response to a widespread popular movement" after Baltimore was "arbitrarily excluded by Organized Baseball from what is known as Major League Baseball." They then detailed how the franchise was injured by the "illegal, oppressive and coercive acts and conduct of" the major leagues, actions that were "intended to cripple and injure" the club. Later, they would contend that the Federal League "was exterminated as a penalty for its attempt" to compete with organized baseball.[31]

The team also stressed the importance of the court "distinguish[ing] between baseball as a sport and baseball as a business or industry," noting that Baltimore was not attacking the national pastime in its "amateur form." As for the professional game, however, they argued that interstate commerce was its "very essence and foundation," insofar as the business required the formation of a league of teams from different cities and states to maintain fan interest. Indeed, Baltimore's counsel insisted, baseball depended upon a "great stream of commerce between the states created by the transportation of the players, the umpires, the equipment of the teams, the thousands and hundreds of thousands of persons to and from the games, [and] the transmission of telegraphic and post and newspaper intelligence of the games," without all of which the sport "would be annihilated."[32]

Having introduced the case, the team then turned its attention to summarizing the facts that were established at trial. Launching into a nearly one-hundred-page discussion of the evidence, the brief discussed the creation and operation of organized baseball's monopoly, the eventual formation of the Federal League, and its ultimate destruction. Along the way, Baltimore's counsel focused the court's attention on the ways in which the National Agreement protected major league teams "from competition from another member in the league or from any sources outside of organized baseball." The brief emphasized the reserve clause in particular, spending thirteen pages walking through the various provisions in the National Agreement and standard player contract that established and fortified the restraint. It also highlighted testimony from Edward Hanlon, Connie Mack, and August Herrmann illustrating the effect the clause had on players.[33]

Despite devoting nearly twenty pages to its discussion of the reserve clause, Baltimore never effectively rebutted organized baseball's contention that the provision was essential to the survival of the professional game. For example, although the brief cited Hanlon's testimony regarding the operation and effect of the provision, it failed to include the portion of his testimony suggesting that in lieu of the reserve clause, teams could instead use multiyear contracts to lock up their players. Though Baltimore's attorneys did include a quick, passing reference to such a possibility later in the brief, they failed to emphasize the point, and thus never persuasively countered the major leagues' argument regarding the essentiality of the reserve clause.[34] Therefore, despite its detrimental effects on professional players, Baltimore left the appellate court to assume that the reserve clause was in fact a reasonably necessary provision, and not simply an unjust, anticompetitive restraint.

Meanwhile, with respect to the destruction of their circuit, the BaltFeds identified the various ways in which the major leagues had dissuaded players from signing with the Federal League, before discussing the circumstances leading up to the 1915 peace agreement. In particular, the team contended that organized baseball had wrecked the rival circuit to destroy any potential competition with its monopoly, noting that the major leagues dismantled the majority of stadiums they acquired in the settlement, and stressing Ban Johnson's testimony regarding his desire to "knock out" the Federals.[35]

Turning to the actual legal issues disputed in the appeal, the BaltFeds addressed each of the major leagues' arguments in turn. First, the team explained its basis for asserting that professional baseball was engaged in interstate commerce. Rather than directly rebut Pepper's argument that the individual baseball games themselves were not commerce, Baltimore's counsel instead conceded the point while nevertheless maintaining that the business "taken as an entirety, is interstate commerce." Thus, the team hoped that it could convince the appellate court to focus its analysis on the entire structure of organized baseball—as Justice Stafford had apparently done during the trial below—rather than just the actual exhibitions staged by the major leagues. Indeed, Baltimore accused the defendants of ignoring "every element and every detail in their business except the playing of their baseball teams in the baseball field."[36]

The brief continued by insisting that there was "scarcely any business more inherently interstate in character" than professional baseball, arguing that the "interstate element in it is fundamental, essential and indispensable." Focusing in particular on the recurrent transportation of players and equipment across state lines, the BaltFeds asserted that "in its essence [baseball] is the same kind of business which has over and over again been held to be interstate commerce." Specifically, the team cited various U.S. Supreme Court precedents holding that transportation constituted interstate commerce, including *Hoke v. United States*—in which Congress's authority to penalize the transportation of persons across state lines for immoral purposes was affirmed—as well as the *Pigg* case finding that correspondence courses were interstate commerce.[37]

However, Baltimore's counsel failed to address the grounds upon which both cases could potentially be distinguished from professional baseball. For instance, in *Hoke,* the Court merely held that Congress could regulate the interstate transportation of people, not that it was authorized to address the immoral acts themselves occurring at the local level. Thus, though the decision may have provided Congress with the authority to restrict the transportation of baseball players across state lines, it did not necessarily follow that the Sherman Act reached other elements of the professional baseball business. Similarly, the fact that the *Pigg* case involved the shipment of textbooks across state lines arguably brought the correspondence courses more closely in line with the traditional definition of commerce than the baseball exhibitions staged by major league teams in a single state.

Baltimore also relied on the district court opinion in the *Marienelli* case involving the brokerage of theater contracts, providing a lengthy, four-page quotation from the decision.[38] The brief neglected to respond to organized baseball's argument that the case was inapposite, though, insofar as it merely dealt with the negotiation of contracts, rather than the underlying, local theatrical performances themselves. Baltimore's counsel could have rebutted this argument by drawing upon Justice Stafford's observation during the trial that the American and National League offices acted similarly to the contract broker in *Marienelli* by scheduling and coordinating games between teams from various states.

Following its discussion of the interstate commerce issue, Baltimore's counsel turned to organized baseball's argument that it had not created an illegal monopoly. In particular, they stressed that the National Agreement was formed to eliminate competition between the American and National Leagues, with the two leagues having built a "perpetual barrier to entry" preventing new competitors from entering the field by restraining all professional players through the reserve clause. The brief also rejected the major leagues' argument that the National Agreement was essential to professional baseball. To the contrary, rather than forming a single, comprehensive organization controlling the entire industry, Baltimore instead asserted that independent leagues could manage their own affairs while competing with one another.[39]

Third, Baltimore contested the notion that it had in any way waived its right to sue the major leagues, pointing out that the June 1917 letter emphasized by the defendants had in fact specifically stated that the peace agreement was illegal. Thus, the club contended, the letter could not reasonably be construed as ratifying the settlement agreement. The team also rejected the defense's suggestion that Carroll Rasin's failure to object during the Waldorf-Astoria conference precluded its right to sue, noting that even if his silence had misled organized baseball during the meeting, the major leagues had nevertheless clearly become aware of the BaltFeds' objections to the settlement before it was formally executed. Therefore, Baltimore claimed, the defense could not credibly assert that organized baseball had acted in good faith when carrying out the peace agreement.[40]

Finally, Baltimore's counsel dismissed organized baseball's argument that the jury's damages award was speculative, noting that Justice Stafford had clearly instructed the jurors that damages could not be based on conjecture, but must be proven specifically. Moreover, they asserted that the defense's argument that damages could not be definitively established because the BaltFeds had never operated absent interference from the major leagues "would practically nullify the Sherman Act" in any case in which the illicit activity resulted in "exterminating a competitor."[41]

Following the submission of each side's brief, the parties awaited the date of their oral argument before the court of appeals, tentatively scheduled for mid-October. Days after Baltimore filed its brief, however, organized baseball was rocked by perhaps the most serious scandal it had ever faced. Specifically, in late-September 1920, news broke that a grand jury had been assembled in Chicago to investigate whether the 1919 World Series had been fixed. In what came to be known as the "Black Sox" scandal, eight players from the heavily favored Chicago White Sox would eventually be indicted on charges of conspiring with gamblers to throw the series. The resulting media and public uproar over the controversy would envelop the sport in the ensuing weeks, raising serious doubt about baseball's continued viability as the national pastime.[42]

Given the timing, it was not immediately clear what impact, if any, the Black Sox scandal would have on organized baseball's appeal in the BaltFeds' suit. Some have speculated that the controversy would have been a cause for "panic" for the major leagues as they prepared to argue their appeal, on the assumption that the appellate court would be hesitant to rule that the Sherman Act was inapplicable to professional baseball at a time when current events evidenced the need for greater regulation of the game.[43] On the other hand, it is also possible that the controversy may have actually bolstered organized baseball's case on appeal. Indeed, the magnitude of the scandal helped illustrate the need for the type of centralized, uniform control over the sport that the major leagues stressed was necessary. In other words, even if the current organization of the major leagues was not strictly in conformance with the antitrust laws, perhaps the appellate court would nevertheless determine that a unified managerial structure was necessary to re-establish order and discipline in the national pastime. Ultimately, one can thus only speculate whether the controversy had any effect on the outcome of the major leagues' appeal.

On October 12, 1920, less than three weeks after the news of the Black Sox scandal broke, the Court of Appeals for the District of Columbia convened to hear oral arguments in the major leagues' appeal. The parties argued their case before a three-judge panel consisting of the court's chief justice, Constantine Smyth, as well as Justices Charles Robb and Josiah Van Orsdel. Chief Justice Smyth in particular was well-versed in the Sherman Act, having served as the special assistant in charge of antitrust cases for the U.S. attorney general from 1913 to 1917.[44] As a result, Smyth was likely involved in the Department of Justice's review of the National Agreement in 1913, as well as its subsequent consideration of the 1915 peace agreement, when it twice declined to launch an antitrust investigation of organized baseball in connection with the Federal League dispute.

Though no transcript of the oral argument exists, based on contemporaneous reports both George Pepper and Benjamin Minor spoke on behalf of organized baseball, while William Rawls—co-counsel to William Marbury and Charles Douglas during the trial—handled Baltimore's argument. The *Washington Post* reported that organized baseball's counsel focused their efforts on the contention that the transportation of players from city to city was not interstate commerce, while Rawls stressed that the judgment should be affirmed because the major leagues had violated the Sherman Act.[45] Following the hearing, Baltimore was confident regarding its prospects, with the team's officials reportedly having "no fear of the outcome" of the appeal. Meanwhile, Pepper was also optimistic about his clients' chances, telling John Heydler that while "[i]t is of course impossible to forecast the action of the court," both he and Minor had "gained the impression . . . that the judges were favorable to our contentions." Pepper was also hopeful based on his observation that "[t]he atmosphere [in the appellate court] was very different from that of Judge Stafford's court room," presumably referring to his perception that the mood in the trial court had been "unfriendly" toward his clients.[46] Despite Pepper's confidence, however, the parties would have to wait several weeks before the court of appeals announced its decision.

As the parties awaited the appellate court's ruling, the fallout from the Black Sox scandal began to place additional strain upon the National Commission's increasingly tenuous control over the sport. Even before the gambling controversy erupted, pressure had continued to build on the commission following its controversial decisions regarding George Sisler and Scott Perry in 1916 and 1918, respectively. Specifically, Ban Johnson came under attack in 1919 for interfering with a trade that sent pitcher Carl Mays from Boston to the New York Yankees just days after he deserted the Red Sox (Mays was reportedly frustrated by the support he was receiving from his teammates). Believing that allowing Mays to pitch for New York would reward him for his desertion, Johnson suspended the pitcher, in the process infuriating the Yankees' ownership. Eventually, the American League's board of directors—a five-member committee heavily influenced by the New York and Boston owners—overturned the suspension, thereby significantly undercutting Johnson's authority.[47]

With his power waning, Johnson was no longer in a position to support his longtime ally August Herrmann's hold on the chairmanship of the National Commission. Herrmann continued to remain the subject of a withering attack from a group of National League owners still harboring resentment over his decision to award George Sisler to the American League. Without Johnson's support, Herrmann was finally forced to resign as chairman in January 1920; the position would remain vacant throughout the 1920 season.[48]

Consequently, the Black Sox controversy was hitting baseball at a particularly inopportune moment, with the sport's management in flux. In the midst of this leadership vacuum, and with public outrage over the scandal growing, the major league owners convened in November 1920 to reform the game's management. Over the objection of Ban Johnson—who opposed ceding power to a non-baseball man—the owners ultimately agreed to appoint Judge Kenesaw Mountain Landis as the first commissioner of baseball. Landis's name had been floated from time to time over the years as a possible replacement for August Herrmann on the National Commission following the judge's favorable handling of the Federal League's 1915 antitrust suit in Chicago. Given the major league owners' fragile position, Landis was able to demand a $50,000 annual salary and absolute control over the game. Thus began Landis's twenty-four-year reign as the "benevolent despot" of professional baseball. Indeed, the following summer, baseball's new commissioner permanently suspended the eight Black Sox players from the sport, just a day after a jury found them not guilty on charges of conspiracy.[49]

Against that turbulent backdrop, the court of appeals' decision came as welcome relief to the major leagues when it was announced on December 6, 1920. In a unanimous opinion authored by Chief Justice Smyth, the court granted organized baseball a sweeping victory, overturning the lower court judgment in its entirety. The appellate court focused its decision on Baltimore's monopolization claim, construing the trial court as having concluded that the defendants monopolized the industry "principally through what

Chief Justice Constantine Smyth wrote the D.C. Court of Appeals' decision in Baltimore's case (Library of Congress, Prints & Photographs Division, LC-DIG-npcc-23788)

is called the 'reserve clause'."[50] Though the reserve clause was of course central to the BaltFeds' case, Smyth nevertheless disregarded the team's other grounds for the monopoly claim, including the evidence presented at trial regarding the major leagues' exclusive territorial restrictions and the destruction of Federal League stadiums following the execution of the peace agreement.

Smyth framed the legal issue at stake in the appeal as follows: "Did the giving of exhibitions of baseball . . . constitute trade or commerce within the meaning of the Sherman Act?" To answer this question, he examined the prevailing judicial definitions of the relevant terms, finding that courts had consistently concluded that trade and commerce "require the transfer of something, whether it be persons, commodities, or intelligence, from one place or person to another." Applying this definition to professional baseball, he held that "[a] game of baseball is not susceptible of being transferred. . . . Nothing is transferred [during the game] to those who patronize it."[51]

Further expanding upon his reasoning, Smyth analogized professional baseball to a Washington law firm sending one of its attorneys to a different state to argue a case, or a Chautauqua lecturer traveling across state lines to deliver a speech, neither of which he believed was an act of commerce. "The fact that the [major leagues] produce baseball games as a source of profit, large or small, cannot change the character of the games," he maintained. "They are still sport, not trade."[52] In support of this conclusion, Smyth relied on two of the precedents cited by the defendants in their brief: the *Hammerstein* case holding that theatrical exhibitions were not commerce, and the *Chase* court's "carefully prepared opinion" determining "that the production of exhibitions of baseball did not constitute trade or commerce." Moreover, the appellate court distinguished two of the primary precedents advanced by Baltimore, finding that the *Marienelli* case was inapplicable because it dealt only with "the negotiation of a contract to travel and perform," rather than the underlying theatrical performances themselves, while the *Pigg* correspondence course case involved the sale "of intelligence through instrumentalities of commerce."[53]

Not only did the court of appeals thus determine that the business of providing exhibitions of baseball to the public was not commerce, it also concluded that the business was not interstate in nature: "The players, it is true, travel from place to place in interstate commerce, but they are not the game. Not until they come into contact with their opponents on the baseball field and the contest opens does the game come into existence. It is local in its beginning and in its end." Thus, the court rejected Baltimore's emphasis on the overall structure of organized baseball, including the routine transportation of players and equipment across state lines. Instead, Smyth adopted Pepper's characterization of the business, focusing solely on the actual games themselves: "The transportation in interstate commerce of the players and the paraphernalia used by them was but an incident to the main purpose of the appellants, namely the production of the game. It was for it they were in business—not for the purpose of transferring players, balls, and uniforms. The production of the game was the dominant thing in their activities."[54]

For good measure, the court of appeals closed its opinion by focusing on the reserve clause itself, which it characterized as "the gravamen of [Baltimore's] case." Because major league rules prevented clubs from using the clause to retain more than the minimum number of players they needed to field a team, the court concluded that the provision was reasonable. It also believed that the clause was essential to the sustainability of professional baseball: "If the reserve clause did not exist, the highly skillful players would be absorbed by the more wealthy clubs, and thus some clubs in the league would so far outstrip others in playing ability that the contests between the superior and inferior clubs would be uninteresting, and the public would refuse to patronize them."[55] Consequently, the appellate court reversed Justice Stafford's judgment and remanded the case back to the trial court for further proceedings consistent with its opinion. Because Baltimore's counsel had agreed to waive all but its federal monopoly claims during the trial's closing argument, the lower court would thus be forced to formally dismiss the case pursuant to the court of appeals' ruling (which foreclosed any possibility of relief under the Sherman Act).

Organized baseball was thrilled with the decision. John Heydler released a statement praising the opinion the afternoon it was issued: "Coming at this time, the value of the decision cannot be measured in dollars and cents. There is nothing which has happened in baseball in years, which has given me greater pleasure, and after we have received so many knocks lately it is good to get good news for a change." Heydler emphasized the court's discussion of the reserve clause in particular, stating: "What is especially vital in the Washington decision is that for the first time in baseball history, the legality of the reserve clause is upheld by a high court."[56] Ban Johnson also applauded the news: "No more sweeping victory ever was won by Organized Baseball, and it will prove a great benefit to the sport. This decision clears the decks for a reorganization along the existing lines that will put the game on a strong foundation for the future."[57]

The *Sporting News* celebrated the opinion as well, regarding it as "a very clear, sensible decision." "The antitrust laws were meant to apply to trade in commodities and to prevent monopolization of the necessaries of life," it continued. "Baseball and theatrical entertainments are not necessaries and no one need buy admission to them unless he wants to. Therefore, the anti-trust laws are not applicable to them."[58]

The paper was less enthusiastic, however, about the passage of the opinion sustaining the validity of the reserve clause. "We cannot share the enthusiasm of some of our baseball contemporaries when they hail the District of Columbia court of appeals' decision in the suit of the Baltimore Federals as establishing the legality of the reserve clause in the player contract." Specifically, it believed "[t]he real test of the reserve clause in a baseball contract would come if a player should [argue] that . . . to get a contract for a season he had to give a mortgage on his services for life." "We doubt if any court, if it were put up to it that way, would uphold the reserve clause in a baseball contract."[59]

Finally, the *Sporting News* also took one last jab at the trial court: "This Judge Stafford of the District of Columbia court who ruled that baseball is interstate commerce and subject to penalties under the anti-trust law, must feel like a bone-headed base runner who has stolen third with all the bags filled, after the decision of the court of appeals telling him what an ivory-head he is."[60]

Nevertheless, the court of appeals' decision was not without its detractors. A commentary published in the *Michigan Law Review* shortly after the opinion was released criticized Chief Justice Smyth's reasoning. Indeed, in light of both organized baseball's overall structure and the frequent travel by players across state lines for road games, the author believed that Baltimore had the better argument on the interstate commerce issue: "[D]oes it not seem that when a baseball player signs to play not only at the home grounds, but on the fields of the other league members as well . . . the contract has the interstate feature as such an 'essential' element as to come within the Sherman Anti-Trust Act?"[61] Subsequent scholars have been similarly critical of the decision, with legal historian G. Edward White arguing years later that Smyth's conclusions that baseball was "local" rather than "interstate," and "sport" not trade or commerce, "seem merely assertive or conclusory."[62]

On the other hand, a 1921 commentary published in the legal periodical *Law Notes* complimented Smyth's opinion as being "well considered." In particular, the article praised the court's discussion of the reserve clause: "It is perfectly clear as a business proposition that the reserve clause is not only essential to the clubs but operates in the long run to the benefit of players and the public. It is therefore to be hoped that this decision will be generally accepted as establishing its validity."[63]

The *New York Herald* predicted that the court of appeals' opinion would mark the end of the case, believing that the "decision rendered yesterday will take all the wind out of the Baltimore sails. The Federal League stockholders of that city are not likely to throw any more good money after bad." Baltimore's counsel quickly shot down any notion that the team would accept the appellate court's ruling, however, with William Rawls announcing that "[t]he case will go to the United States Supreme Court. When we receive a copy of the opinion we will take steps to perfect the appeal." Indeed, Rawls's co-counsel, Charles Douglas, believed that his side would be vindicated on appeal: "We are absolutely confident that the United States Supreme Court will take our view of the matter, and will reverse the findings of the Court of Appeals."[64] In response, the *Sporting News* decried the possibility of continued litigation with a sub-headline announcing "Pestiferous Oriole City Feds Won't Let Dead Dog Lie." "[T]he pesky guerillas still seemed disposed to make trouble," a related story continued, "with every indication that they will get most of it themselves."[65]

Under the typical judicial procedure of the day, Baltimore's case would normally have returned to the trial court for Justice Stafford to formally dismiss it before it could then be appealed back up to the U.S. Supreme Court, a process that could have taken months to complete. To expedite the process, Baltimore's counsel instead asked the court of appeals to enter a final judgment itself in favor of the major leagues, so that the team could immediately appeal the decision.[66] The appellate court agreed in January 1921, paving the way for a direct appeal to the Supreme Court. Nevertheless, given the backlog of cases on the Court's docket, Baltimore's appeal would not be heard for nearly sixteen months.[67] As a result, the case would languish for more than a year without any significant developments.

Despite Douglas's confidence, Baltimore had its work cut out to convince the Supreme Court to overrule the appellate court's decision. By the time the case would be heard in 1922, the Court was headed by its recently appointed chief justice, William Howard Taft. The only man in history to serve as both president of the United States and chief justice of the Supreme Court, Taft finally realized his life's ultimate ambition in 1921 when he was tapped by President Warren G. Harding to lead the nation's highest court (Taft had long desired the position because it offered "power without worry").[68]

Taft's presence on the Court presented several challenges for Baltimore. First, although the chief justice had formerly held progressive political leanings, by the time he was appointed to the Supreme Court he had become a rather consistent judicial conservative. In particular, he frequently voted to interpret the commerce clause narrowly to protect private property rights.

Moreover, with specific regard to the Sherman Act, Taft had publicly adopted President Theodore Roosevelt's distinction between "good" and "bad" trusts, believing that the antitrust laws should only be used to defeat the latter, more pernicious forms of combination.[69] Together, these philosophies lent support to organized baseball's narrow reading of the Sherman Act's reach, especially considering that the major leagues would emphasize the beneficial aspects of the National Agreement in their brief.

Perhaps even more significantly, though, Taft's history with organized baseball and its legal counsel should also have worried Baltimore. Although Taft is popularly portrayed as a big baseball fan—he famously became the first U.S. president to throw out the ceremonial first pitch on baseball's opening day in 1910—and is rumored to have been a former player during his college years at Yale, in reality there is little evidence that he played the sport or maintained more than casual interest in it.[70] Nevertheless, the chief justice had extensive connections to the major leagues and their legal counsel, some of which likely shaped his view of Baltimore's claims. Most notably, Taft's half-brother Charles was the former owner of the Chicago Cubs, having sold the team to Charles Weeghman in 1915 as part of organized baseball's settlement with the Federal League.[71] Thus, Taft's own brother was himself a central party to the very peace agreement at issue in the case.

Second, the major leagues consulted with the former president in 1913 regarding the legality of the reserve clause—in anticipation of the forthcoming challenge from the Federal League—with Taft reportedly expressing his belief that the provision was legally enforceable.[72] Third, several major league owners reportedly approached Taft in 1918 to ascertain whether he would be willing to replace August Herrmann as chairman of the National Commission.[73] Fourth, the American and National Leagues each sent the chief justice a 1922 season pass—entitling him to free admission in any major league ballpark—just weeks before Baltimore's appeal was heard by the Supreme Court. In fact, during the Court's deliberations in May 1922, John Heydler sent a follow-up letter to Taft's secretary to confirm that the National League pass had been received (Taft had inadvertently sent his earlier thanks only to New York Giants owner Horace Stoneham).[74]

Finally, Taft was also a longtime acquaintance of George Pepper, having offered organized baseball's lead counsel a seat on the Third Circuit Court of Appeals during his presidency.[75] More recently, Taft was corresponding with the major leagues' attorney around the time that the Supreme Court considered Baltimore's appeal.[76] In January 1922, Pepper was appointed to the U.S. Senate on an interim basis by Pennsylvania's governor, following the death of Senator Boies Penrose, an office Pepper would hold until being defeated for re-election in 1927. Taft viewed Pepper as a potential ally in the chief justice's attempts to lobby Congress to pass legislation comprehensively reforming the organization and operation of the federal judiciary, with Taft even pushing for the celebrated litigator to be named to the Senate Judiciary Committee.[77]

Despite these apparent conflicts of interest, Taft did not recuse himself from the case, but instead fully participated in the Court's consideration of Baltimore's appeal. Taft's participation potentially placed the BaltFeds at a distinct disadvantage given the significant influence that he wielded over his colleagues. In the words of historian David H. Burton, "Taft dominated the Court for a decade," working to shape the Court's opinions so that they supported his personal jurisprudential beliefs. In fact, the chief justice had himself appointed two of his fellow justices—Willis Van Devanter and Mahlon Pitney—to the Court during his single term in the White House.[78]

Besides Taft, several other justices also potentially appeared predisposed to favor the major leagues in the case, for various reasons. For example, both Justices Joseph McKenna and William Day were known baseball fans, with Justice Day in particular considered by the press to be "[a] baseball fan of the first caliber." Not only did he know "the big league players by name," but Day also kept "up to the minute on their batting averages." Known to frequently rush "from the court to the ball park as soon as he could lay aside his robe," Day arranged for the Court's pages to provide him with inning-by-inning updates from the World Series when the Court was in session.[79] Though such baseball fandom did not render McKenna or Day incapable of judging Baltimore's case fairly, of course, the team nevertheless should have worried that it might factor into their consideration of the appeal. Meanwhile, Justice James McReynolds had reportedly met with Federal League officials in 1913 while serving as United States attorney general to discuss a potential antitrust investigation of organized baseball, but ultimately declined to take action.[80]

Finally, legendary Supreme Court Justice Oliver Wendell Holmes Jr. presented a different challenge for Baltimore. Specifically, Holmes subscribed to the contemporaneous social Darwinist belief that monopolies were merely part of the inevitable evolution of a market-based economy, with any attempt to curb them "flying in the face of the organization of the world." As a result, he famously abhorred the Sherman Act, considering it an "absurd" and "noxious humbug" that was "based on economic ignorance and incompetence," while listing antitrust cases among the "things I loathe."[81]

On the other hand, the personal histories of at least two members of the Court seemingly made them more amenable to Baltimore's case. For instance, the notably liberal Justice Louis Brandeis was an outspoken critic of trusts and monopolies, having worked to formulate the theory of regulated competition incorporated in the Federal Trade Commission Act of 1914 prior to his appointment to the Supreme Court.[82] Similarly, Justice Mahlon Pitney was known to possess an "antimonopoly bias," and as a result frequently voted to give "vitality to the [Sherman] Act" by dissenting in cases where he believed the Court was resorting to "'strained and unusual' interpretations . . . to uphold the legality of challenged practices."[83]

Despite the apparently unfavorable composition of the Court, as well as the fact that they had lost decisively at the court of appeals, Baltimore's counsel nevertheless elected to stay the course when filing their brief with the Supreme Court on February 27, 1922. Indeed, the brief was substantially the same as the one Baltimore had submitted to the appellate court below. For example, the franchise once again urged the Court "to distinguish between the business of providing exhibitions of baseball . . . and the sport

The Supreme Court justices that decided Baltimore's appeal (seated, from left to right): Justices William R. Day, Joseph McKenna, Chief Justice William Howard Taft, and Justices Oliver Wendell Holmes Jr. and Willis Van Devanter; (standing, from left to right): Justices Louis D. Brandeis, Mahlon Pitney, James C. McReynolds, and John Hessin Clarke (Photograph by Clinedinst Studio, Collection of the Supreme Court of the United States)

of baseball."[84] The brief also included the same, nearly one-hundred-page summary of the facts of the case, once more describing the organization and development of the two major leagues, the formation of the National Agreement, the operation of the reserve clause, organized baseball's interference with the Federal League, and the resulting peace agreement of 1915.

Baltimore's counsel presumably hoped that this discussion would highlight the injustice of the major leagues and their treatment of the Federals. Along these lines, the brief once again included heightened rhetoric describing organized baseball's "complete and despotic control" over the game through its "oppressive, intimidating and coercive course of treatment." Baltimore further characterized the 1915 peace agreement as a transaction amounting "to nothing less than bribery," while describing the major leagues' motives in forming the National Agreement of 1903 as little more than the "eliminat[ion of] the possibility of competition by establishing an absolute monopoly."[85]

Turning to its legal arguments, Baltimore's counsel followed the same structure used in the team's earlier brief to the court of appeals. Specifically, the attorneys first addressed the central issue of the appeal, namely whether professional baseball constituted interstate commerce. Once again, rather than contest the status of the individual games themselves under antitrust law, they emphasized the organization of the major leagues as a whole. Contending that "[t]he interstate element" of professional baseball "is fundamental, essential, indistinguishable and predominant," the attorneys argued that "[i]n its primary conception, in its original organization, throughout its entire existence, and in its every essential operation, this business contemplates, requires and avails itself of, travel, intercourse and commerce among a large number of the States of the Union." As a result, they insisted that "[i]n no other business that can now be recalled is there such a close inter-relationship and inter-dependence between persons in one state and persons in another." To further highlight the interstate nature of professional baseball, Baltimore added several maps to its brief illustrating the complete circuits of the two major leagues, the Federal League, and eight different minor leagues.[86]

Baltimore's brief also relied on the same legal precedents it had cited to the appellate court. Specifically, it once again provided an extensive, four-page quotation from the district court's opinion in *Marienelli,* while also emphasizing the Supreme Court's decisions in *Hoke* and *Pigg*. The team did add a brief reference to the revenue both the American and National Leagues received from their contracts with baseball manufacturers and Western Union, but otherwise simply repeated its prior assertion that the consistent and necessary travel by major league teams rendered the business interstate commerce under *Marienelli, Hoke,* and *Pigg*.[87] Baltimore thus did not provide any meaningful rebuttal of the grounds upon which the court of appeals had distinguished these legal precedents. The brief also failed to address either the *Hammerstein* or *Chase* decisions, a particularly glaring omission given the emphasis that the appellate court had placed on the two opinions. Consequently, Baltimore was never able to formulate an effective rebuttal to Pepper's argument that because the underlying baseball games themselves were not commerce, the industry as a whole could not constitute interstate commerce, regardless of how frequently baseball players were transported across state lines.

Next, Baltimore repeated its prior argument regarding organized baseball's monopolization of the baseball industry. The team once more contended that although a league of teams was necessary to maintain professional baseball, there was no need for a single organization controlling each of the various professional leagues under the National Agreement. The brief also took issue with the court of appeals' characterization of the case, noting that Baltimore had not based its monopolization claim solely on the reserve clause, but had also alleged that the major leagues conspired to destroy the Federal League through "coercion of both clubs and players and other unlawful practices." Finally, the club reasserted its belief that it had not waived the right to sue organized baseball, and that the trial court's damages verdict was supported by proper evidence.[88]

Whether the result of time or budget constraints, or mere hubris, Baltimore's counsel thus elected to rely on practically the exact same argument it had unsuccessfully pressed at the court of appeals less than a year and a half before. Instead, the team would have been better served if its attorneys had reworked their argument on the interstate commerce issue by placing greater emphasis on the revenues the major leagues received from equipment manufacturers and telegraph providers, thereby illustrating a way in which organized baseball profited from the production of tangible goods and the dissemination of information across state lines, both of which served to more closely align the industry with existing definitions of trade and commerce. Baltimore's counsel also could have drawn upon Justice Stafford's observation that the American and National Leagues' schedule-making authority was analogous to the theatrical contract brokerage activity at issue in the *Marienelli* case, thereby reaffirming the applicability of its most favorable precedent.

Organized baseball filed its brief in response a little more than a month later, on April 4, 1922. Like Baltimore, the major leagues also relied on substantially the same arguments they had presented to the court of appeals. Given the appellate court's decision, however, Pepper's decision to stay the course was more prudent and reasonable. Specifically, the brief began with the same discussion regarding the general structure and operation of professional baseball, again insisting that competitive sport requires a high degree of organization to maintain discipline, order, and competition. It also once more discussed the history of the Federal League and the ensuing peace agreement. In the process, organized baseball again characterized the reserve clause as "absolutely necessary" to the sport, and described the transportation of players as merely "incidental and subsidiary" to the "end in view," namely the actual games themselves.[89]

With respect to the legal arguments, Pepper again asserted that baseball was not subject to the Sherman Act for several reasons. First, he argued, "[i]t is believed that in no decided case has it ever been held that personal effort, considered apart from production, is a subject of commerce."[90] Years later, Pepper would recollect that he had chosen this language because he "knew that Justice Holmes had a keen appreciation for a well-turned phrase. And I thought that if I could implant such a phrase in his mind, it might affect the court's decision." In reality, though, this line was merely copied in its entirety from the brief organized baseball previously filed with the court of appeals.[91]

From there, the brief advanced several of the same analogies Pepper had previously used, comparing baseball to other activities that courts had ruled were not interstate commerce, such as acting, singing, and selling insurance contracts. In the process, it cited many of the same cases, emphasizing the holdings in *Hammerstein* and *Chase* in particular, while once more distinguishing the opinions in *Marienelli, Hoke,* and *Pigg*. Pepper also advanced the same two additional reasons why he believed baseball was not subject to the Sherman Act, contending that sporting events should only be subject to local, not national, regulation and insisting that the National Agreement was necessary to preserve the immensely popular World Series. Thus, he concluded, federal antitrust law should not apply to baseball absent express instruction from Congress.[92]

In addition to the interstate commerce arguments, the major leagues also advanced the other points they had made to the appellate court, once more arguing that organized baseball had acted in good faith when negotiating the settlement with the Federal League, that Baltimore had waived its right to sue, and that there had been insufficient evidence of damages presented during the trial. Finally, the defendants added one new argument, briefly contending that Baltimore lacked standing to sue because any injury inflicted by the major leagues harmed the Federal League in its entirety, and not the

BaltFeds specifically. As a result, they argued, the Federal League corporate entity itself should have brought the suit, and not a mere league shareholder like the Baltimore franchise.[93] This new argument was unlikely to be taken seriously by the Court, considering the major leagues had not only waited much too late in the litigation to assert it, but had also ignored the fact that the BaltFeds had indeed presented evidence at trial showing that organized baseball's actions had harmed the franchise itself—such as by driving up the price the team was forced to pay its players—and not just the league as a whole.

A week after the major leagues filed their brief, Baltimore submitted a short supplemental brief to the Supreme Court addressing several of the defendants' arguments. For example, the team took issue with organized baseball's contention that the National Agreement was essential to staging the World Series, noting that the series was never even mentioned in the agreement. Regardless, the BaltFeds insisted, the World Series alone did not justify the major leagues having complete control over the entire industry. Similarly, Baltimore rejected the defendants' argument that they had not monopolized the industry because the major league teams had only signed the minimum number of players they needed, arguing that organized baseball controlled all professional players through the reserve clause—including those in the minor leagues—and excluded rival leagues like the Federal from making routine trades or transactions for players. The supplemental argument closed with a final emotional appeal to the justices, framing the case as raising "the simple question as to whether [the defendants] are above the law or is the law above them?"[94]

Oral argument before the Supreme Court was scheduled for April 19, 1922. Pepper would later recall that he "was confident of the ultimate outcome" as the hearing approached, but nevertheless "awaited the third and final round of the fight with no little anxiety."[95] As was the case with the appellate court's oral argument, unfortunately no transcript of the Supreme Court's hearing remains. Nevertheless, much of the scene was captured in contemporaneous press reports, correspondence from baseball's attorneys, and Pepper's later recollections in his memoirs.

Indeed, Pepper would subsequently describe "[t]he situation [as being] dramatic. The courtroom was full of interested onlookers who realized that the continuance of the World Series games was at stake."[96] Heading into the argument, Pepper and Minor had "anticipated that [Baltimore's counsel] Mr. Douglass [*sic*] would open with a vitriolic attack on the methods of Organized Base-Ball and would focus attention upon the utterances of [Ban] Johnson as reported in the Evening Sun, which had made such a powerful impression upon the jury." They further expected Douglas's co-counsel "Mr. Marbury [to] prepare his closing argument on the theory that [Pepper] would attempt to answer Mr. Douglass [*sic*] and that the two of them would catch [him] between the upper and the lower mill-stone." Pepper was thus prepared to ignore his opponent's attacks in order to avoid spending all his time rebutting Douglas's characterizations of the major leagues at the expense of asserting his own legal arguments to the Court. He was subsequently relieved when his predictions regarding Baltimore's strategy "worked out exactly as we anticipated."[97]

According to Pepper, Douglas began the argument by using "all the epithets in the dictionary and stressed the Johnson interview for all it was worth."[98] Press reports at the time noted that Baltimore's attorney characterized the major league magnates as "highway men," while describing the players as being held in "peonage" where they were "bought and sold" like "chattels and slaves." Douglas would go on to discuss how his client was "betrayed" by its fellow league members, with the rest of the Federal League "selling out" to organized baseball. As a result, he explained, "[t]he Baltimore club was left with no club to play with and suffered heavy damages." He concluded by urging the Court to decide whether organized baseball is "above the law, or the law is above them," repeating the closing line from Baltimore's supplemental brief.[99] "When he finished," Pepper reported, "the Court was obviously impressed. There was a tense moment in the crowded court room before our side was presented."[100]

Rather than respond to Douglas's argument in kind, Pepper instead began his address by "quietly [telling] the Court that this was a battle between adjectives and nouns and that while the Federal League called us names we would answer only by reviewing the facts." Pepper then "proceeded to ignore everything Mr. Douglass [*sic*] had said and aroused the interest of the Court by picturing a World Series game, indicating the investment represented in the grounds, tracing through the minor leagues the history of each participating player, describing the interest and excitement of the crowd and explaining the necessity for the rules and regulations governing the draft, the reserve-right and the playing of the game." The strategy worked just as Pepper had hoped, "securing the lively interest of the justices and [making] them forget Mr. Douglass's [*sic*] indictment."[101]

Pepper then turned to the legal merits of the case. He stressed that any transportation was merely incidental, with the key facet of the business being the playing of baseball games in a single state. The "mere fact that the players habitually and necessarily cross State lines is not legally a material circumstance," he insisted. "Players move from one city to another under schedule . . . but a baseball game is not a part of commerce," he urged, just as "Mr. Marbury came here from Baltimore as per schedule today to argue this case, but he is not a part of interstate commerce." Pepper also pressed his argument that professional sports necessarily required a high degree of organization, contending that "[n]o statute can be construed as applying to combinations to regulate sport, unless Congress has plainly indicated an intention that this should happen." Finally, he cautioned, should the National Agreement be held unlawful, the World Series would have to be "done away with."[102]

Pepper would later report that by the time he had finished, "Mr. Marbury was taken by surprise. He rose to reply, tried to re-emphasize what Mr. Douglass [*sic*] had said but was told by Mr. Justice McKenna that he had better cut out the adjectives and get down to the nouns." Consequently, because "his argument had been prepared on an adjective basis he was unable to switch."[103]

Marbury would go on to emphasize the transportation of players across state lines, insisting that "[i]t is absolutely essential to the success of baseball that there be interstate transportation and intercourse." He also focused the Court's attention on the anticompetitive aspects of the major leagues, stressing "that the life of the business of providing exhibitions of professional baseball as [organized baseball] conducts it, depends not upon competition, but upon the complicated and complete restraint and regulation thereof." Continuing, he alleged that "[o]rganized baseball today presents the most peculiar and complete monopoly in this country, and I merely ask the court to go over its contracts, its reserve clauses and its draft arrangements to show that not one of the 8,000 players in this country have a chance to play ball unless they become a part of the system."[104]

Nevertheless, Pepper believed that Justice McKenna's interruption had caused Marbury to lose "his usual force and when he sat down [organized baseball's] case was won." The major leagues' attorney would later criticize Baltimore's strategy in his memoirs, stating that the team's counsel had "made the grave mistake of minimizing the real point of the case (the question, namely, whether interstate commerce was involved) and sought to inflame the passions of the Court by a vehement attack on the evils of the organization. . . ."[105]

Notwithstanding Pepper's confidence, the parties would have to wait several weeks for the Supreme Court to hand down its decision. Under the Court's typical procedure, the nine justices would have met in conference shortly after the argument to discuss the case and cast their initial votes regarding how it should be decided. One justice would then be assigned the task of writing the majority opinion by the chief justice (assuming the chief had voted in the majority).

Although no record of the initial vote remains, we know, based on contemporaneous correspondence between the justices, that Oliver Wendell Holmes Jr. drew the assignment to draft the majority opinion in the case. Before the opinion was announced publicly, Holmes circulated a draft of his decision among his fellow justices. In response to the draft, at least two justices wrote to Holmes to let him know they were changing their initial dissenting votes and now supported his majority opinion. Specifically, Justice Brandeis informed Holmes, "I have [great] doubt but shall acquiesce," while Justice McKenna wrote, "I voted the other way but I have resolved on amiability & concession, so submit. I am not [sure] that I am not convinced."[106] Thus, rather than reaching at best a 7–2 decision, the Court would be issuing a unanimous decision in the case.

Although unusual by present-day standards, at the time it was relatively common for justices to join decisions with which they personally disagreed. Indeed, Chief Justice Taft made it a priority to "mass" the court (that is, build a unanimous majority), believing that the Supreme Court should issue undivided rulings as often as possible given its standing as the court of last resort. As a result, more than 92 percent of the decisions rendered by the Court in 1922 were unanimous, an unimaginable figure today. In particular, the liberal Justice Brandeis would regularly forgo dissenting in what he deemed to be merely "ordinary cases," instead acquiescing to the decision adopted by his more conservative colleagues.[107]

The Supreme Court announced its decision on May 29, 1922. Following the usual custom, Justice Holmes read the unanimous majority opinion from the bench. The *Washington Post* described the scene by noting that Holmes "held the crowded courtroom in suspense as he gave 'a summary statement of the nature of the business involved' in the attack made upon organized baseball."[108] Reading from his characteristically concise written opinion—Holmes routinely omitted all but what he believed to be the essential elements of the decision—he began by explaining the context for the case, noting that Baltimore had accused the two major leagues of "conspir[ing] to monopolize the base ball business." Believing that it was "unnecessary to repeat" the specific ways in which organized baseball was alleged to have violated the law, Holmes praised "[t]he decision of the Court of Appeals" for having cut "to the root of the case," stating, "we are of the opinion that the Court of Appeals was right."[109]

Specifically, Holmes explained, "[t]he business is giving exhibitions of base ball," which he characterized as being "purely state affairs." "It is true," he conceded, "that in order to attain for these exhibitions the great popularity that they have achieved, competitions must be arranged between clubs from different cities and States." Nevertheless, he insisted, "the fact that in order to give the exhibitions the Leagues must induce free persons to cross state lines and must arrange and pay for their doing so is not enough to change the character of the business."[110] Thus, the Supreme Court adopted Pepper's characterization of the case, focusing on the status of the individual games themselves rather than the framework of the business in its entirety, as Baltimore had urged.

Continuing on, Holmes cited the Supreme Court's 1895 decision in *Hooper v. California*—a case dealing with interstate insurance contracts—as establishing the proposition that "the transport is a mere incident, not the essential thing."[111] Instead, he maintained, the proper focus should be placed on the exhibitions themselves, which "although made for money would not be called trade or commerce in the commonly accepted use of those words. As it is put by defendant, personal effort, not related to production, is not a subject of commerce." Holmes then adopted the analogies utilized by the court of appeals, noting that "a firm of lawyers sending out a member to argue a case, or the Chautauqua lecture bureau sending out lecturers, does not engage in such commerce because the lawyer or lecturer goes into another state." He concluded the opinion by reaffirming that the "conduct charged against the defendants [was] not an interference with commerce among the States."[112]

Thus, organized baseball had won the case.

The decision was, of course, celebrated by the major leagues. Curiously, the newly appointed commissioner of baseball, Judge Landis, does not appear to have issued a public statement regarding the decision. However, National League president John Heydler praised the opinion, declaring that "[i]t is, of course, most gratifying to all of us to know that the game as conducted is legally as well as morally sound." He characterized the ruling as "a tribute to the foresight and wisdom of the men who laid the foundations of the sport," predicting that it would "prove a great stimulus to the future development of baseball." "After years of litigation," he continued, "we finally have the clear-cut ruling of the highest court that baseball is a sport and not a trade, and that the Sherman Anti-Trust act has no application to our games as played under our interleague agreements and form of players' contract."[113]

Privately, Heydler congratulated Pepper "on this splendid termination of your untiring efforts," expressing his relief "to finally have this matter out of the way."[114] Meanwhile, Heydler himself received a perceptive note of congratulations from Julian Curtiss—president of the National League's official baseball manufacturer, Spalding—pointing out that "[t]he National League should pass a vote of thanks to the Baltimore Federal League crowd for carrying this matter to a final decision. . . . [I]t makes base ball stronger, and it will be a great help to the game." Curtiss closed his letter by noting, "Best of all too, it was a unanimous decision," obviously unaware of the Court's internal maneuverings prior to its announcement of the ruling.[115]

The *Sporting News* also predictably hailed the Supreme Court's decision, calling it "one of the biggest events in the history of the game." "The opinion of the court presents the matter in a very clear, common sense way," it observed, "indicat[ing] a much better knowledge of professional baseball than is usual among men not connected with the game. Perhaps the fact that Chief Justice Taft and Justice Day are veteran fans had something to do with this."[116] The paper closed its discussion of the case by declaring, "Now Organized Baseball knows definitely where it stands, and the baseball magnates, as well as the millions of fans, may well give thanks for this wonderful decision."[117] On the other hand, an editorial in the *Baltimore Sun* criticized the Court's decision, posing the rhetorical question: "[S]hould the legal status of a trust depend entirely upon the intangibility of its products? Should it not depend, in fairness, upon whether its chief purpose is to make money, and whether in conducting its business it destroys or injures the business of others?"[118]

Meanwhile, although the baseball establishment applauded the finality of Justice Holmes's opinion, Baltimore nevertheless prepared one last-ditch effort to revive its suit. Specifically, the club filed a Petition for Rehearing with the Supreme Court on July 1, 1922, asking the justices to set aside their earlier decision and reconsider the case, a drastic measure the Court would normally adopt only when it had made some sort of fundamental error in its opinion. Rather than identify any such mistake, however, Baltimore merely sought to reargue its case on the same grounds it had already asserted. Stating that it was apparent "we have altogether failed to make clear to the Court the nature of the business," the team's counsel once again insisted that transportation was not incidental to professional baseball—as Justice Holmes's opinion had concluded—but was in fact essential. The team asked rhetorically, "How can it be seriously denied that this business, as we have described it . . . is not interstate commerce in view of the repeated decisions of this Court"? In the process, Baltimore also challenged Holmes's characterization of the business as "giving exhibitions of base ball," arguing that major league teams were actually involved in the business of selling "to the public seats in said baseball parks."[119]

At a minimum, the club pleaded, the Court should amend its passing reference in the decision to baseball players as "free persons," to avoid giving "this monopoly such sanction and stamp of approval." Far from being free, Baltimore's counsel insisted, the players were actually subject to "a system of involuntary servitude . . . such as has not been witnessed since the enactment of the Thirteenth Amendment." The only reason that players would submit themselves to such a system, the petition closed, was "the passionate love which the boys of America have for the playing of this game."[120]

As one would expect, the Supreme Court promptly denied Baltimore's request for a rehearing upon reconvening in October. On October 9, 1922, the Court's clerk unceremoniously wrote to Baltimore's counsel, William Marbury, as follows: "I am instructed by the court to inform you that your petition for rehearing in the case of The Federal Base Ball Club of Baltimore, Inc. vs. The National League of Professional Baseball Clubs et al., No. 204 of the October Term, 1921, has been denied."[121]

Baltimore's case was officially over.

EPILOGUE

Scholars have not been kind to Justice Holmes's decision in *Federal Baseball.* The opinion ranks among the most frequently criticized in Supreme Court history, with commentators declaring it "unsatisfactory," "irrational," and "absurd."[1] These critics typically argue that "Holmes was clearly wrong" given the regularity with which professional baseball players traveled between states, and thus write the decision off as a reflection of the justice's "utter misunderstanding of the nature of the business of baseball."[2] One author has even gone so far as to speculate that the decision may have resulted from a secret conspiracy between Chief Justice William Howard Taft and baseball's first commissioner, Judge Kenesaw Mountain Landis (there is no sign of any such scheme in Taft's correspondence from the period).[3] As a result, the decision is generally considered "one of Holmes's worst," with the justice having had "one of the all-time worst days in Supreme Court history."[4]

These criticisms are largely unfair. Although *Federal Baseball* would unquestionably be decided differently today, at the time Holmes wrote the opinion it actually "represented a fairly orthodox application of then-prevalent constitutional doctrine," as U.S. Supreme Court Justice Samuel Alito noted in 2009.[5] Indeed, as the foregoing analysis has shown, when Baltimore's lawsuit was pending, courts interpreted the phrase "interstate commerce" much more narrowly than they do today. Although the Supreme Court would eventually transform its interstate commerce jurisprudence in the 1930s and 1940s—radically expanding the concept to encompass almost all commercial activity—at the time Baltimore's suit reached the Supreme Court, the judicial system was still adhering to traditional definitions limiting commerce to just the production or sale of tangible goods.

Viewed in that light, Holmes's opinion appears much more reasonable. As George Pepper shrewdly argued throughout the litigation, the industry's revenue at the time derived almost entirely from selling tickets to local exhibitions of baseball. Organized baseball neither produced any physical products itself nor received any income directly from the transportation of its players. Although the major leagues did earn some revenue from their contracts with equipment manufacturers and telegraph companies, these profits were not emphasized by Baltimore in its briefing, and in any event were relatively modest. Meanwhile, many of the features that would clearly render professional baseball to be interstate commerce today—such as the nationwide broadcasts of games over radio, television, and the Internet, and the major leagues' extensive merchandising activities—were years away from being adopted in 1922 (or, in the case of radio broadcasting, only in their experimental infancy).[6] Therefore, Holmes's focus on the status of the actual baseball games themselves in *Federal Baseball* was more than justifiable at the time.

Indeed, much of the criticism of Holmes's decision is based on the erroneous belief that *Federal Baseball* simply holds that the business of professional baseball was not sufficiently interstate in nature to fall within the ambit of the Sherman Act.[7] In actuality, however, the opinion was premised on two related, but ultimately separate grounds: (i) that organized baseball was not engaged in commerce, and (ii) that the relevant aspects of its business (that is, the games themselves) were not transacted across state lines (with the transportation of players being merely incidental to the overall scheme).[8] Nor did Holmes formally "exempt" baseball from antitrust law, as many commonly believe; instead, he merely determined that the Sherman Act did not apply to the sport under contemporaneous judicial interpretations of the law, a ruling that was subject to reconsideration should the Court modify its interstate commerce jurisprudence in the future. Thus, to argue that Holmes's decision was "absurd" or "clearly wrong" reflects a misunderstanding of the jurist's actual holding and/or the state of the law in 1922.

Meanwhile, some scholars have argued that the soundness of the *Federal Baseball* decision was undermined a year later by Holmes's opinion in *Hart v. B.F. Keith Vaudeville Exchange,* an antitrust case involving the vaudeville industry (notably featuring George Pepper arguing for the defense).[9] In *Hart,* the lower court had dismissed the plaintiff's complaint before trial, concluding that vaudeville was not interstate commerce and therefore that the defendants could not be liable under the Sherman Act. Despite the similarities between vaudeville and professional baseball, Holmes nevertheless reversed the lower court, instructing it to hold a trial in the case. The justice contended that it was possible the plaintiff could establish that the transportation of the vaudeville performers across state lines was central to the performances, and not merely "incidental" as in *Federal Baseball,* thereby potentially bringing the *Hart* defendants within the scope of federal antitrust law.[10]

Subsequent commentators have argued that the only way the *Hart* and *Federal Baseball* decisions "can be reconciled is by concluding that one involved baseball and the other involved vaudeville," suggesting that the Supreme Court was unusually deferential to the national pastime.[11] However, Holmes's decision in *Hart* can be distinguished from *Federal Baseball* in two other, more significant respects. First, by the time *Federal Baseball* reached the Supreme Court, Baltimore had already had a full trial on the merits, and therefore had had an opportunity to present its evidence regarding the aspects of the baseball industry that it believed subjected the sport to the Sherman Act. Holmes could thus rely upon a full record in the case when deciding that organized baseball was not engaged in interstate commerce and not within the scope of federal antitrust law. In contrast, the trial court dismissed *Hart* before the plaintiff could develop its evidence establishing the interstate elements of the defendants' vaudeville operations.[12] Therefore, Holmes's decision in the latter case can be read as holding that the plaintiff should at least receive an opportunity to prove that the defendants were engaged in interstate commerce, even if he was ultimately unlikely to succeed given the *Federal Baseball* precedent.[13]

Second, *Hart* is also potentially distinguishable from *Federal Baseball* insofar as the defendants in the vaudeville case were allegedly engaged in the brokering of contracts between performers and theaters in different states.[14] This facet of their business brought the *Hart* suit more closely in line with the *Marienelli* precedent Baltimore had relied on throughout the litigation, arguably providing a stronger basis to assert that the vaudeville defendants were engaged in interstate commerce than Baltimore was able to muster in its appeal. Therefore, Holmes's opinion in *Hart* does not necessarily contradict his conclusion in *Federal Baseball,* as some commentators have suggested.

Given the relatively orthodox nature of the Supreme Court's decision in *Federal Baseball,* it is fair to ask whether there was anything Baltimore could have done to win the suit. Although Holmes's opinion was consistent with the then-prevailing judicial precedent, that does not necessarily mean the case's eventual outcome was inevitable. Considering that at least two Supreme Court justices (Brandeis and McKenna), as well as a highly respected trial court judge (Stafford), all initially voted the other way—concluding that organized baseball was engaged in interstate commerce—shows that the proper characterization of the industry was a difficult question at the time. Thus, although the BaltFeds faced an uphill battle in prevailing under federal antitrust law, the team nevertheless could have presented a stronger case on appeal.

Most significantly, Baltimore's attorneys never formulated an effective strategy to counter George Pepper's focus on the status of the individual baseball games themselves as commerce. Although the team may not have been able to completely rebut this argument, it could have bolstered its case by highlighting different elements of the major leagues' operations to show that professional baseball was engaged in activities that were more conventionally considered to be interstate commerce at the time. For example, Baltimore could have illustrated organized baseball's involvement in both the production of tangible goods and the dissemination of information across states lines by placing greater emphasis on its contracts with the manufacturers of its official baseballs and telegraph provider Western Union. Similarly, the club's attorneys also could have done a better job of emphasizing the American and National Leagues' schedule-making authority. As Justice Stafford observed during the Washington trial, this activity arguably rendered the two major leagues (and their presidents, who were both defendants in the case) more closely analogous to the theatrical contract brokers in *Marienelli,* and thus would have made the club's presentation of its most favorable precedent more compelling.

Baltimore's failure to present its strongest argument was most glaring in its brief to the Supreme Court. Indeed, despite suffering a resounding defeat at the court of appeals, the team did not modify its interstate commerce argument in any meaningful respect for the final appeal. At a minimum, its attorneys should have addressed the grounds upon which the court of appeals had distinguished its precedents, and attempted to differentiate the opinions relied on by the appellate judges. Admittedly, these arguments may not have been enough to sway a majority of the Supreme Court, but they nevertheless would have improved Baltimore's chances of prevailing in the suit.

Not only did Baltimore thus fail to present its most compelling case on the threshold issue of baseball's status as interstate commerce, but its briefs also failed to effectively rebut organized baseball's arguments regarding the necessity of the reserve clause. Although this shortcoming likely was not fatal to its case, given the central role that the reserve clause played in the litigation the team's position nevertheless would have been strengthened had it done a better job explaining why the provision was not essential to the professional game. For instance, Baltimore could have highlighted Edward Hanlon's testimony from the trial in which he argued that in lieu of a reserve clause, major league teams could instead sign players to multiyear contracts, thereby providing the same roster stability benefits without imposing undue hardship on players or rival leagues. Had the club emphasized this point, it would have painted the reserve clause in a more nefarious, anticompetitive light, enabling the team to argue that far from being necessary, the provision was merely the most expedient means for the major leagues to reduce players' salaries and prevent the formation of competing leagues.

Moreover, well before the case reached the appellate stage, Baltimore's counsel made a critical mistake that likely cost the team its chance to prevail in the lawsuit, irrespective of the Supreme Court's ultimate decision regarding the applicability of the Sherman Act. Specifically, in addition to its federal antitrust claims, the team originally asserted both common-law monopoly and conspiracy claims in its Washington complaint. During the trial's closing arguments, however, Baltimore attorney William Marbury waived the common-law claims, resting his case entirely on the Sherman Act.[15] In hindsight, this was a significant mistake. Though Marbury presumably hoped to emphasize Baltimore's conviction in its interstate commerce argument, the decision to forgo its other grounds for relief was unlikely to have any appreciable impact on Justice Stafford's ultimate resolution of the issue.

Had the team preserved its other claims, it may have been victorious in the case despite the Supreme Court's decision. For example, to prevail on its common law conspiracy claim, Baltimore would have simply had to prove that the major league teams had schemed together to injure the team. Given the substantial evidence the club presented during the trial regarding organized baseball's efforts to destroy the Federal League—not only via the 1915 peace agreement, but also throughout the entire lifespan of the organization—the jury likely would have rendered a verdict in favor of the team on the conspiracy claim had it had the chance. Significantly, the Supreme Court's eventual decision in the case would have had little bearing on such a conspiracy finding because the claim did not require any proof of interstate activity or an effect on commerce.

Meanwhile, given that Justice Stafford ruled that baseball was an illegal monopoly under the Sherman Act, he likely would have ruled that its monopolization violated the common law as well if he had been allowed to consider the claim. Although that portion of the hypothetical verdict may also have been overturned on appeal—on the basis that professional baseball was not commerce under the common law for the same reasons as under federal law—such an outcome was not necessarily inevitable. Indeed, the New York state court in *Chase* held that organized baseball was not interstate commerce, and thus not governed by the Sherman Act, but nevertheless was an illegal monopoly under the common law.[16] Therefore, it is possible that a higher court would have reached the same result in Baltimore's suit, especially given the D.C. Court of Appeals' determination that *Chase* was a "carefully prepared opinion."[17]

Baltimore's legal counsel thus made several critical mistakes in the suit. Not only did the team fail to present its case as effectively as possible on appeal, but it also needlessly waived additional potential bases for relief during the trial. Although it is impossible to know for sure how events would have unfolded had these errors not occurred, they nevertheless significantly reduced the team's chances of victory in the suit.

Meanwhile, even though legal commentators have been overwhelmingly critical of Holmes's opinion in *Federal Baseball,* subsequent courts have—with a few notable exceptions discussed below—generally treated the decision quite deferentially. Remarkably, the opinion is still binding precedent today, despite the subsequent expansion of the Supreme Court's interstate commerce jurisprudence and the significant evolution of the major leagues' business operations.

After Baltimore's lawsuit, organized baseball did not face another antitrust challenge for more than a quarter of a century, until the 1948 case of *Gardella v. Chandler*. The facts giving rise to the *Gardella* case are similar to *Federal Baseball*. Following World War II, the owners of the Mexican League disregarded organized baseball's reserve clause and tried to sign current major leaguers by offering them substantial contracts in the hope of improving their circuit's reputation. One of the few players the league successfully recruited was Danny Gardella, a relatively undistinguished outfielder from the New York Giants, who signed a $10,000 contract with Veracruz for the 1946 season. Although Gardella returned to the United States the next year, he was unable to resume playing in the major leagues because of a five-year suspension baseball commissioner Happy Chandler—Judge Landis's successor—had imposed on every player defecting to the Mexican League. Gardella eventually sued the major leagues under the Sherman Act, alleging that they had illegally monopolized the industry and conspired to deprive him of his livelihood as a professional player.[18]

Although the district court dismissed Gardella's case—determining that the Supreme Court's decision in *Federal Baseball* precluded the suit—the Second Circuit Court of Appeals reversed the decision, allowing Gardella to proceed with his claim. In particular, the appellate court characterized *Federal Baseball* as an "impotent zombi," concluding that the advent of radio and television broadcasts of baseball games, as well as the Supreme Court's expanded definition of interstate commerce, now brought baseball within the scope of the Sherman Act. Before the case could proceed any further, however, the major leagues settled the dispute by reinstating Gardella and paying him $60,000, thereby ending the litigation.[19]

The Supreme Court would not have to wait long for another opportunity to reconsider the *Federal Baseball* precedent, though. Shortly after Gardella's suit, three minor league players each individually sued the major leagues, alleging that the reserve clause was an illegal restraint of trade in violation of the Sherman Act. All three suits were dismissed by their respective trial courts pursuant to *Federal Baseball,* decisions that were affirmed on appeal. The Supreme Court then agreed to hear the consolidated appeals, resulting in its 1953 opinion in *Toolson v. New York Yankees.*[20]

In *Toolson,* the Supreme Court rejected the players' challenge by a seven-to-two margin, determining that the suits were precluded by Holmes's decision in *Federal Baseball.* In a short, one-paragraph opinion, the Court noted that despite the significant expansion of its interstate commerce jurisprudence and the growth of baseball's commercial operations, the sport had nevertheless "been left for thirty years to develop on the understanding that it was not subject to existing antitrust legislation." Although "Congress [had] had the [*Federal Baseball*] ruling under consideration" for some time, it had "not seen fit to bring [baseball] under these laws by legislation," the opinion continued. Consequently, the Court concluded, "if there are evils in this field which now warrant application to it of the antitrust laws, it should be by legislation," rather than a judicial decision retroactively overturning a long-standing precedent. The Supreme Court thus affirmed the lower court decisions on the basis of *Federal Baseball,* "so far as that decision determines that Congress had no intention of including the business of baseball within the scope of the federal antitrust laws."[21]

Holmes, of course, never mentioned congressional intent in his *Federal Baseball* decision, despite George Pepper asserting that very argument on behalf of the major leagues in the appeal. As a result, one commentator has called the *Toolson* court's interpretation of *Federal Baseball* "the greatest bait-and-switch scheme in the history of the Supreme Court."[22] Nevertheless, this closing passage had significant practical implications, transforming the *Federal Baseball* holding from "a rule subject to change pending future developments in the law or the business of baseball" to "a permanent exemption grounded in Congress's purported original intent when passing the Sherman Act."[23] Thus, it was actually *Toolson,* rather than Holmes's opinion in *Federal Baseball,* that formally established an enduring antitrust exemption for professional baseball.

Shortly after *Toolson,* other, seemingly analogous industries sought to extract their own antitrust protection from the 1953 decision, to no avail.

For example, in 1955 the Supreme Court refused to extend baseball's antitrust exemption to professional boxing.[24] Then, in a 1957 case involving the National Football League, the Court held that *Federal Baseball* and *Toolson* applied only to the "business of baseball."[25] In the process, the Court acknowledged that *Federal Baseball* "was of dubious validity," and that it would be decided differently if being raised "for the first time upon a clean slate."[26] Nevertheless, the justices refused to overturn the decision or extend it to professional football.

The Supreme Court considered baseball's antitrust status for the third and (to date) final time in 1972, in the case of *Flood v. Kuhn*.[27] The suit arose after St. Louis traded its star center fielder, Curt Flood, to the Philadelphia Phillies in 1969. Flood refused to report to Philadelphia and instead requested that he be given the right to sign with any team of his choice. When baseball commissioner Bowie Kuhn refused, Flood opted to file suit, attacking the reserve clause under antitrust law.[28]

Flood's lawsuit was eventually dismissed by both the trial and appellate courts on the basis of *Federal Baseball* and *Toolson*. The Supreme Court then agreed to hear the case in order "to look once again at this troublesome and unusual situation." In a controversial decision authored by Justice Harry Blackmun—the opinion has been criticized in particular for its initial, three-page "sentimental journey" through baseball history, identifying more than eighty former players by name while praising baseball's status as the national pastime—the Court acknowledged that "baseball is a business and it is engaged in interstate commerce." The opinion also admitted that baseball's antitrust exemption was "an exception and an anomaly." Nevertheless, the Court was "loath, 50 years after *Federal Baseball* and almost two decades after *Toolson*, to overturn those cases judicially when Congress, by its positive inaction, has allowed those decisions to stand for so long."[29] In other words, because Congress had permitted baseball to develop on the assumption it was immune from antitrust law, a five-to-three majority of the Supreme Court decided not to revoke the exemption even though the original basis for the doctrine had long since been eviscerated.

Following *Flood*, courts have generally continued to hold that the major leagues are exempt from antitrust law, with most judges interpreting the Supreme Court's decisions as broadly shielding the entire business of baseball from the Sherman Act. In the mid-1990s, however, several courts tried to restrict baseball's antitrust exemption by limiting its scope to encompass only the reserve clause. These decisions interpreted *Flood* as merely protecting the reservation practice itself from antitrust law based on an overemphasis of a few passing references to the provision in the decision.[30] Meanwhile, because *Flood* explicitly stated that baseball was "engaged in interstate commerce"—thereby directly repudiating the central logic of Justice Holmes's opinion—these lower courts believed it had stripped *Federal Baseball* of "any precedential value . . . beyond the particular facts there involved."[31] Put differently, rather than continue to provide baseball with a broad exemption from antitrust law, these lower courts believed that the Supreme Court's three baseball precedents now only shielded those specific activities that were at issue in the respective litigations.

While both the *Toolson* and *Flood* suits were primarily premised on the reserve clause, these lower courts also determined that *Federal Baseball* itself dealt exclusively with the provision. Given Holmes's relatively terse opinion, the courts turned to the D.C. Court of Appeals' decision in the case—which characterized the reserve clause as the "gravamen of [Baltimore's] case"—and concluded that the provision was the only basis for Baltimore's lawsuit.[32] Because major league players had freed themselves of the reserve clause through collective bargaining and arbitration in 1976, the implication of these lower court decisions was that baseball's antitrust exemption was effectively dead.[33]

As the foregoing analysis has revealed, this interpretation of *Federal Baseball* was clearly erroneous. Although the reserve clause was central to Baltimore's case, it was not the sole basis for the team's antitrust claims. Indeed, the club also alleged that the major leagues violated the Sherman Act in other ways, including the 1915 peace agreement and the National Agreement's territorial restrictions granting teams exclusive control over their home markets.[34] Moreover, though not sufficiently stressed by the team, Baltimore's brief to the Supreme Court also argued that the major leagues' contracts with their official equipment manufacturers and Western Union brought professional baseball within the scope of the Sherman Act.[35] Thus, while the reserve clause played an important role in the case, it was not the only activity at issue in the suit. As a result, these recent attempts to limit the scope of baseball's antitrust exemption to just the reserve clause are contrary to the actual history of the *Federal Baseball* case.[36]

Because later courts have largely ignored these three lower court decisions limiting the scope of baseball's antitrust immunity, the exemption remains largely intact today. Although scholars have debated the significance of the exemption on baseball's development and operations, at a minimum most commentators agree that the doctrine provides valuable protection to the minor league system, preventing any potential antitrust challenges to the major league teams' significant control over their minor league affiliates.[37] As a result, Major League Baseball closely guards its unique antitrust status, having even gone so far as to refrain from asserting the exemption in several antitrust recent cases, presumably to avoid the risk of an adverse decision limiting the scope of its protection.[38] Consequently, it appears unlikely that the Supreme Court will get another opportunity to re-evaluate the *Federal Baseball* precedent anytime soon.

Ironically, Justice Holmes himself would likely be among the harshest critics of the continued vitality of his decision in *Federal Baseball.* Prior to joining the Supreme Court, he wrote that "[i]t is revolting to have no better reason for a rule of law than that so it was laid down in the time of Henry IV. It is still more revolting if the grounds upon which it was laid down have vanished long since, and the rule simply persists from blind imitation of the past."[39] Revolting or not, the legacy of the Federal League and Baltimore's lawsuit nevertheless continues to live on today.

NOTES

INTRODUCTION

1. For example, see Roger I. Abrams, *Legal Bases: Baseball and the Law* (Philadelphia: Temple University Press, 1998); Jerold J. Duquette, *Regulating the National Pastime: Baseball and Antitrust* (Westport, Conn.: Prager, 1999), Ed Edmonds, "Over Forty Years in the On-deck Circle: Congress and the Baseball Antitrust Exemption," *Thurgood Marshall Law Review* 19 (1994); Gordon Hylton, "Why Baseball's Antitrust Exemption Still Survives," *Marquette Sports Law Journal* 9 (1999); Andrew Zimbalist, "Baseball Economics and Antitrust Immunity," *Seton Hall Journal of Sport Law* 4 (1994).

2. For example, see Gary Hailey, "Anatomy of a Murder: The Federal League and the Courts," *National Pastime* (Spring 1985): 73.

CHAPTER 1. THE RIVALRY BEGINS

1. "Federal League Will War On Majors to the Finish," *Atlanta Constitution,* October 16, 1913, 10.

2. Daniel R. Levitt, *The Battle that Forged Modern Baseball: The Federal League Challenge and Its Legacy* (Lanham, Md.: Ivan R. Dee, 2012), 34; Robert Peyton Wiggins, *The Federal League of Base Ball Clubs: The History of an Outlaw Major League, 1914–1915* (Jefferson, N.C.: McFarland, 2009), 6; "Columbian League Awards Franchise," *Milwaukee Sentinel,* February. 13, 1912, 2.

3. Levitt, *The Battle that Forged Modern Baseball,* 36–37; Wiggins, *The Federal League of Base Ball Clubs,* 10.

4. Levitt, *The Battle that Forged Modern Baseball,* 38; Wiggins, *The Federal League of Base Ball Clubs,* 10–11, 17.

5. Levitt, *The Battle that Forged Modern Baseball,* 42; "This Federal Child Renounces Father," *Sporting News,* August 7, 1913, 1.

6. Levitt, *The Battle that Forged Modern Baseball,* 42.

7. Ibid., 42–43; Wiggins, *The Federal League of Base Ball Clubs*, 22, 26.

8. Lee Lowenfish, *The Imperfect Diamond: A History of Baseball's Labor Wars* (Lincoln: University of Nebraska Press, 1980, 2010), 16.

9. Killefer Answer, Weeghman v. Killefer, Exhibit A, National Archives, Chicago, Illinois.

10. Ibid.

11. Ibid.

12. Abrams, *Legal Bases*, 33.

13. G. Edward White, *Creating the National Pastime: Baseball Transforms Itself 1903–1953* (Princeton, N.J.: Princeton University Press, 1996), 48.

14. Ibid., 49.

15. Abrams, *Legal Bases*, 19.

16. 9 N.Y.S. 779 (1890).

17. Ibid.

18. *Brooklyn Baseball Club v. McGuire*, 116 F. 782 (E.D. Pa. 1902); *Metropolitan Exhibition Company v Ewing*, 42 F. 198 (S.D.N.Y. 1890); *Philadelphia Ball Club v. Hallman*, 8 Pa.C.C. 57 (1890); *American Association Base-Ball Club of Kansas City v. Pickett*, 8 Pa.C.C. 232 (1890); *Harrisburg Base-Ball Club v. American Association*, 8 Pa.C.C. 337 (1890).

19. 202 Pa. 210 (1902).

20. Abrams, *Legal Bases*, 40.

21. E. G. Barrow to August Herrmann, November 26, 1913, Federal League Suit Papers, Box 2, Folder 1, National Baseball Hall of Fame Library, Cooperstown, New York (hereafter FLSP).

22. 15 U.S.C. § 1; Duquette, *Regulating the National Pastime*, 10.

23. 15 U.S.C. § 2.

24. Wiggins, *The Federal League of Base Ball Clubs*, 5; Lowenfish, *The Imperfect Diamond*, 70.

25. Eugene C. Murdock, *Ban Johnson: Czar of Baseball* (Westport, Conn.: Greenwood Press, 1982), 18–19, 31; Charles C. Alexander, *Our Game: An American Baseball History* (New York: MJF Books, 1991), 76.

26. Alexander, *Our Game*, 75; Levitt, *The Battle that Forged Modern Baseball*, 16–18.

27. Lowenfish, *The Imperfect Diamond*, 70.

28. "Anti-Trust Law in Baseball War," *New York Times*, December 31, 1913, 12.

29. Ibid.

30. Ibid.

31. "Are the Ball Leagues in Restraint of Trade?" *Christian Science Monitor*, March 14, 1912, 16.

32. "Congress is After the Baseball Trust," *New York Times*, April 20, 1913, 1; Charles C. Alexander, *Ty Cobb* (New York: Oxford University Press, 1985), 112, 133; "Capitol Sneers at 'Baseball Inquiry'," *Washington Herald*, May 13, 1913.

33. "Congressional Probe for Organized Baseball," *Pittsburgh Gazette,* March 22, 1913; John Toole to T. J. Lynch, June 17, 1913, August "Garry" Herrmann Papers, Box 114, Folder 3, National Baseball Hall of Fame Library, Cooperstown, New York (hereafter HP); "Federal League Protests," *New York Times,* June 16, 1913, 7.

34. National Commission Confidential Memorandum, Undated, HP, Box 114, Folder 2.

35. Ibid.

36. Ban Johnson to August Herrmann, May 23, 1913, HP, Box 114, Folder 3.

37. "Baseball in House," *Washington Post,* April 23, 1913, 1.

38. William A. Cook, *August "Garry" Herrmann: A Baseball Biography* (Jefferson, N.C.: McFarland, 2008), 1; Levitt, *The Battle that Forged Modern Baseball,* 24; Wiggins, *The Federal League of Base Ball Clubs,* 29.

39. "Major Leagues Would Not Suffer From 'Trust' Probe," *Cincinnati Enquirer,* April 24, 1913.

40. Mitchell Nathanson, "Who Exempted Baseball Anyway? The Curious Development of the Antitrust Exemption That Never Was," *Harvard Journal of Sports & Entertainment Law,* 4 (2013):5.

41. "Big Ban in Capital; Does Not Fear Probe," *Washington Herald,* June 14, 1913, 10.

42. "Ready for Issue When It Arises," *Sporting Life,* May 31, 1913.

43. Quinn to Johnson, May 29, 1913, FLSP, Box 2, Folder 1.

44. Hedges to Johnson, June 4, 1913, FLSP, Box 2, Folder 1.

45. Johnson to August Herrmann, May 31, 1913, FLSP, Box 2, Folder 1.

46. Barnard to Johnson, August 4, 1913, FLSP, Box 2, Folder 1.

47. Johnson to Herrmann, August 5, 1913, FLSP, Box 2, Folder 1.

48. Ibid.

49. Cook, *August "Garry" Herrmann,* 195; Galvin and Kinkead to August Herrmann, January 3, 1914, 3–5, HP, Box 82, Folder 12.

50. Ibid., 12.

51. 15 U.S.C. § 1–2 (1890).

52. Galvin and Kinkead to Herrmann, January 3, 1914, 17.

53. Ibid., 25; "Clubs to Enjoin Contract Jumpers," *New York Times,* December 29, 1913, 5.

54. Bulletin from Herrmann to Major League Club Owners, February 18, 1914, FLSP, Box 2, Folder 2.

55. "Federal League Raids Stir Tener," *New York Times,* January 8, 1914, 12.

56. Levitt, *The Battle that Forged Modern Baseball,* 6; Robert C. Gallagher, "John Tener's Brilliant Career," *Baseball Research Journal* 20 (1990): 36–37.

57. "Did Commission Make a Break?" *Sporting News,* January 15, 1914, 1.

58. Levitt, *The Battle that Forged Modern Baseball,* 104.

59. "Clubs to Enjoin Contract Jumpers," *New York Times,* December 29, 1913, 5

60. Ibid.

Chapter 2. The Opening Salvos

1. Levitt, *The Battle that Forged Modern Baseball,* 8–10.

2. Wiggins, *The Federal League of Base Ball Clubs,* 32–33, 91; "Dope on Bank Roll Weeghman of Feds," *Sporting News,* January 29, 1914, 7; Patrick E. Mears, "The Catcher, 'The Quick Lunch King' and Baseball's Reserve Clause: Major League Litigation in Grand Rapids," *Stereoscope* (Winter 2003): 4.

3. "Take No Action Against Tinker," *Washington Post,* December 29, 1913, 8; "Will Back Its Players," *Washington Post,* December 29, 1913, 8; Levitt, *The Battle that Forged Modern Baseball,* 10.

4. Ibid., 10, 181; "Cincinnati Now Becomes Center of Ball Matters," *Christian Science Monitor,* January 5, 1914, 16; "Federal League Jumps Too Great," *Atlanta Constitution,* January 2, 1914, 8.

5. "Herrmann Again Heads Commission," *Atlanta Constitution,* January 6, 1914, 9.

6. Wiggins, *The Federal League of Base Ball Clubs,* 35–36; Levitt, *The Battle that Forged Modern Baseball,* 62.

7. Ibid., 67, 112.

8. Wiggins, *The Federal League of Base Ball Clubs,* 48; Mears, "The Catcher," 4.

9. "Killifer Comes Back and Magee Signs His Contract," *Sporting News,* January 29, 1914, 1.

10. Ibid.; Levitt, *The Battle that Forged Modern Baseball,* 92.

11. Levitt, 93.

12. Ibid.

13. Ibid.

14. Harold Seymour, *Baseball: The Golden Age* (New York: Oxford University Press, 1971, 1989), 204.

15. "Federals Ready to Sue," *New York Times,* February 9, 1914, 8.

16. "President Gilmore Announces Plans," *Sporting News,* January 29, 1914, 5.

17. "Their Action Shows Fear, He Asserts," *Washington Post,* January 23, 1914, 8.

18. Levitt, *The Battle that Forged Modern Baseball,* 92, 96.

19. Ibid., 96.

20. "Ebbets Will Try to Restrain Tinker," *New York Times,* February 7, 1914, 12; Levitt, *The Battle that Forged Modern Baseball,* 93.

21. "Baseball Reserve Clause is Legal," *New York Times,* January 31, 1914, 9; "Big Leagues Plan to Thwart Federal," *New York Times,* February 5, 1914, 7; "Ball Players In Court," *New York Times,* January 27, 1914, 10; "Much Ball to be Played in Court," *Sporting News,* February 5, 1914, 1.

22. "Federals Get 'Dan' Murphy," *Washington Post,* March 10, 1914, 8; "Federals Will War on Organized Ball," *Atlanta Constitution,* March 9, 1914, 6.

23. "Federals Will War on Organized Ball," *Atlanta Constitution,* March 9, 1914, 6.

24. Levitt, *The Battle that Forged Modern Baseball,* 104.

25. A copy of the injunction order is attached to a letter from James Gaffney to John Tener, March 18, 1914, FLSP, Box 3, Folder 1.

26. Mears, "The Catcher," 2.

27. Complaint, Weeghman v. Killefer, 2–7, HP, Box 110, Folder 8.

28. "Federal Goes Into Court for Killifer," *New York Times,* March 21, 1914, 11; "With Phillies Says Killifer," *Washington Post,* March 21, 1914, 8.

29. Wiggins, *The Federal League of Base Ball Clubs,* 119; Levitt, *The Battle that Forged Modern Baseball,* 105.

30. Complaint, Pittsburgh Athletic Company v. Federal League Base Ball Club of Pittsburgh, 2–3, HP, Box 108, Folder 23.

31. Johnson to Herrmann, March 28, 1914, FLSP, Box 2, Folder 2; Levitt, *The Battle that Forged Modern Baseball,* 105.

32. Herrmann to Johnson, March 30, 1914, FLSP, Box 2, Folder 2.

33. Answer, Pittsburgh Athletic Company v. Federal League Base Ball Club of Pittsburgh, 2–5, HP, Box 108, Folder 23.

34. Herrmann to Johnson, March 30, 1914, FLSP, Box 2, Folder 2.

35. "Contracts in Court," *New York Times,* April 3, 1914, 9; Ellis Kinkead to August Herrmann, April 6, 1914, HP, Box 108, Folder 21.

36. Opinion, Pittsburgh Athletic Company v. Federal League Base Ball Club of Pittsburgh, 3–5, 7, HP, Box 108, Folder 21.

37. Kinkead to August Herrmann, April 6, 1914, HP, Box 108, Folder 21.

38. Johnson to Herrmann, April 8, 1914, HP, Box 111, Folder 8.

39. Answer of Killefer, Weeghman v. Killefer, 2–4, National Archives, Chicago, Illinois (hereafter National Archives, Chicago); Answer of Philadelphia, Weeghman v. Killefer, National Archives, Chicago.

40. "Federal League Put on Defensive," *New York Times,* April 5, 1914, S1; Levitt, *The Battle that Forged Modern Baseball,* 40; Leander J. Monks, ed., *Courts and Lawyers of Indiana* (Indianapolis: Federal Publishing, 1916), 1, 257–58.

41. "Federal League Put on Defensive," *New York Times,* April 5, 1914, S1; Levitt, *The Battle that Forged Modern Baseball,* 113–14; George Wharton Pepper, *Philadelphia Lawyer: An Autobiography* (Philadelphia: J. B. Lippincott, 1944), 81–82, 141.

42. "Federal League Put on Defensive," *New York Times,* April 5, 1914, S1.

43. Ibid.

44. Levitt, *The Battle that Forged Modern Baseball,* 115; "Courts Question Fed Moral Rights," *Sporting News,* April 9, 1914, 2.

45. "Federal League on Defensive At Opening of Legal Fight," *Atlanta Constitution,* April 7, 1914, 13; "'Feds' Get Setback," *Washington Post,* April 5, 1914, S1; "Killifer Case is Undecided," *Washington Post,* April 8, 1914, 8.

46. "Opinions on Killifer Decision," *Sporting News,* April 16, 1914, 3.

47. "Insures Feds, He Declares," *Washington Post,* April 3, 1914, 8.

48. Tener to Herrmann, April 2, 1914, HP, Box 70, Folder 3.

49. "Court League May Hang on Awhile," *Sporting News,* April 16, 1914, 2.

50. *Weegham v. Killefer*, 215 F. 168, 170–71 (W.D. Mich. 1914).

51. Ibid., 171–73.

52. "Baseball Reserve Clause is Invalid," *New York Times,* April 11, 1914, 12.

53. "Opinions on Killifer Decision," *Sporting News,* April 16, 1914, 3; "Killifer Injunction Denied," *Atlanta Constitution,* April 11, 1914, 11; "Baseball Reserve Clause is Invalid," *New York Times,* April 11, 1914, 12; "No Court Fights for Feds," *New York Times,* April 25, 1914, 16.

54. "Reserve Rule 'Is Not Valid'," *Washington Post,* April 11, 1914, 8.

55. "Killifer Injunction Denied," *Atlanta Constitution,* April 11, 1914, 11.

56. Ibid.

57. Kinkead to Herrmann, April 13, 1914, 2–4, HP, Box 110, Folder 8.

58. The suit noted that John Quinn's real name was John Picus. Declaration, Boston National League Baseball Company v. Hanlon, 5–7, National Archives, Philadelphia, Pennsylvania (hereafter National Archives, Philadelphia); "Gaffney Sues Federal Heads in Quinn Case," *Christian Science Monitor,* April 13, 1914, 16

59. "Federals Sued," *Washington Post,* April 14, 1914, 8.

60. "Two $25,000 Suits Aimed at Federals," *New York Times,* April 14, 1914, 9.

61. Complaint, Philadelphia National League Club v. Weeghman, 2–4, National Archives, Chicago.

62. Answer, Philadelphia National League Club v. Weeghman, 2, National Archives, Chicago.

63. "No Date for Federal Hearings," *New York Times,* April 15, 1914, 11.

64. "Commission to Mix in Fight on Feds," *New York Times,* April 20, 1914, 10.

65. Bulletin from National Commission to Major League Club Owners, April 23, 1914, FLSP, Box 2, Folder 3.

66. Complaint, Federal Base Ball Company of Kansas City v. Blanding, Case No. 295, Circuit Court of St. Louis Records Department, St. Louis, Missouri; Petition for Damages, Federal Baseball Company of Kansas City v. Hamilton, Case No. 82557, Circuit Court of Jackson County, Missouri. Hamilton eventually removed his case from state court to the United States district court for the Western District of Missouri in September 1914.

67. Levitt, *The Battle that Forged Modern Baseball,* 116; Wiggins, *The Federal League of Base Ball Clubs,* 49.

68. Levitt, *The Battle that Forged Modern Baseball,* 116–17.

69. Wiggins, *The Federal League of Base Ball Clubs,* 75.

70. Herrmann Affidavit, Cincinnati Exhibition Company v. Johnson, 2–3, HP, Box 109, Folder 5; Complaint, Cincinnati Exhibition Company v. Johnson, Case No. B2356, Cook County Circuit Court Archives, Chicago, Illinois (hereafter Cook County Archives.).

71. Complaint, Cincinnati Exhibition Company v. Johnson, 2, HP, Box 109, Folder 4.

72. Complaint, Cincinnati Exhibition Company v. Madison, 3, 6, Case No. 308197, Cook County Archives; Complaint, Cincinnati Exhibition Company v. Madison, Case No. B2357, Cook County Archives.

73. Herrmann to John Tener, April 29, 1914, FLSP, Box 2, Folder 3.

74. Galvin to August Herrmann, April 28, 1914, HP, Box 109, Folder 8.

75. Galvin to Herrmann, May 16, 1914, FLSP, Box 1, Folder 3; Herrmann to Galvin, May 18, 1914, FLSP, Box 1, Folder 3.

76. Answer, Cincinnati Exhibition Company v. Johnson, 1–2, HP, Box 109, Folder 1.

77. Ibid., 2–3.

78. Appellate Brief, Cincinnati Exhibition Company v. Johnson, 4, FLSP, Box 5, Folder 6.

79. Answer, Cincinnati Exhibition Company v. Johnson, 3–4.

80. John Galvin and Ellis Kinkead to August Herrmann, May 20, 1914, HP, Box 109, Folder 8.

81. John Healy to John Galvin, May 25, 1914, HP, Box 111, Folder 3.

82. Opinion, Cincinnati Exhibition Company v. Johnson, 5–7, 20, HP, Box 109, Folder 8.

83. Ibid., 3, 5, 7–8.

84. "Federals Dealt Severe Blow by Court Decision," *Chicago Tribune,* June 4, 1914, 15.

85. "Federal League Gets Hard Blow," *New York Times,* June 4, 1914, 9; "'Chief' Johnson Restrained From Playing With Federals," *Washington Post,* June 4, 1914, 8.

86. "Indian Turns Against Reds," *Chicago Tribune,* June 4, 1914, 15.

87. Statement of August Herrmann, Undated, HP, Box 109, Folder 8.

88. "Federals Dealt Severe Blow by Court Decision," *Chicago Tribune,* June 4, 1914, 15; "Federal League Gets Hard Blow," *New York Times,* June 4, 1914, 9.

89. Herrmann to Johnson and Tener, May 27, 1914, FLSP, Box 2, Folder 3; Levitt, *The Battle that Forged Modern Baseball,* 116.

Chapter 3. The Federal League Strikes Back

1. Levitt, *The Battle that Forged Modern Baseball,* 127; Peter T. Toot, *Armando Marsans: A Cuban Pioneer in the Major Leagues* (Jefferson, N.C.: McFarland, 2004), 8, 13, 94; Wiggins, *The Federal League of Base Ball Clubs,* 126.

2. Toot, *Armando Marsans,* 94.

3. Levitt, *The Battle that Forged Modern Baseball,* 127.

4. Wiggins, *The Federal League of Base Ball Clubs,* 127.

5. Galvin to John Healy, June 17, 1914, 2, HP, Box 109, Folder 18.

6. Ellis Kinkead to August Herrmann, June 9, 1914, 2–3, HP, Box 109, Folder 18.

7. Toot, *Armando Marsans,* 100–102; Levitt, *The Battle that Forged Modern Baseball,* 127; Wiggins, *The Federal League of Base Ball Clubs,* 127.

8. Bill for Injunction, Federal Baseball Co. of Kansas City v. Blanding, Case No. 308988, Cook County Archives; Answer of Fred Blanding, 6, Federal Baseball Co. of Kansas City v. Blanding, Case No. 308988, Cook County Archives; "Federals Would Enjoin Blanding," *Chicago Tribune,* June 5, 1914, 13.

9. "Becomes a Fed," *Washington Post,* June 16, 1914, 8.

10. Ibid., 129.

11. Ibid., 129–30.

12. David Pietrusza, *Major Leagues: The Formation, Sometimes Absorption and Mostly Inevitable Demise of 18 Professional Baseball Organizations, 1871 to Present* (Jefferson, N.C.: McFarland, 1991), 231.

13. Martin Donell Kohout, *Hal Chase: The Defiant Life and Turbulent Times of Baseball's Biggest Crook* (Jefferson, N.C.: McFarland, 2001), 130.

14. Ibid., 131.

15. Wiggins, *The Federal League of Base Ball Clubs,* 130.

16. Complaint, Cincinnati Exhibition Company v. Marsans, 5–6 (included as part of the appellate record in the case filed with the United States Circuit Court of Appeals for the Eighth Circuit, Case No. 4562, available from the National Archives, Kansas City, Missouri).

17. Toot, *Armando Marsans,* 105.

18. Kinkead to August Herrmann, June 18, 1914, 1, HP, Box 109, Folder 18.

19. Opinion, Cincinnati Exhibition Company v. Marsans, HP, Box 109, Folder 13.

20. Toot, *Armando Marsans,* 106.

21. Bill for Injunction, American League Baseball Club of New York, Inc. v. Schulz, Case No. 309300, Cook County Archives; "Suit to Restrain Schulz," *New York Times,* June 21, 1914, S1.

22. Wiggins, *The Federal League of Base Ball Clubs,* 130; Kohout, *Hal Chase,* 134–35.

23. Wiggins, *The Federal League of Base Ball Clubs,* 131; Kohout, *Hal Chase,* 135.

24. Ibid., 137.

25. "Chase's Side of His Case," *New York Times,* July 2, 1914, 10.

26. American League Baseball Club of Chicago v. Chase, 149 N.Y.S. 6, 17 (1914).

27. Untitled, *New York Times,* July 2, 1913, 10.

28. Plaintiff's Brief, American League Baseball Club of Chicago v. Chase, 4–5, 9, 24, 39, FLSP, Box 5, Folder 6.

29. Ibid., 6, 18, 29, 41, 56–57.

30. Ibid., 47–49.

31. Wiggins, *The Federal League of Base Ball Clubs,* 131; Kohout, *Hal Chase,* 137.

32. Ellis Kinkead to August Herrmann, July 14, 1914, 2–3, HP, Box 108, Folder 24; "Chase Verdict July 18," *New York Times,* July 11, 1914, 9.

33. Ibid.; Ellis Kinkead to August Herrmann, July 14, 1914, 2.

34. Brief for Appellants, *Weeghman v. Killefer,* 29, National Archives, Chicago.

35. Brief for Appellees, *Weeghman v. Killefer,* 12–13, National Archives, Chicago

36. "Phelon's Pickups," *Sporting News,* June 18, 1914, 4.

37. Weeghman v. Killifer, 215 F. 289, 292 (6th Cir. 1914).

38. "Is Feds' Weapon," *Washington Post,* July 2, 1914, 8.

39. Opinion, Cincinnati Exhibition Company v. Johnson, 3–5, HP, Box 109, Folder 8.

40. "Federal League Wins Big Victory," *Atlanta Constitution,* July 17, 1914, 8.

41. Levitt, *The Battle that Forged Modern Baseball,* 129.

42. "Federal League Wins Big Victory," *Atlanta Constitution,* July 17, 1914, 8; "Appellate Court Changes Ruling in Johnson Case," *Christian Science Monitor,* July 16, 1914, 1.

43. Ellis Kinkead to August Herrmann, July 17, 1914, 2, HP, Box 109, Folder 8; Ellis Kinkead to August Herrmann, July 16, 1914, 2–3, HP, Box 109, Folder 8.

44. *American League Baseball Club of Chicago v. Chase,* 149 N.Y.S. 6, 7, 10–14 (1914).

45. Ibid., 17.

46. "Chase Declared Free Agent by New York Court, Which Rules Ten-Day Clause Creates Monopoly," *Washington Post,* July 22, 1914, 8.

47. "Chase Injunction Set Aside; Feds Win Another Victory," *Atlanta Constitution,* July 22, 1914, 8.

48. Pietrusza, *Major Leagues,* 232.

49. Kohout, *Hal Chase,* 140.

50. Kinkead to George Williams, August 3, 1914, 2, HP, Box 109, Folder 7.

51. Ellis Kinkead to August Herrmann, July 21, 1914, 1–2, HP, Box 109, Folder 7; Lambert to Moot and Marcy, August 1, 1914, HP, Box 108, Folder 24.

52. George Williams to Ellis Kinkead, July 2, 1914, 1, HP, Box 109, Folder 18.

53. Answer, Cincinnati Exhibition Company v. Marsans, 6, HP, Box 109, Folder 15.

54. Ibid., 7; Ellis Kinkead to August Herrmann, June 18, 1914, 1, HP, Box 109, Folder 18.

55. Cornelius Roach to Cincinnati Exhibition Company, September 1, 1914, HP, Box 109, Folder 7.

56. Answer, Cincinnati Exhibition Company v. Marsans, 8–9, 14, 15, 17, 18–19, 24.

57. John Galvin and Ellis Kinkead to August Herrmann, October 7, 1914, at 10–12, HP, Box 109, Folder 7.

58. Kinkead to George Williams, August 3, 1914, 2, HP, Box 109, Folder 7.

59. Pittsburgh Order, Cincinnati Exhibition Company v. Johnson, HP, Box 109, Folder 8.

60. John Galvin to August Herrmann, July 30, 1914, 2–4, HP, Box 109, Folder 8.

61. Ibid., 5.

62. John Galvin to Watson and Freeman, August 13, 1914, 1, HP, Box 109, Folder 7.

63. Pittsburgh Transcript, Cincinnati Exhibition Company v. Johnson, 3–5, HP, Box 109, Folder 7.

64. Ibid., 6.

65. John Galvin to August Herrmann, September 2, 1914, 2, HP, Box 109, Folder 7.

66. Pittsburgh Opinion, Cincinnati Exhibition Co. v. Johnson, 5, HP, Box 109, Folder 7.

67. "A Victory For What?" *Sporting News,* July 23, 1914, 4.

68. Ibid.

69. "The War of the Leagues," *Baseball Magazine,* August 1914, 33, 35–36.

70. "Fans Tired of Baseball War; Sport Itself Interests Them," *Washington Post,* August 11, 1914, 8.

71. Herrmann to Ban Johnson and John Tener, July 22, 1914, FLSP, Box 2, Folder 3.

72. Johnson to August Herrmann, July 23, 1914, FLSP, Box 2, Folder 3.

73. "Feds Ready to Seek Truce, Says St. Louis Club Head," *Chicago Tribune,* September 25, 1914.

74. Wiggins, *The Federal League of Base Ball Clubs,* 163–64.

75. Cook, *August "Garry" Herrmann,* 195.

76. Johnson to Herrmann, October 29, 1914, HP, Box 111, Folder 19.

77. Galvin Ellis Kinkead to Herrmann, October 7, 1914, at 16, HP, Box 109, Folder 7.

78. Ibid., 16–17.

79. August Herrmann to Ban Johnson, October, 17, 1914, 2, 4–5, FLSP, Box 2, Folder 4; August Herrmann to Ban Johnson and John Tener, October 24, 1914, FLSP, Box 2, Folder 4; August Herrmann to John Tener, November 2, 1914, 4–6, FLSP, Box 2, Folder 4.

80. Levitt, *The Battle that Forged Modern Baseball,* 156; Herrmann to John Tener, November 2, 1914, 6.

81. "Barney Dreyfuss Flays Federals," *New York Times,* Dec. 7, 1914, 12; "Prospects of Early Peace Fade as Issues are Joined," *Sporting News,* November 19, 1914, 1.

82. August Herrmann to M. H. Cantillon, September 9, 1914, 1, FLSP, Box 2, Folder 3.

83. "Barney Dreyfuss Flays Federals," *New York Times,* December 7, 1914, 12; Levitt, *The Battle that Forged Modern Baseball,* 158; "Prospects of Early Peace Fade as Issues are Joined," *Sporting News,* November 19, 1914, 1.

84. "Braves Withdraw Damage Suit Against Feds," *Atlanta Constitution,* December 8, 1914, 12.

85. Seymour, *Baseball,* 152–53.

86. Levitt, *The Battle that Forged Modern Baseball,* 172; "Feds Can't Use Johnson Declares A. L. President," *Washington Post,* December 15, 1914, 10; "Weeghman Warned in Plenty of Time, *Sporting News,* December 17, 1914, 1.

87. Benjamin Minor to Ban Johnson, December 4, 1914, 1, HP, Box 109, Folder 7.

88. "Feds Can't Use Johnson Declares A. L. President," *Washington Post,* December 15, 1914, 10; "Johnson Convinced that Option Clause is Valid; This is What Brought Him Back, Asserts Griffith," *Washington Post,* December 21, 1914, 8.

89. "Johnson is to Stay," *Washington Post,* December 20, 1914, 1; "Johnson Convinced that Option Clause is Valid; This is What Brought Him Back, Asserts Griffith," *Washington Post,* December 21, 1914, 8.

90. Pietrusza, *Major Leagues,* 234–35.

91. "Johnson is to Stay," *Washington Post,* December 20, 1914, 15.

Chapter 4. The Landis Case

1. "The Famous Federal Suit," *Baseball Magazine,* March 1915, 65.

2. Bill of Complaint, Federal League of Professional Baseball Clubs v. National League of Professional Baseball Clubs, FLSP, Box 9.

3. Ibid., 1–3, 4–9, 16.

4. Ibid., 38.

5. Ibid., 10–11.

6. Ibid., 11–13, 24.

7. Ibid., 17.

8. Ibid., 19, 21.

9. Ibid., 22.

10. Ibid., 22–23.

11. Ibid., 26–36.

12. Ibid., 38–39.

13. Ibid., 39–40. Exhibits attached to the pleading included copies of the National Agreement, the National Commission's Rules and Regulations, and Walter Johnson's 1914 contract with Washington.

14. James R. Devine, "The Racial Re-Integration of Major League Baseball: A Business Rather Than Moral Decision; Why Motive Matters," *Seton Hall Journal of Sport Law* 11 (2001): 21; J. G. Taylor Spink, *Judge Landis and Twenty-Five Years of Baseball* (Binghamton, N.Y.: Vail-Ballou Press, 1947), 26, 29; Wiggins, *The Federal League of Base Ball Clubs,* 174; David Pietrusza, *Judge and Jury: The Life and Times of Judge Kenesaw Mountain Landis* (South Bend, Ind.: Diamond Communications, 1998), 39–40; Shayna M. Sigman, "The Jurisprudence of Judge Kenesaw Mountain Landis," *Marquette Sports Law Journal* 15 (2005): 282.

15. Wiggins, *The Federal League of Base Ball Clubs,* 174.

16. Pietrusza, *Judge and Jury,* 3; Spink, *Judge Landis and Twenty-Five Years of Baseball,* 18.

17. "Baseball Defense Raises New Point," *New York Times,* January 20, 1915, 10; "Press Box Pickups and Landis Park," *Sporting News,* January 28, 1915, 3.

18. Herrmann to Griffith, January 5, 1915, HP, Box 105, Folder 7.

19. Griffith to Herrmann, January 8, 1915, HP, Box 105, Folder 7.

20. Minor to Herrmann, January 12, 1915, 1, HP, Box 105, Folder 7.

21. "Federals File Suit to Enjoin Majors as a Trust," *Chicago Tribune,* January 6, 1915, 9.

22. Ibid.

23. "Federal League in Suit Against the Commission," *Christian Science Monitor,* January 5, 1915, 1.

24. "Federals File Suit to Enjoin Majors as a Trust," *Chicago Tribune,* January 6, 1915, 9.

25. Ibid.

26. "Case to Landis; Johnson Happy," *Chicago Tribune,* January 7, 1915, 9.

27. "Federals File Suit to Enjoin Majors as a Trust," *Chicago Tribune,* January 6, 1915, 9; "Reply Will Charge Fraud," *New York Times,* January 6, 1915, 14.

28. "Tener Engages Pepper," *New York Times,* January 9, 1915, 9.

29. "O. B. is Strictly Legal Declares N. L. President," *Washington Post,* January 9, 1915, 8.

30. Bulletin from Herrmann to Major League Club Owners, January 6, 1915, FLSP, Box 1, Folder 4.

31. August Herrmann to Gaffney, December 16, 1914, FLSP, Box 2, Folder 4; C. H. Ebbets to August Herrmann, January 3, 1915, FLSP, Box 1, Folder 4.

32. August Herrmann to Ban Johnson and John Tener, January 5, 1915, FLSP, Box 1, Folder 4.

33. Herrmann to Tener, January 6, 1915, 1–2, HP, Box 112, Folder 21.

34. "Federal League Charges a Trust," *New York Times,* January 6, 1915, 14.

35. "Federals File Suit to Enjoin Majors as a Trust," *Chicago Tribune,* January 6, 1915, 9.

36. "Feds Pull Greatest Bone in All Their Erratic Career," *Sporting News,* January 14, 1915, 1; "Our Own Part in It," *Sporting News,* January 14, 1915, 4.

37. "Feds Pull Greatest Bone in All Their Erratic Career," *Sporting News,* January 14, 1915, 1.

38. "Limit on Affidavits in Baseball Battle," *Washington Post,* January 10, 1915, S1.

39. "Discuss Baseball Suit," *New York Times,* January 13, 1915, 10; August Herrmann to Ban Johnson and John Tener, January 15, 1915, FLSP, Box 1, Folder 4; "'Business Men' In Baseball Must Go," *New York Times,* January 8, 1915, 9.

40. "O. B. is Strictly Legal Declares N. L. President," *Washington Post,* January 9, 1915, 8; Herrmann to John Tener, January 7, 1915, FLSP, Box 1, Folder 1.

41. Kinkead to Miller, January 9, 1915, 2, HP, Box 105, Folder 7.

42. 15 U.S.C. § 17.

43. Kinkead to Miller, January 9, 1915, 4, HP, Box 105, Folder 7.

44. All citations to the affidavits from *Federal League of Professional Baseball Clubs v. National League of Professional Baseball Clubs* (hereafter "Chicago Suit") refer to copies of the statements prepared by the National Commission, on file with the National Baseball Hall of Fame Library, FLSP, Box 9. Brown Affidavit, Chicago Suit, 23.

45. Bresnahan Affidavit, Chicago Suit, 260–62.

46. Brown Affidavit, Chicago Suit, 20.

47. "Watkins and His Affidavit," *Sporting News,* January 21, 1915, 4.

48. Watkins Affidavit, Chicago Suit, 5–6.

49. Ibid., 7

50. "Watkins and His Affidavit," *Sporting News,* January 21, 1915, 4.

51. Knabe Affidavit, Chicago Suit, 25–27; Oakes Affidavit, Chicago Suit, 13–15, 16–17; Tinker Affidavit, Chicago Suit, 37–38.

52. Herrmann Affidavit in Opposition to Injunction, Chicago Suit, 8, 12, 13, 19, 20–22, 26–27.

53. Ibid., 24–25, 26, 29, 30.

54. Ibid., 18, 31, 32.

55. Herrmann Affidavit regarding Allegations in Paragraph Six of the Complaint, Chicago Suit.

56. Comiskey Affidavit, Chicago Suit, 92; Griffith Affidavit, Chicago Suit, 117, 121–22.

57. Baker Affidavit, Chicago Suit, 204.

58. Gilmore Reply Affidavit, Chicago Suit, 6, 10–12, 13–19.

59. Ibid., 4–5, 21, 26, 34.

60. "Rival Baseball Leaders Expect Speedy Action," *Chicago Tribune,* January 14, 1915, 9.

61. "Moguls Mold Shells for Big Legal Battle," *Chicago Tribune,* January 16, 1915, 9.

62. "Organized Ball and Feds in Big Legal 'Game' Today," *Chicago Tribune,* January 20, 1915, 9; "Interest in Organized Baseball," *Christian Science Monitor,* January 21, 1915, 16.

63. "Press Box Pickups and Landis Park," *Sporting News,* January 28, 1915, 3; "Federal League Opens Court Battle Against O.B.," *Chicago Tribune,* January 21, 1915, 9.

64. Ibid.; Levitt, *The Battle that Forged Modern Baseball,* 185; "Press Box Pickups and Landis Park," *Sporting News,* January 28, 1915, 3.

65. Transcript, Chicago Suit, 2–4, HP, Box 105, Folders 5 and 6.

66. Ibid., 4, 7–8, 13.

67. Ibid., 14–15, 16.

68. Ibid., 27–29, 31, 32.

69. Ibid., 23, 81–82.

70. Ibid., 52–62.

71. "Federal League Opens Court Battle Against O.B.," *Chicago Tribune,* January 21, 1915, 9.

72. Transcript, Chicago Suit, 29–31, 34–36, 37–40, 82–83.

73. "Press Box Pickups and Landis Park," *Sporting News,* January 28, 1915, 3.

74. Transcript, Chicago Suit, 123.

75. "Minor Leagues and Players Oppressed," *New York Times,* January 21, 1915, 10.

76. "Doubts Jurisdiction in Baseball Suit," *New York Times,* January 22, 1915, 12.

77. "Landis Excuses 'Commy'," *Chicago Tribune,* January 24, 1915, III–1.

78. Transcript, Chicago Suit, 126–29.

79. Ibid., 145–49.

80. 235 U.S. 133 (1914).

81. Transcript, Chicago Suit, 150.

82. "O.B. Attorney Goes to Plate in Feds' Suit," *Chicago Tribune,* January 22, 1915, 14; Transcript, Chicago Suit, 150, 158–66.

83. Transcript, Chicago Suit, 164, 188.

84. Ibid., 191–92; "O.B. Attorney Goes to Plate in Feds' Suit," *Chicago Tribune,* January 22, 1915, 14.

85. Ibid.; Transcript, Chicago Suit, 194–97, 204.

86. Ibid., 207, 208, 211.

87. Ibid., 198–99, 200–201, 214–15.

88. Ibid., 210, 218.

89. Ibid., 220, 229.

90. Ibid., 231.

91. Ibid., 246–48.

92. Ibid., 242–43.

93. 147 N.Y.S. 532 (1914).

94. Transcript, Chicago Suit, 239, 240–42, 244.

95. Ibid., 251–52.

96. Ibid., 256. On this point, Pepper attempted to distinguish the *Chase* court's ruling that baseball was commerce for purposes of state antitrust law by noting that the court there simply found that the defendants' actions precluded the issuance of injunctive relief on their behalf, not that the Federal League would itself have a basis under the law on which to sue organized baseball. Ibid., 260.

97. Ibid., 264.

98. Ibid., 265–66.

99. Ibid., 268–70.

100. Ibid., 273.

101. Jason M. Pollack, "Take My Arbitrator, Please: Commissioner 'Best Interests' Disciplinary Authority in Professional Sports," *Fordham Law Review* 67 (1999): 1651; L. A. Powe Jr., "What Does Bo Know?" *Virginia Law Review* 82 (1996): 1390; White, *Creating the National Pastime,* 106.

102. Pietrusza, *Judge and Jury,* 156.

103. "Federal League Closes Its Case With E.E. Gates," *Christian Science Monitor,* January 23, 1915, 26.

104. Transcript, Chicago Suit, 280–320, 322–23, 347, 350–58.

105. Ibid., 325–27, 331, 334–35, 339.

106. Ibid., 359–61, 368–73.

107. Ibid., 374, 376–78.

108. "Federal League Closes Its Case With E.E. Gates," *Christian Science Monitor,* January 23, 1915, 26; "Attorneys Fire Hot Shot at Feds in Defense Plea," *Chicago Tribune,* January 23, 1915, 11.

109. "Ban Grilled by Attorney in Ball War," *Chicago Tribune,* January 24, 1915, III–1.

110. Transcript, Chicago Suit, 379–80, 381–82.

111. Ibid., 382; "Why Did Feds Start Their Trust Busting Suit Anyway?" *Sporting News,* January 28, 1915, 1.

112. Transcript, Chicago Suit, 386, 387, 392; "Ban Grilled by Attorney in Ball War," *Chicago Tribune,* January 24, 1915, III–2.

113. Transcript, Chicago Suit, 394–402.

114. Ibid., 403–8.

115. Ibid., 420–22, 425–26.

116. "Baseball Fans Await Decision of Judge Landis," *Christian Science Monitor,* January 25, 1915, 14; "Ban Grilled by Attorney in Ball War," *Chicago Tribune,* January 24, 1915, III–1; Transcript, Chicago Suit, 456, 458–59, 465, 502.

117. Ibid., 524; Walsh Affidavit, Chicago Suit, 22; Lichtenhein to Herrmann, January 29, 1915, 2, HP, Box 106, Folder 1.

118. Transcript, Chicago Suit, 469, 476–81.

119. "Ban Grilled by Attorney in Ball War," *Chicago Tribune,* January 24, 1915, III–1; Transcript, Chicago Suit, 472.

120. Ibid., 524–26.

121. Ibid., 528.

122. Ibid., 532.

123. "Sliced Off a Few Requests," *Cincinnati Enquirer,* January 25, 1915, 8.

124. "Federals Will Abide By Ruling of Judge Landis," *Christian Science Monitor,* January 26, 1915, 20.

125. "Two Pitchers Let Go By Manager Griffith," *Washington Post,* January 26, 1915, 8; "Why Did Feds Start Their Trust Busting Suit Anyway?" *Sporting News,* January 28, 1915, 1; "Baseball Fans Await Decision of Judge Landis," *Christian Science Monitor,* January 25, 1915, 14.

Chapter 5. The Long Wait

1. August Herrmann to Ban Johnson and John Tener, January 25, 1915, FLSP, Box 1, Folder 4.

2. Joint Answer of August Herrmann, Byron Bancroft Johnson and John K. Tener, Chicago Suit, FLSP, Box 9; Separate Answer of the Cincinnati Exhibition Company, Chicago Suit, FLSP, Box 9.

3. Ibid., 32–38.

4. For example, see Separate Answer of the Brooklyn Ball Club, Chicago Suit, National Archives, Chicago, Box 4, Folder 12; Separate Answer of the American Baseball Club of Philadelphia, Chicago Suit, National Archives, Chicago, Box 4, Folder 12; Separate Answer of National Exhibition Company, Chicago Suit, National Archives, Chicago, Box 4, Folder 13; John Galvin to August Herrmann, February 15, 1915, FLSP, Box 1, Folder 1.

5. No reply to the counterclaims was contained in the case file for the litigation at the National Archives, Chicago, nor was any mentioned in the press.

6. "Judge Landis Will Hand Down Decision in Feds' Suit by Next Saturday," *Atlanta Constitution,* February 4, 1915, 9; "No Decision on Baseball Case Given This Week," *Christian Science Monitor,* February 6, 1915, 14.

7. "Rumor Factory is Doing Double Time," *Sporting News,* February 11, 1915, 1; "Judge Landis to Speak This Week," *Washington Post,* February 24, 1915, 20.

8. Levitt, *The Battle that Forged Modern Baseball,* 197, 264; Wiggins, *The Federal League of Base Ball Clubs,* 186.

9. Ibid., 186–92.

10. "Desertions Stir Up Federals' Wrath," *New York Times,* March 4, 1915, 10. These players included Jimmy Austin, Ray Caldwell, Rip Hagerman, W. P. Perritt, and Ivy Wingo.

11. "Newark Feds to Stay," *New York Times,* March 13, 1915, 11; "Landis' Delay is an Ever Present Alibi," *Sporting News,* February 18, 1915, 5.

12. "Baseball Peace Rumor in Chicago," *New York Times,* April 24, 1915, 12.

13. George Williams to Ellis Kinkead, April 24, 1915, FLSP, Box 1, Folder 1; "Johnson to Aid Feds at Expense of Tener," *Washington Post,* April 26, 1915, 8; "Peace Terms Signed," *New York Times,* May 5, 1915, 11.

14. "Judge Landis May End Baseball War," *New York Times,* April 27, 1915, 10; "Feds' New Boogie Man," *Sporting News,* May 6, 1915, 4.

15. August Herrmann to Ban Johnson and John Tener, April 10, 1915, FLSP, Box 2, Folder 5.

16. Tener to August Herrmann, May 19, 1915, 1, HP, Box 109, Folder 19.

17. George Williams to August Herrmann, June 4, 1914, FLSP, Box 1, Folder 1.

18. Deposition Transcript, Cincinnati Exhibition Company v. Marsans, 21, 38. The deposition transcript is attached to the petition filed by the St. Louis Federal League club with Judge Landis on June 28, 1915. Petition of St. Louis Federal League Base Ball Company, Chicago Suit, National Archives, Chicago, Box 4, Folder 15 (hereafter "St. Louis Petition").

19. Kinkead to August Herrmann, May 4, 1915, 3, FLSP, Box 1, Folder 1.

20. St. Louis Petition, 4–5.

21. Ellis Kinkead to August Herrmann, June 29, 1915, 1–2, HP, Box 109, Folder 19.

22. "Landis Baseball Decision Soon," *New York Times,* June 29, 1915, 11.

23. "Let Judge Landis Speak," *Sporting News,* July 8, 1915, 4.

24. John Healy to Ellis Kinkead, July 29, 1915, FLSP, Box 1, Folder 1; John Healy to Ellis Kinkead, August 7, 1915, FLSP, Box 1, Folder 5.

25. "Will Try Ten-Cent Baseball to Draw 'Fed' Fans in Newark," *Washington Post,* August 5, 1915, 8.

26. Levitt, *The Battle that Forged Modern Baseball,* 217.

27. Ellis Kinkead to August Herrmann, August 14, 1915, 4, HP, Box 109, Folder 19.

28. Montague Lyon to Ellis Kinkead, April 5, 1915, HP, Box 109, Folder 19; John Galvin and Ellis Kinkead to August Herrmann, April 6, 1915, HP, Box 109, Folder 19.

29. Ellis Kinkead to August Herrmann, August 14, 1915, 2, 6–7, HP, Box 109, Folder 19.

30. Ellis Kinkead to August Herrmann, August 17, 1915. Kinkead's letter is contained in a compilation entitled "Marsans Case at St. Louis, on file with the Hall of Fame Library, HP, Box 109, Folder 16 (hereafter "Marsans Case Compilation").

31. Opinion, Cincinnati Exhibition Co. v. Marsans, Marsans Case Compilation.

32. Ibid., 46–47.

33. Ellis Kinkead and John Galvin to Ban Johnson, John Tener, and August Herrmann, August 21, 1915, 1–2, 4–5, Marsans Case Compilation.

34. "Delay Baseball Suit," *New York Times,* October 3, 1915, 40; "Baseball This Winter," *New York Times,* October 16, 1915, 12; Levitt, *The Battle that Forged Modern Baseball,* 224, 227.

35. "Robert Ward, Fed Backer, is Dead," *Sporting News,* October 21, 1915, 1.

36. August Herrmann to John Tener, August 4, 1915, FLSP, Box 2, Folder 5.

37. "National Said to Have Agreed to Let Federals Buy Into Their Circuit," *Washington Post,* December 15, 1915, 8; Wiggins, *The Federal League of Base Ball Clubs,* 276–77; Levitt, *The Battle that Forged Modern Baseball,* 226.

38. Pepper to Tener, November 8, 1915, 2, FLSP, Box 1, Folder 1; Pepper to Tener, October 29, 1915, FLSP, Box 1, Folder 1; Pepper to Tener, November 3, 1915, FLSP, Box 1, Folder 1.

39. Galvin and Kinkead to August Herrmann, November 8, 1915, 2–4, FLSP, Box 1, Folder 1.

40. Testimony of James Gilmore, Washington Trial Transcript, Federal League Baseball Club of Baltimore, Inc. v. National League of Professional Baseball Clubs, 1161, FLSP, Boxes 6 and 7 (hereafter "Transcript, Washington Suit").

41. Levitt, *The Battle that Forged Modern Baseball,* 228–29, 241.

42. August Herrmann to John Tener, December 29, 1915, FLSP, Box 2, Folder 5.

43. Transcript, Washington Suit, 1163.

44. "End of Baseball War Now Assured," *New York Times,* December 16, 1915, 12.

45. Levitt, *The Battle that Forged Modern Baseball,* 230.

46. Specifically, Gilmore and others would later contend that Baltimore president Carroll Rasin moved to vest a negotiating committee with full authority to finalize the settlement terms with organized baseball, while Baltimore's representatives strenuously denied that they had proposed the formation of such a committee, or that it had been duly authorized to act on behalf of the league. Transcript, Washington Suit, 568, 1167–68, 1171–72.

47. Stenographic minutes of the December 17, 1915, meeting at the Waldorf-Astoria appear as an appendix to the brief submitted by organized baseball to the United States Supreme Court on April 4, 1922. Brief on Behalf of Defendants in Error, *Federal Baseball Club of Baltimore v. National League of Professional Baseball Clubs,* 107–8, 109–13, Supreme Court Records and Briefs, 259 U.S. 200 (1922) (No. 1922-204).

48. Ibid., 113–14, 116.

49. Ibid., 118–26, 133.

50. Ibid., 144–47, 150.

51. Ibid., 151–52.

52. Ibid., 153–54.

53. Ibid., 155–56.

54. Ibid., 157, 161–62.

55. Ibid., 163–66.

56. Ibid., 168, 172, 174, 176–77.

57. "Federals Fail to Withdraw Suit," *New York Times,* December 21, 1915, 11; "Goes to Peace Meeting," *New York Times,* December 21, 1915, 11.

58. Cook, *August "Garry" Herrmann,* 199; "Sinclair Controls Many of the Federals Players, Has Disposal of Entire Roster of Three Clubs," *Washington Post,* December 24, 1915, 8; Levitt, *The Battle that Forged Modern Baseball,* 243.

59. Levitt, *The Battle that Forged Modern Baseball,* 242.

60. Transcript, Washington Suit, 895.

61. Ibid. Jim Gilmore would later dispute this account, insisting that he had made an offer of $75,000 to the team during the phone call. Transcript, Washington Suit, 1227.

62. Levitt, *The Battle that Forged Modern Baseball,* 243; Wiggins, *The Federal League of Base Ball Clubs,* 288.

63. "Agreement for Baseball Peace Finally Signed," *Christian Science Monitor,* December 23, 1915, 14.

64. Tener to Pepper, December 28, 1915, 1–2.

65. Ritchie, Janney and Griswold to August Herrmann, January 3, 1916, FLSP, Box 3, Folder 6; "Gives $500,000 For 9–10 of Cubs," *Washington Post,* January 6, 1916, 8.

66. "Yanks Issue Call for Training Trip," *New York Times,* January 12, 1916, 11; "National Baseball Commission to Stay," *New York Times,* January 14, 1916, 10.

67. "Baltimore Feds to Fight Peace Pact," *New York Times,* January 28, 1916, 7.

68. "The Trouble Baltimore Breeds," *Sporting News,* January 13, 1916, 4; "Real Facts Behind Baltimore Move," *Sporting News,* February 3, 1916, 1.

69. "O.B. Magnates Worried," *Baltimore Sun,* January 29, 1916, 9; "Hears BaltoFeds in Baseball Suit," *Washington Post,* February 5, 1916, 8.

70. "Terps Soon to Open Up," *Baltimore Sun,* January 12, 1916, 5; "Baseball Monopoly is Within the Law," *Washington Post,* January 11, 1916, 9; Levitt, *The Battle that Forged Modern Baseball,* 245.

71. "Outlaw Anti-Trust Suit is Dismissed by Judge Landis," *Sporting News,* February 10, 1916, 1; "Baltimore Club Heard Monday," *Christian Science Monitor,* February 4, 1916, 16.

72. 1916 Transcript, Chicago Suit, 2–3. The transcript of the hearing follows a letter from William Harridge to August Herrmann dated February 9, 1916, on file with the Hall of Fame Library, FLSP, Box 1, Folder 2.

73. "Outlaw Anti-Trust Suit is Dismissed by Judge Landis," *Sporting News,* February 10, 1916, 1.

74. 1916 Transcript, Chicago Suit, 3.

75. "Judge Landis Dismisses the Baseball Suit," *Christian Science Monitor,* February 7, 1916, 16; "Outlaw Anti-Trust Suit is Dismissed by Judge Landis," *Sporting News,* February 10, 1916, 1.

76. "The Tribune from Landis," *Sporting News,* February 17, 1916, 4.

77. For example, see Eldon L. Ham, "The Immaculate Deception: How the Holy Grail of Protectionism Led to the Great Steroid Era," *Marquette Sports Law Review* 19 (2008): 216.

78. Herrmann to Johnson, February 14, 1916, 2, FLSP, Box 3, Folder 6.

Chapter 6. An Aborted Trial

1. Herrmann to Johnson, February 14, 1916, 1–2, FLSP, Box 3, Folder 6.

2. Ritchie et al. to August Herrmann, February 23, 1916, FLSP, Box 3, Folder 6.

3. Johnson to Herrmann, February 28, 1916, FLSP, Box 3, Folder 6; Herrmann to Johnson and John Tener, 25, 1916, FLSP, Box 3, Folder 6.

4. Tener to Pepper, February 18, 1916, 1–2, FLSP, Box 4, Folder 8.

5. Pepper to Tener, February 19, 1916, 1–2, FLSP, Box 4, Folder 8.

6. Charles Knapp to Ed Barrow, February 29, 1916, FLSP, Box 3, Folder 8.

7. Ed Barrow to August Herrmann, March 1, 1916, FLSP, Box 3, Folder 8.

8. Ed Barrow to August Herrmann, March 3, 1916, FLSP, Box 3, Folder 6.

9. Charles Knapp to Ed Barrow, March 4, 1916, 1, FLSP, Box 3, Folder 6.

10. "Baseball Disputes Still Unsettled," *New York Times,* March 5, 1916, S4.

11. Herrmann to Ban Johnson and John Tener, March 8, 1916, FLSP, Box 3, Folder 6.

12. Ritchie et al. to Herrmann, March 7, 1916, FLSP, Box 3, Folder 8.

13. Herrmann to Ban Johnson and John Tener, March 8, 1916, FLSP, Box 3, Folder 8.

14. "Shoot, Baltimore, and Be Done," *Sporting News,* March 16, 1916, 4; "Glasgow Gets Papers," *Baltimore Sun,* March 18, 1916, 15; "Terrapins May File $900,000 Suit Today," *Baltimore Sun,* March 17, 1916, 10.

15. Plaintiff's Statement of Claim, Federal League Baseball Club of Baltimore, Inc. v. National League of Professional Baseball Clubs, 1–2, 3–4, 5–6, 8, National Archives, Philadelphia. The BaltFeds' Philadelphia lawsuit is generally hereafter referred to as "Philadelphia Suit."

16. Ibid., 9–10, 12, 14, 18, 25.

17. Ibid., 27, 29, 30.

18. Ibid., 31–32.

19. "Ask Huge Damages of Ball Magnates," *New York Times,* March 30, 1916, 10.

20. "Baseball Suit May Result in Federal Action," *Christian Science Monitor,* March 30, 1916, 18.

21. "Ask Huge Damages of Ball Magnates," *New York Times,* March 30, 1916, 10.

22. "Facts Combat Baltimore Suit," *Sporting News,* April 6, 1916, 4.

23. "'Conspiracy' Hard to Believe," *Sporting News,* April 6, 1916, 4.

24. "Joe Vila Hurls Shafts at Damage Seeking BaltFeds," *Sporting News,* April 6, 1916, 1.

25. John Tener to Barney Dreyfuss, March 31, 1916, FLSP, Box 4, Folder 8; John Tener to George Pepper, April 3, 1916, FLSP, Box 4, Folder 8.

26. "Peace Payments to Feds Held Up," *New York Times,* April 28, 1916, 12.

27. "Feds Shift Blame, of Course," *Sporting News,* May 4, 1916, 1; John Toole to Ban Johnson, April 26, 1916, 2, FLSP, Box 3, Folder 8.

28. Praecipe for Summons in Trespass, Philadelphia Suit, National Archives, Philadelphia; Alias Summons Trespass, Philadelphia Suit, National Archives, Philadelphia.

29. "Aftermath of the Baltimore Club's Suit," *Sporting Life,* April 15, 1916, 9; Transcript, Philadelphia Suit, 125.

30. Petition to Set Aside Service, Philadelphia Suit, National Archives, Philadelphia.

31. Petition of the Federal Baseball Club of Baltimore, Philadelphia Suit, National Archives, Philadelphia; Petition of St. Louis American League Base Ball Company, Philadelphia Suit, National Archives, Philadelphia.

32. For example, see Affidavit of Defense of the Brooklyn National League Baseball Club, Philadelphia Suit, National Archives, Philadelphia; Affidavit of Defense of John K. Tener, Philadelphia Suit, National Archives, Philadelphia; Affidavit of Defense of the New York National League Baseball Club, Philadelphia Suit, National Archives, Philadelphia.

33. Affidavit of Defense of American Baseball Club of Philadelphia, 4, 6, 7–8, 8–9, 11, 12, Philadelphia Suit, National Archives, Philadelphia.

34. "Scribbled by Scribes," *Sporting News,* April 13, 1916, 4; "Abortive Peace Proving a Plague," *Sporting News,* November 23, 1916, 1; "To Avert a Big Legal Tangle," *Sporting Life,* November 25, 1916, 10; "Scribbled by Scribes," *Sporting News,* December 21, 1916, 4.

35. "To Avert a Big Legal Tangle," *Sporting Life,* November 25, 1916, 10; "Goat, Yes, But Savior, Too," *Sporting News,* November 30, 1916, 4.

36. "Scribbled by Scribes," *Sporting News,* December 21, 1916, 4.

37. Tener to August Herrmann, April 7, 1916, FLSP, Box 3, Folder 8.

38. "Baltimore Suit is Not Trifling Thing," *Sporting News,* December 28, 1916, 1.

39. "Postpone Federal League Suit," *Christian Science Monitor,* January 25, 1917, 10; "Baseball Suit Listed," *Washington Post,* March 22, 1917, 8; "Baltimore Suit Again Postponed, *Sporting Life,* April 7, 1917, 7.

40. Petition for Subpoena Duces Tecum, Philadelphia Suit, National Archives, Philadelphia.

41. "John G. Johnson, Noted Lawyer, Dies," *New York Times,* April 15, 1917; Ban Johnson to August Herrmann, August 17, 1917, FLSP, Box 3, Folder 11; Evelyn Bodek Rosen, *The Philadelphia Fels, 1880–1920: A Social Portrait* (Madison, N.J.: Fairleigh Dickinson University Press, 2000), 119.

42. "Federals' Suit for $900,000," *Sporting Life,* December 1916, 5; Amendment to Statement of Claim, Philadelphia Suit, National Archives, Philadelphia; "Glasgow Gets Papers," Baltimore Sun, March 18, 1916, 15; Transcript, Washington suit, 1122.

43. Ibid.; Eugene Fauntleroy Cordell, *University of Maryland, 1807–1907* (New York: Lewis Publishing, 1907), 169.

44. "No Compromise with Feds, O.B. Moguls Say," *Washington Post,* June 11, 1917, 6.

45. "Moguls Gather for Baltimore Trial," *Sporting News,* June 7, 1917, 1.

46. "Baltimore Feds Begin the Fight," *Philadelphia Inquirer,* June 12, 1917, 12.

47. Federal Judicial Center, "Biographical Directory of Federal Judges, Oliver Booth Dickinson"; "Scribbled by Scribes," *Sporting News,* December 21, 1916, 4.

48. "Cost O.B. A Million to Put Out Federals," *Baltimore Sun,* June 12, 1917, 8; "Baltimore Feds Begin the Fight," *Philadelphia Inquirer,* June 12, 1917, 12.

49. "Claims Baltimore Club Was Ignored," *New York Times,* June 12, 1917, 10; "Cost O.B. A Million to Put Out Federals," *Baltimore Sun,* June 12, 1917, 8; "Baltimore Feds Begin the Fight," *Philadelphia Inquirer,* June 12, 1917, 12.

50. Transcript, Philadelphia Suit, 13, FLSP, Box 8.

51. Ibid., 14, 18, 26–27.

52. Ibid., 12, 35–36.

53. Ibid., 15, 17.

54. Ibid., 37.

55. Ibid., 40–41, 64.

56. Ibid., 48–49, 50–51, 53–54.

57. Ibid., 61–62, 85.

58. Ibid., 93, 94, 97.

59. Ibid., 100.

60. "Baltimore Feds Begin the Fight," *Philadelphia Inquirer,* June 12, 1917, 12; "Pickups," *Christian Science Monitor,* June 12, 1917, 10.

61. Transcript, Philadelphia Suit, 115, 121, 122–29, 130–31.

62. Ibid., 131–33, 134–39.

63. Ibid., 155–56, 174.

64. "'Herrmann asked Blacklist,'—Fultz," *Philadelphia Inquirer,* June 13, 1917, 14.

65. Transcript, Philadelphia Suit, 183–93, 193–94, 195–98, 199.

66. "'Herrmann asked Blacklist,'—Fultz," *Philadelphia Inquirer,* June 13, 1917, 14.

67. Transcript, Philadelphia Suit, 229, 238.

68. Ibid., 230–33.

69. Ibid., 213, 224.

70. "O.B. Aids Players, Herrmann Avers," *Philadelphia Inquirer,* June 14, 1917, 12.

71. Transcript, Philadelphia Suit, 249–50, 252, 307.

72. Ibid., 256, 260–62.

73. Ibid., 270, 271, 275.

74. Ibid., 281, 284–87, 301–2.

75. Ibid., 334, 339, 344–46.

76. Ibid., 347–51, 363.

77. Ibid., 374.

78. "Federal League Suit is Dropped," *Christian Science Monitor,* June 15, 1917, 14; "Baltimore Club Rests Its Case," *Philadelphia Inquirer,* June 15, 1917, 14.

79. "Collapse of Baltimore Suit Removes Last Real Menace," *Sporting News,* June 21, 1917, 1.

80. Transcript, Philadelphia Suit, 377–81, 386–86 ½.

81. Ibid., 400–401, 402, 405.

82. Ibid., 423–23 ½, 425.

83. Ibid., 426, 429.

84. Ibid., 440, 443–44.

85. Ibid., 446, 447, 450, 453–54.

86. Ibid., 467–69, 470–71, 472; "Baltimore Club Rests Its Case," *Philadelphia Inquirer,* June 15, 1917, 14.

87. Transcript, Philadelphia Suit, 473.

88. "Collapse of Baltimore Suit Removes Last Real Menace," *Sporting News,* June 21, 1917, 1; Washington Transcript, 1122.

89. "Baltimore Feds Drop Damage Suit," *Philadelphia Inquirer,* June 16, 1917, 14; Washington Transcript, 1122.

90. "Collapse of Baltimore Suit Removes Last Real Menace," *Sporting News,* June 21, 1917, 1; *Transcript*, Philadelphia Suit, 473, 475.

91. "BaltFeds Drop Suit Against Baseball; No Compromise is Made," *North American,* June 16, 1917, 16.

92. "Collapse of Baltimore Suit Removes Last Real Menace," *Sporting News,* June 21, 1917, 1.

93. "One Man Who Will Not be Bluffed," *Sporting News,* June 21, 1917, 1; "Beaten By Own Evidence, Baltimore Feds Drop Suit," *Sporting News,* June 21, 1917, 4.

Chapter 7. Baltimore Goes to Trial, Again

1. Chester Farr et al. to Prichard et al., June 15, 1917, 1–2, FLSP, Box 3, Folder 6.

2. Pepper to John Toole, June 15, 1917, 1–2, FLSP, Box 3, Folder 16.

3. "Terps Will Fight On," *Baltimore Sun,* June 20, 1917, 8.

4. George Pepper to John Toole, July 5, 1917, FLSP, Box 3, Folder 4.

5. "Feds May Sue O.B. Again," *Washington Post,* July 26, 1917, 8; "Baseball Suit to be Settled by J.C. Toole," *Christian Science Monitor,* August 7, 1917, 10.

6. George Pepper to John Tener, August 28, 1917, FLSP, Box 4, Folder 1.

7. Herrmann to Tener, September 4, 1917, FLSP, Box 3, Folder 12.

8. Pepper to John Tener, July 9, 1917, FLSP, Box 3, Folder 14.

9. Declaration, Federal League Baseball Club of Baltimore, Inc. v. National League of Professional Baseball Clubs, National Archives, Washington, D.C. The BaltFeds' Washington lawsuit is generally hereafter referred to as "Washington Suit."

10. Ibid., 27, 53.

11. Ibid., 27.

12. Ibid., 8–13, 27–28, 53.

13. William L. Marbury, *In the Catbird Seat* (Baltimore: Maryland Historical Society, 1988), 21, 27, 34, 53.

14. "C.A. Douglas Rites to Be Held Today," *Washington Post,* November 1, 1939, 9.

15. "Terps Again Sue O.B.," *Baltimore Sun,* September 21, 1917, 9.

16. "Another $900,000 Fed Suit," *Washington Post,* September 21, 1917, 8; "Baltimore Feds Sue Again," *New York Times,* September 22, 1917, 12; "Baltimore Feds Sue Again," *Sporting News,* September 27, 1917, 2.

17. "Federal League Again in Action," *Christian Science Monitor,* September 2, 1917, 14.

18. August Herrmann to John Tener, November 16, 1917, FLSP, Box 4, Folder 1; Johnson to John Heydler, February 21, 1919, 1–2, FLSP, Box 4, Folder 2.

19. George Pepper to John Tener, October 22, 1917, 3, FLSP, Box 4, Folder 2; John Tener to Ban Johnson, October 25, 1917, FLSP, Box 4, Folder 1.

20. Pepper to John Tener, February 8, 1918, FLSP, Box 3, Folder 11; John Tener to Pepper, February 14, 1918, FLSP, Box 3, Folder 11.

21. "Third Big League May Settle Suit," *New York Times,* October 31, 1917, 10.

22. Herrmann to Johnson, November 5, 1917, FLSP, Box 4, Folder 3.

23. Johnson to Herrmann, November 3, 1917, FLSP, Box 4, Folder 1; John Toole to Herrmann, December 29, 1917, 2, FLSP, Box 3, Folder 12.

24. Frank Prichard et al. to Herrmann et al., July 16, 1917, 2, FLSP, Box 3, Folder 11; Herrmann to John Tener, September 24, 1917, FLSP, Box 3, Folder 12; Herrmann to John Tener, September 4, 1917, FLSP, Box 3, Folder 12.

25. "Federal Baseball League to be Paid," *New York Times,* February 7, 1918, 12. A copy of the draft agreement is attached to a letter from John Toole to John Tener, September 19, 1917, FLSP, Box 3, Folder 12.

26. "Baseball Leaders to Assemble Here," *New York Times,* February 10, 1918, 32; "Terms Not Made Public, May Use Newark Park for Sunday Games," *Washington Post,* February 16, 1918, 8.

27. Seymour, *Baseball,* 259–63.

28. Ibid., 262.

29. Ibid., 263.

30. August Herrmann to Ban Johnson, December 19. 1917, 1, FLSP, Box 3, Folder 12; Pleas of Defendants, Washington Suit, National Archives, Washington, D.C.

31. Herrmann to Johnson and Heydler, January 21, 1919, FLSP, Box 4, Folder 2; Johnson to Herrmann, February 17, 1919, FLSP, Box 4, Folder 2.

32. Pepper to John Heydler, March 5, 1919, 1–2, FLSP, Box 4, Folder 3.

33. Herrmann to John Heydler, March 8, 1919, FLSP, Box 4, Folder 2; Johnson to John Heydler, February 26, 1919, FLSP, Box 4, Folder 2.

34. Bulletin from John Heydler to National League Club Presidents, February 19, 1919, 1, FLSP, Box 3, Folder 4; John Heydler to Johnson, February 19, 1919,

FLSP, Box 4, Folder 3; Johnson to John Heydler, February 21, 1919, 2, FLSP, Box 4, Folder 2.

35. Notice to Produce Documents, Washington Suit, National Archives, Washington, D.C.; Notice to Produce, Washington Suit, National Archives, Washington, D.C.; "Terps to Meet Today," *Baltimore Sun,* March 20, 1919, 10.

36. John Heydler to P.T. Power, February 28, 1919, FLSP, Box 4, Folder 2; Benjamin Minor to John Heydler, March 8, 1919, FLSP, Box 4, Folder 2.

37. John Heydler to George Pepper, March 7, 1919, FLSP, Box 4, Folder 3; John Heydler to August Herrmann, March 15, 1919, HP, Box 107, Folder 3.

38. "By All Means Let's Have It," *Sporting News,* February 20, 1919, 4; "Big News May Come Out of Washington," *Sporting News,* March 6, 1919, 1; "Baltimore Fed Suit Ordered to Trial," *Sporting News,* March 27, 1919, 1.

39. "See Bitter Fight in $900,000 Suit," *Washington Post,* March 6, 1919, 8; "Suit of Baltimore Feds Against O.B. Opens Here Today," *Washington Post,* March 24, 1919, 8.

40. "Baseball Hearing Today," *New York Times,* March 25, 1919, 14; Federal Judicial Center, "Biographical Directory of Federal Judges, Wendell Phillips Stafford"; Hailey, "Anatomy of a Murder," 62; "Terps Prove O.B. Monopoly," *Baltimore Sun,* April 10, 1919.

41. "Calls O.B. a Monopoly," *Baltimore Sun,* March 26, 1919, 14; Transcript, Washington Suit, 3, 5, 9.

42. Ibid., 8, 10–29.

43. Ibid., 30–41, 45.

44. Ibid., 43–44.

45. Ibid., 49.

46. Ibid., 68, 85–87, 81–84.

47. Ibid., 138, 143, 155–56, 180–87, 197–98, 204, 211–14.

48. Ibid., 214, 219, 226, 229–34, 241–42, 259.

49. Ibid., 264–65, 272.

50. Ibid., 368–71.

51. Ibid., 373–86, 386–93.

52. Ibid., 394, 397–99, 400–12.

53. Ibid., 394, 414–16.

54. Ibid., 458–59, 465–68.

55. Ibid., 420–28, 470–76, 478–83, 485–88.

56. Heydler to All National League Club Presidents, March 29, 1919, HP, Box 107, Folder 3.

57. Stipulations of Counsel, Washington Suit, National Archives, Washington, D.C.

58. Transcript, Washington Suit, 503, 522–29. George Pepper objected strenuously to the admissibility of the newspaper article, asserting that at most it defamed the Federal League as a whole, not the Baltimore team specifically, and therefore was not relevant to the plaintiff's claim. Ibid., 531. Baltimore's counsel effectively rebutted this argument, noting that not only was Baltimore a member of the group attacked

by Johnson, but that the team was specifically mentioned in his comments. Ibid., 551. As a result, Justice Stafford ruled that the article was admissible as a statement made in furtherance of organized baseball's conspiracy to monopolize the baseball industry. Ibid., 556, 562.

59. Ibid., 563–69, 572–601, 602–8, 609–10, 611–12, 613, 614–20. The witnesses were Robert Garrett, Carroll Rasin, Philip Poe, Frank Webb, Ellis Nordlinger, Harry Neepier, and Leonard Weil.

60. Ibid., 573.

61. Ibid., 576–78.

62. Ibid., 578, 585–86, 588, 590.

63. Ibid., 592, 596.

64. Ibid., 621.

65. Heydler to All National League Club Presidents, March 29, 1919, 1–2, HP, Box 107, Folder 3.

66. "So Much for Court Baseball," *Sporting News,* April 3, 1919, 4.

67. Transcript, Washington Suit, 635–41, 642–45, 646–54, 654–730, 745–47, 747–48, 749–53. These witnesses included Harry Busick, John Fahey, Otto Simonson, Edward Hanlon, David Landreth, Edwin Poe, and George Scheunnes.

68. Ibid., 735–38.

69. Ibid., 742–45.

70. Ibid., 666–77, 681, 683–85, 687; "Baltimore an Outcast," *Baltimore Sun,* April 1, 1919, 16.

71. Transcript, Washington Suit, 667, 700.

72. Ibid., 709–13.

73. Ibid., 826–39.

74. Ibid., 850–58, 859–70.

75. Ibid., 874–75, 878–79, 880–81, 889–90.

76. Ibid., 891–92, 895.

77. Ibid., 926, 928–29, 934–35.

78. Ibid., 1031, 1037–38.

79. Ibid., 1064–66.

80. Ibid., 1079, 1082–84, 1119–20.

81. Ibid., 1116, 1122–24.

82. Ibid., 1128; "Baltimore on Griddle When O.B. Starts Its Testimony," *Sporting News,* April 10, 1919, 2.

Chapter 8. The Defense and Verdict

1. Transcript, Washington Suit, 1129–30.

2. Ibid., 1130–31.

3. Ibid., 1137–38, 1140.

4. Ibid., 1141–44.

5. Ibid., 1144 45, 1147–48.

6. Ibid., 1155–56.

7. Ibid., 1157–59.
8. Ibid., 1160–63.
9. Ibid., 1164–72.
10. Ibid., 1174–75, 1187–1200, 1203–5, 1210–27.
11. Ibid., 1227–31.
12. "League Wrecking Denied by Gilmore," *Washington Post,* April 4, 1919, 10; "Froze Out Baltimore," *Baltimore Sun,* April 4, 1919, 12.
13. Transcript, Washington Suit, 1252–53, 1262–63, 1278, 1286.
14. Ibid., 1264, 1266, 1288–92.
15. Ibid., 1297–98, 1303.
16. Ibid., 1310–11, 1313.
17. "Froze Out Baltimore," *Baltimore Sun,* April 4, 1919, 12.
18. Transcript, Washington Suit, 1323, 1327, 1337.
19. Ibid., 1343, 1347, 1349.
20. Ibid., 1334–35.
21. Ibid., 1330–33, 1349.
22. Ibid., 1370, 1372–75, 1385–93; "Not Afraid, says Garry," *Baltimore Sun,* April 5, 1919, 5.
23. Transcript, Washington Suit, 1383, 1396–98, 1402, 1413.
24. Ibid., 1427–29, 1436–37, 1969; "Jury Awards Feds $240,000," *Baltimore Sun,* April 13, 1919, 14.
25. Transcript, Washington Suit, 1440, 1444–45, 1447–48.
26. Ibid., 1451–52, 1473–75.
27. Ibid., 1477, 1495, 1498.
28. Ibid., 1507–11, 1513–14.
29. Ibid., 1525–26.
30. Ibid., 1536, 1538–40.
31. Ibid., 1546.
32. Ibid., 1546–47.
33. Ibid., 1555–60, 1563–69.
34. Ibid., 1579–80, 1582.
35. Ibid., 1595–96, 1599.
36. Ibid., 1614–15.
37. Ibid., 1615.
38. Ibid., 1616–17.
39. Ibid., 1626, 1638, 1641.
40. Ibid., 1661, 1663, 1668–70.
41. Ibid., 1706, 1709, 1729.
42. Ibid., 1744.
43. Ibid., 1747, 1756–59.
44. Ibid., 1761–62, 1769.
45. Ibid., 1759–60, 1772.
46. Ibid., 1772, 1774, 1776.
47. Ibid., 1778, 1780–83, 1785; *Paul v. Virginia,* 75 U.S. 168 (1869).

48. 227 F. 165 (S.D.N.Y. 1914).
49. Transcript, Washington Suit, 1786.
50. Ibid., 1787, 1790–91.
51. 162 A.D. 691 (1914).
52. Ibid., 693; Transcript, Washington Suit, 1800–1804.
53. Ibid., 1804–7, 1809.
54. Ibid., 1809–10.
55. Ibid., 1816–21.
56. Ibid., 1823–25, 1827–28.
57. Ibid., 1836; Chester Farr et al. to Frank Prichard et al., June 15, 1917, 2, FLSP, Box 3, Folder 6.
58. Transcript, Washington Suit, 1840, 1843, 1845–46, 1848–49, 1881.
59. Ibid., 1866–69, 1884–85, 1924; *International Textbook Co. v. Pigg,* 217 U.S. 91 (1910).
60. Transcript, Washington Suit, 1840–42, 1889, 1889–90, 1901. Ironically, the U.S. Supreme Court would adopt Pepper's reasoning in the 1953 case of *Toolson v. New York Yankees,* 346 U.S. 356 (1953), holding "that Congress had no intention of including the business of baseball within the scope of the federal antitrust laws." Ibid., 357.
61. Transcript, Washington Suit, 1897–99.
62. Ibid., 1902, 1911.
63. Ibid., 1922–23, 1926–27.
64. Ibid., 1933, 1936.
65. Ibid., 1933–34.
66. Ibid., 1934–35.
67. Ibid., 1933.
68. "Terps Prove O.B. Monopoly," *Baltimore Sun,* April 10, 1919, 1; "O.B. is Badly Beaten," *Baltimore Sun,* April 10, 1919, 14; "Jury Awards Feds $240,000," *Baltimore Sun,* April 13, 1919, 1.
69. "Terps Prove O.B. Monopoly," *Baltimore Sun,* April 10, 1919, 1.
70. Heydler to All National League Club Presidents, April 14, 1919, 1, FLSP, Box 4, Folder 13; Heydler to Caylor, April 9, 1919, 1, FLSP, Box 4, Folder 5.
71. Transcript, Washington Suit, 1942–43.
72. Ibid., 1943–44, 1946–47.
73. Ibid., 1948, 1979.
74. Ibid., 1953–57, 1964.
75. Ibid., 1964, 1974, 1980.
76. Ibid., 1981.
77. Ibid., 1981–83.
78. Ibid., 1984–87, 1990.
79. Ibid., 1991, 1993, 1998–99.
80. Ibid., 2002–3.
81. Ibid., 2020–21, 2040, 2043; "Jury Will Get Fed Case Today," *Washington Post,* April 12, 1919, 10.

82. Transcript, Washington Suit, 2052–53.

83. "And Jury Will Get Federals' Case This Morning," *Baltimore Sun,* April 12, 1919.

84. Transcript, Washington Suit, 2071, 2073–74.

85. Ibid., 2076–80.

86. Ibid., 2080–81.

87. Ibid., 2084–86.

88. Ibid., 2089; Herrmann to Benjamin Minor, April 17, 1919, Box 5, Folder 3.

89. Transcript, Washington Suit, 2093; "Fate of Baseball is in Hands of Judges," *Sporting News,* October 21, 1920, 2. Before awarding Baltimore the attorneys' fees, Stafford denied the defendants' motion for a new trial, as organized baseball's counsel had anticipated. Benjamin Minor to John Heydler, April 15, 1919, FLSP, Box 5, Folder 3.

90. "Playing the Game," *Baltimore Sun,* April 13, 1919, 14.

91. "Jury Awards Feds $240,000," *Baltimore Sun,* April 13, 1919, 14.

92. Herrmann to George Pepper, April 21, 1919, 1, FLSP, Box 4, Folder 5; Heydler to Benjamin Minor, April 16, 1919, FLSP, Box 5, Folder 3.

93. "Baseball Moguls See Dire Changes," *New York Times,* April 14, 1919, 10.

94. Ibid.

95. Ibid.; "All Baseball Dazed Over Feds' Verdict," April 20, 1919 (attached to a letter from John Heydler to George Pepper, April 26, 1919, FLSP, Box 4, Folder 5).

96. Pepper, *Philadelphia Lawyer,* 357.

97. Herrmann to Clark Griffith, April 14, 1919, FLSP, Box 4, Folder 5.

98. "Baseball Leaders Bound Fed Case Shall Go to the Limit," *Sporting News,* April 24, 1919, 2.

99. "The Status of Organized Baseball," *Sporting News,* April 24, 1919, 4.

100. "All Baseball Dazed Over Feds' Verdict," April 20, 1919 (attached to a letter from John Heydler to George Pepper, April 26, 1919, FLSP, Box 4, Folder 5); Seymour, *Baseball,* 272.

101. Herrmann to Pepper, April 21, 1919, 1, FLSP, Box 4, Folder 5; Heydler to Pepper, April 26, 1919, FLSP, Box 4, Folder 5.

102. Johnson to Herrmann, May 19, 1919, 1–2, HP, Box 107, Folder 5.

103. Heydler to Pepper, April 26, 1919, FLSP, Box 4, Folder 5; Heydler to All National League Club Presidents, April 14, 1919, 2, FLSP, Box 4, Folder 13.

Chapter 9. The Appeal and Final Decision

1. John Heydler to Ban Johnson, June 25, 1919, 1, FLSP, Box 4, Folder 10; Order Extending Time, Washington Suit, National Archives, Washington, D.C.; Assignments of Error, Washington Suit, 11–15, National Archives, Washington, D.C.

2. Pepper to John Heydler, May 5, 1919, FLSP, Box 4, Folder 5.

3. Heydler to Ban Johnson, June 25, 1919, 2, FLSP, Box 4, Folder 10.

4. "Congress May Help O.B.," *Washington Post,* August 13, 1919, 10.

5. Pepper to John Heydler, November 8, 1919, 1–2, FLSP, Box 4, Folder 5.

6. Ibid., 2.

7. Johnson to Heydler, November 28, 1919, FLSP, Box 4, Folder 13; Heydler to Pepper, November 14, 1919, FLSP, Box 4, Folder 5.

8. Heydler to Ban Johnson, December 3, 1919, FLSP, Box 4, Folder 13.

9. Rawls to Pepper, November 25, 1919, 2–3, FLSP, Box 4, Folder 5.

10. Pepper to Rawls, December 2, 1919, FLSP, Box 4, Folder 5.

11. Clement to John Heydler, December 9, 1919, FLSP, Box 4, Folder 5.

12. Heydler to Ban Johnson, December 10, 1919, FLSP, Box 4, Folder 5; Heydler to Ban Johnson, December 20, 1919, FLSP, Box 4, Folder 5.

13. Pepper to Herrmann, January 6, 1920, FLSP, Box 4, Folder 6.

14. Veeck to Heydler, December 1, 1919, FLSP, Box 4, Folder 13.

15. "Baseball War Not Over Yet," *Baltimore American,* December 7, 1920.

16. Minor to Ban Johnson, February 3, 1920, FLSP, Box 4, Folder 6.

17. Pepper and Samuel Clement to John Heydler, February 6, 1920, FLSP, Box 4, Folder 6.

18. Heydler to Pepper and Samuel Clement, February 21, 1920, FLSP, Box 4, Folder 6.

19. Benjamin Minor to John Heydler, December 10, 1920, FLSP, Box 4, Folder 13.

20. Brief on Behalf of Appellants, National League of Professional Baseball Clubs v. Federal League Baseball Club of Baltimore, Inc., 21, 24, National Archives, Washington, D.C., Appellate Case File (hereafter "Appellants' Brief"). The Court of Appeals proceedings are here referred to as "Appellate Case."

21. Ibid., 19.

22. Ibid., 28–29, 30–37.

23. Ibid., 44–45, 47–48, 60–63.

24. Ibid., 48–50, 52, 56, 57–59; *Metropolitan Opera Co. v. Hammerstein,* 162 A.D. 691 (1914); *Marienelli v. United Booking Offices,* 227 F. 165 (S.D.N.Y. 1914).

25. Appellants' Brief, 65–67.

26. Ibid., 68.

27. Ibid., 69–72.

28. Ibid., 72–80.

29. Ibid., 80–86, 83.

30. Ibid., 86–96.

31. Brief on Behalf of Appellee, Appellate Case, 3–4, 7, National Archives, Washington, D.C., Appellate Case File (hereafter "Appellee's Brief").

32. Ibid., 9–11.

33. Ibid., 25–26, 27–40, 40–45.

34. Ibid., 147.

35. Ibid., 102–3.

36. Ibid., 108, 125.

37. Ibid., 108, 109, 119, 116–21; *Hoke v. United States,* 227 U.S. 308 (1913).

38. Appellee's Brief, 129–34.

39. Ibid., 142, 146.

40. Ibid., 161, 167–68.

41. Ibid., 174–75, 176.

42. Eliot Asinof, *Eight Men Out: The Black Sox and the 1919 World Series* (New York: Holt, Rinehart and Winston, 1963), 168, 198.

43. Ibid., 199.

44. "Fate of Baseball is in Hands of Judges," *Sporting News,* October 21, 1920, 2; Jeffrey Brandon Morris, *Calmly to Poise the Scales of Justice: A History of the Courts of the District of Columbia Circuit* (Durham, N.C.: Carolina Academic Press, 2001), 71.

45. George Pepper to John Heydler, October 15, 1920, 1, FLSP, Box 4, Folder 13; "Baseball Case in Court of Appeals," *Washington Post,* October 14, 1920, 12.

46. "Around the Horn," *Baltimore Sun,* October 14, 1920, 8; Pepper to Heydler, October 15, 1920, 1, FLSP, Box 4, Folder 13; Pepper, *Philadelphia Lawyer,* 357.

47. Seymour, *Baseball,* 264–67, 271; Alexander, *Our Game,* 114.

48. Seymour, *Baseball,* 272–73.

49. Ibid., 312, 314–19, 320, 330; Sigman, "The Jurisprudence of Judge Kenesaw Mountain Landis," 277.

50. *National League of Professional Baseball Clubs v. Federal League Baseball Club of Baltimore, Inc.,* 269 F. 681, 684 (D.C. Cir. 1920).

51. Ibid., 684–85.

52. Ibid.

53. Ibid., 686.

54. Ibid., 684–85.

55. Ibid., 687–88.

56. "Baseball Men Greet Verdict," *Evening Telegram,* December 6, 1920.

57. "Strongest Decision Yet Given Baseball," *Sporting News,* December 9, 1920, 1.

58. "Small Chance That Feds Will Fight On," *Sporting News,* December 16, 1920, 3.

59. "Let the Reserve Clause Rest," *Sporting News,* December 16, 1920, 4.

60. "Baseball By-Plays," *Sporting News,* December 16, 1920, 4.

61. "Constitutional Law—Monopolies—Baseball Club Not Engaged in 'Trade' or 'Commerce'," *Michigan Law Review* 19 (1921): 868.

62. White, *Creating the National Pastime,* 78.

63. "Baseball Law," *Law Notes* 25 (1921): 24.

64. "High Lights and Shadows in All Spheres of Sport," *New York Herald,* December 7, 1920; "Baltimore Loses Case Against O.B.," *Baltimore Sun,* December 7, 1920.

65. "Baltimore Decides to Appeal," *Sporting News,* December 16, 1920, 6; "Balto Feds Plan to Carry Fight Higher," *Sporting News,* December 30, 1920, 2.

66. Petition for Rehearing & Petition to Stay Mandate, Appellate Case, National Archives, Washington, D.C., Appellate Case File (hereafter "Appellate Case").

67. Order Modifying Judgment, Appellate Case, National Archives, Washington, D.C., Appellate Case File; Benjamin Minor to John Heydler, January 8, 1921, FLSP, Box 5, Folder 1. Unlike today, when the Supreme Court generally has the discretion to decide whether to hear a particular appeal, under the procedure in place in 1921,

the Court had to consider Baltimore's appeal. See David H. Burton, *Taft, Holmes, and the 1920s Court: An Appraisal* (Madison, N.J.: Fairleigh Dickinson University Press, 1998), 116.

68. Alpheus Thomas Mason, *William Howard Taft: Chief Justice* (New York: Simon and Schuster, 1964, 1965), 17.

69. Russell W. Galloway Jr., "The Taft Court (1921–1929)," *Santa Clara Law Review* 25 (1985): 4; Paul L. Murphy, *The Constitution in Crisis Times: 1918–1969* (New York: Harper & Row, 1972), 58–59; Donald F. Anderson, "The Anti-trust Act and the Supreme Court," in *The Collected Works of William Howard Taft,* eds. David Potash and Donald F. Anderson (Athens: Ohio University Press, 2003), 5:166.

70. Ross E. Davies, "A Crank on the Court: The Passion of Justice William R. Day," *Baseball Research Journal* 38 (2009): 95.

71. "$500,000 Paid for Cubs," *New York Times,* January 21, 1916, 7.

72. "Clubs to Enjoin Contract Jumpers," *New York Times,* December 29, 1913, 5.

73. Seymour, *Baseball,* 263.

74. Taft to Ban Johnson, April 6, 1922, William Howard Taft Papers, Library of Congress, Washington, D.C., Series 3, Reel 240 (hereafter "Taft Papers"); Taft to Horace Stoneham, April 11, 1922, Taft Papers, Series 3, Reel 241; March to Taft, May 23, 1922, Taft Papers, Series 3, Reel 242; Taft to Heydler, May 28, 1922, Taft Papers, Series 3, Reel 240.

75. Pepper, *Philadelphia Lawyer,* 81–82.

76. Taft to Pepper, March 2, 1922, Taft Papers, Series 3, Reel 239; Taft to Pepper, February 28, 1922, Taft Papers, Series 3, Reel 239.

77. Pepper, *Philadelphia Lawyer,* 138–41; Mason, *William Howard Taft,* 95.

78. Burton, *Taft, Holmes, and the 1920s Court,* 115; Peter G. Renstrom, *The Taft Court: Justices, Rulings, and Legacy* (Santa Barbara, Calif.: ABC-CLIO, 2003), xii.

79. Davies, "A Crank on the Court," 98.

80. John Toole to T. J. Lynch, June 17, 1913, HP, Box 114, Folder 3.

81. Spencer Weber Waller, "The Antitrust Philosophy of Justice Holmes," *Southern Illinois University Law Journal* 18 (1994): 316–17; Alfred S. Neely, "'A Humbug Based on Economic Ignorance and Incompetence'—Antitrust in the Eyes of Justice Holmes," *Utah Law Review* (1993): 10–12.

82. Barak Orbach, and Grace Campbell Reblin, "The Antitrust Curse of Bigness," *Southern California Law Review* 85 (2012): 624; Gerald Berk, *Louis D. Brandeis and the Making of Regulated Competition, 1900–1932* (New York: Cambridge University Press, 2009), 1.

83. Michal R. Belknap, "Mr. Justice Pitney and Progressivism," *Seton Hall Law Review* 16 (1986): 418.

84. Brief on Behalf of Plaintiff in Error, Federal Baseball Club of Baltimore, Inc. v. National League of Professional Baseball Clubs, 12, Supreme Court Records and Briefs, 259 U.S. 200 (1922) (No. 1922–204) (hereafter "Plaintiff in Error's Brief"). The Supreme Court appeal is hereafter referred to as "Supreme Court Appeal."

85. Ibid., 5–6, 9, 25.

86. Ibid., 117, 122, 126–31.

87. Ibid., 134, 146–51, 152–54.

88. Ibid., 164–65, 170, 175–92, 192–201.

89. Brief on Behalf of Defendant in Error, Supreme Court Appeal, 11, 14, Supreme Court Records and Briefs, 259 U.S. 200 (1922) (No. 1922–204) (hereafter "Defendant in Error's Brief").

90. Ibid., 46.

91. "Radio and Video Have Not Altered Game, Says Pepper," *Sporting News,* November 25, 1953, 4; Appellants' Brief, 47.

92. Defendant in Error's Brief, 47–48, 50–62, 66–68, 68–71.

93. Ibid., 72–81, 82–88, 89–102, 102–3.

94. Supplement to Brief for Plaintiff in Error, Supreme Court Appeal, 3, 4–6, 9, Supreme Court Records and Briefs, 259 U.S. 200 (1922) (No. 1922-204).

95. Pepper, *Philadelphia Lawyer,* 359.

96. Ibid.

97. Pepper to John Heydler, December 9, 1922, 2, FLSP, Box 4, Folder 13.

98. Ibid.

99. "Big Leagues are Attacked in Suit," *New York Times,* April 20, 1922, 23.

100. Pepper to John Heydler, December 9, 1922, 2, FLSP, Box 4, Folder 13; "Marbury Assails Big Ball Leagues," *Baltimore Sun,* April 20, 1922, 7.

101. Pepper to John Heydler, December 9, 1922, 2–3, FLSP, Box 4, Folder 13.

102. "Big Leagues are Attacked in Suit," *New York Times,* April 20, 1922, 23; "Marbury Assails Big Ball Leagues," *Baltimore Sun,* April 20, 1922, 7.

103. Pepper to John Heydler, December 9, 1922, 3, FLSP, Box 4, Folder 13.

104. "Big Leagues are Attacked in Suit," *New York Times,* April 20, 1922, 23; "Marbury Assails Big Ball Leagues," *Baltimore Sun,* April 20, 1922, 7.

105. Pepper to John Heydler, December 9, 1922, 3, FLSP, Box 4, Folder 13; Pepper, *Philadelphia Lawyer,* 359.

106. Note from Brandeis to Holmes, Undated, Papers of Oliver Wendell Holmes Jr., Harvard Law School Library, Cambridge, Mass., Reel 71 (hereafter "Holmes Papers"); Note from McKenna to Holmes, Undated, Holmes Papers, Reel 71. The bracketed text reflects portions of the handwritten notes from Brandeis and McKenna that are particularly difficult to decipher; these notes are also interpreted in Robert Post, "The Supreme Court Opinion as Institutional Practice: Dissent, Legal Scholarship, and Decisionmaking in the Taft Court," *Minnesota Law Review* 85 (2001): 1344, 1344 n. 233. In addition, Justice James McReynolds wrote a note to Holmes regarding the case, stating, "Yes. Thanks—many of them. You are the very nicest [nixer] known to history!" Note from McReynolds to Holmes, Undated, Holmes Papers, Reel 71. The context for this communication is unclear, but it is possible that it was written in response to Holmes's rejection of an earlier, proposed modification to the opinion. Meanwhile, Holmes's papers relating to the opinion also contain a note from Justice John Clarke, but based on the case number referenced (108-09),

the note does not appear to relate to Baltimore's appeal (Case No. 204). Note from Clarke to Holmes, Undated, Holmes Papers, Reel 71.

107. Alpheus Thomas Mason, *The Supreme Court From Taft to Warren* (Baton Rouge: Louisiana State University Press, 1958, 1968), 61; Renstrom, *The Taft Court,* 36, 100, 189; Mason, *William Howard Taft,* 192, 212; Post, "The Supreme Court Opinion as Institutional Practice," 1311, 1351; Burton, *Taft, Holmes, and the 1920s Court,* 128.

108. "Not Combination in Restraint of Trade," *Washington Post,* May 30, 1922, 10.

109. *Federal Baseball Club of Baltimore, Inc. v. National League of Professional Baseball Clubs,* 259 U.S. 200, 207–8 (1922); Post, "The Supreme Court Opinion as Institutional Practice," 1290–91.

110. *Federal Baseball,* 259 U.S. at 208–9.

111. Ibid., 209; *Hooper v. California,* 155 U.S. 648 (1895).

112. *Federal Baseball,* 259 U.S. at 209.

113. "'Court Decision a Tribute to Game's Founders'—Heydler," *New York Tribune,* May 30, 1922.

114. Telegram from Heydler to Pepper, May 31, 1922, FLSP, Box 5, Folder 2; Heydler to Pepper, June 1, 1922, FLSP, Box 5, Folder 2.

115. Curtiss to Heydler, May 31, 1922, FLSP, Box 5, Folder 2.

116. "Knockout of Baltimore Feds Red Letter Day for Baseball," *Sporting News,* June 8, 1922, 3.

117. "Casual Comment," *Sporting News,* June 8, 1922, 4.

118. "Some Interesting Questions," *Baltimore Sun,* May 31, 1922, 8.

119. Petition for Rehearing, Supreme Court Appeal, 2–3, 5, 7, National Archives, Washington, D.C., Supreme Court Case File.

120. Ibid., 13–14, 21.

121. William Stansbury to Marbury, October 9, 1922, Supreme Court Appeal, National Archives, Washington, D.C., Supreme Court Case File.

Epilogue

1. William L. Reynolds, "Maryland and the Constitution of the United States: An Introductory Essay," *Maryland Law Review* 66 (2007): 943; Eldon L. Ham, "Aside the Aside: The True Precedent of Baseball in Law," *Marquette Sports Law Review* 13 (2003): 216; Waller, "The Antitrust Philosophy of Justice Holmes," 312.

2. Finkelman, Paul, "Baseball and the Rule of Law," *Cleveland State Law Review* 46 (1998): 246, 247.

3. Ham, "The Immaculate Deception," 220.

4. Jonathan D. Gillerman, "Calling Their Shots: Miffed Minor Leaguers, the Steroid Scandal, and Examining the Use of Section 1 of the Sherman Act to Hold MLB Accountable," *Albany Law Review* 73 (2010): 565; Bruce Johnson, "Why Baseball's

Antitrust Exemption Must Go," in *Stee-Rike Four!: What's Wrong with the Business of Baseball?*, ed. Daniel R. Marburger (Westport, Conn.: Praeger, 1997), 38.

5. Samuel A. Alito Jr., "The Origin of the Baseball Antitrust Exemption: Federal Baseball Club of Baltimore, Inc. v. National League of Professional Baseball Clubs," *Journal of Supreme Court History* 34 (2009): 183.

6. Nathaniel Grow, "Defining the 'Business of Baseball': A Proposed Framework for Determining the Scope of Professional Baseball's Antitrust Exemption," *University of California at Davis Law Review* 44 (2010): 568.

7. For example, see Finkelman, "Baseball and the Rule of Law," 246.

8. Kevin McDonald, "Antitrust and Baseball: Stealing Holmes," *Journal of Supreme Court History* (1998): 95.

9. *Hart v. B.F. Keith Vaudeville Exchange,* 262 U.S. 271 (1923); "Baseball and Vaudeville as Interstate Commerce," *Central Law Journal* (1923): 237.

10. *Hart,* 262 U.S. at 274.

11. Abrams, *Legal Bases,* 59–60. The same argument is made in Ham, "Immaculate Deception," 219–20.

12. McDonald, "Antitrust and Baseball," 116.

13. Indeed, the plaintiff in *Hart* was subsequently unable to develop enough evidence of interstate activity, and thus ultimately had its case dismissed for a second time. *United States v. Shubert,* 348 U.S. 222, 228 n. 10 (1955).

14. *Hart,* 262 U.S. at 272.

15. Declaration, Washington Suit, 28, 53; Transcript, Washington Suit, 1911.

16. *American League Baseball Club of Chicago v. Chase,* 149 N.Y.S. 6 (1914).

17. *National League of Professional Baseball Clubs v. Federal League Baseball Club of Baltimore, Inc.,* 269 F. 681, 686 (D.C. Cir. 1920).

18. McDonald, "Antitrust and Baseball," 97–98; Brad Snyder, *A Well-Paid Slave: Curt Flood's Fight for Free Agency in Professional Sports* (New York: Plume, 2007), 26; *Gardella v. Chandler,* 79 F.Supp. 260, 261–62 (S.D.N.Y. 1948).

19. *Gardella v. Chandler,* 172 F.2d 402, 408–9 (2d Cir. 1949); Snyder, *A Well-Paid Slave,* 26–27.

20. 346 U.S. 356 (1953); Grow, "Defining the 'Business of Baseball'," 569.

21. *Toolson,* 346 U.S. at 357.

22. McDonald, "Baseball and Antitrust," 100.

23. Grow, "Defining the 'Business of Baseball'," 571.

24. *United States v. International Boxing Club,* 348 U.S. 236 (1955).

25. *Radovich v. National Football League,* 352 U.S. 445 (1957).

26. Ibid., 450, 452.

27. 407 U.S. 258 (1972).

28. Grow, "Defining the 'Business of Baseball'," 573–74. For an outstanding history of the *Flood* litigation, see Snyder, *A Well-Paid Slave.*

29. *Flood,* 407 U.S. at 262–64, 269, 282, 283–84; Roger I. Abrams, "Blackmun's List," *Virginia Sports and Entertainment Law Journal* 6 (2007): 182.

30. Grow, "Defining the 'Business of Baseball'," 581, 592–95; *Piazza v. Major League Baseball,* 831 F.Supp. 420 (E.D. Pa. 1993); *Butterworth v. National League*

of Professional Baseball Clubs, 644 So.2d 1021 (1994); *Morsani v. Major League Baseball,* 663 So.2d 653 (1995).

31. *Piazza,* 831 F. Supp. at 436.

32. *National League of Professional Baseball Clubs,* 269 F. at 688; Grow, "Defining the 'Business of Baseball'," 587.

33. Specifically, pitchers Andy Messersmith and Dave McNally challenged the reserve clause in 1975 by playing an entire season without signing a new contract. They then declared themselves free agents at the end of the year, arguing that the reserve clause in their most-recent contracts could only be renewed for a single season. The dispute ultimately went to a panel of arbitrators, who declared the pitchers free agents. The major league owners and players' union then negotiated a new collective bargaining agreement in 1976, officially beginning baseball's free agency era. Ibid., 562 n.16.

34. Declaration, Washington Suit, 12, 27.

35. Plaintiff in Error's Brief, Supreme Court Appeal, 152–54.

36. These decisions can also be attacked on several other grounds, including the fact that Holmes expressly stated that it was "unnecessary to repeat" each of the ways in which Baltimore had alleged the major leagues violated antitrust law, language indicating that the decision was not limited to just the reserve clause. Grow, "Defining the 'Business of Baseball'," 591–600.

37. Nathaniel Grow, "In Defense of Baseball's Antitrust Exemption," *American Business Law Journal* 49 (2012); Mitchell Nathanson, "The Irrelevance of Baseball's Antitrust Exemption: A Historical Review," *Rutgers Law Review* 58 (2005); Zimbalist, "Baseball Economics and Antitrust Immunity," 287; Jeff Friedman, "Antitrust Exemption Vital for Minor League Survival: MLB & Parent Clubs Must Put Money Behind 1991 Stadium Standards," *DePaul Journal of Sports Law & Contemporary Problems* 1 (2003); Gary R. Roberts, "The Case for Baseball's Special Antitrust Immunity," *Journal of Sports Economics* 4 (2003).

38. *Major League Baseball Properties, Inc. v. Salvino,* 420 F.Supp. 2d 212 (S.D.N.Y. 2005); *Garber v. Office of the Commissioner of Baseball,* Case No. 12-Civ-3704 (S.D.N.Y. 2012).

39. Oliver Wendell Holmes Jr., "The Path of the Law," *Harvard Law Review* 10 (1897): 469.

BIBLIOGRAPHY

The most important primary source materials for this project were the original court papers, trial transcripts, and judicial decisions from the relevant lawsuits, as well as the original correspondence between executives from organized baseball, their attorneys, and court officials. In particular, documents from the United States Supreme Court (Case No. 204), Court of Appeals for the District of Columbia (Case No. 3368), and Supreme Court of the District of Columbia (Case No. 60653) proceedings in *Federal Baseball Club of Baltimore, Inc. v. National League of Professional Baseball Clubs, et al.*, are available at the National Archives in Washington, D.C., as well as at the National Baseball Hall of Fame Library in Cooperstown, New York, in the August "Garry" Herrmann Papers ("HP") and the Federal League Suit Papers ("FLSP") collections. The transcript from the Washington trial is on file with the Hall of Fame (FLSP Boxes 6 and 7).

Court documents from the Eastern District of Pennsylvania proceedings in *Federal Baseball Club of Baltimore, Inc. v. National League of Professional Baseball Clubs, et al.* (Case No. 4058) are available at the National Archives in Philadelphia, Pennsylvania, as well as at the Hall of Fame (HP Box 106). The transcript from the Philadelphia trial is on file with the Hall of Fame (FLSP Box 8).

Court documents from the Northern District of Illinois proceedings in *Federal League of Professional Baseball Clubs v. National League of Professional Baseball Clubs* (Case No. 373) are available at the National Archives in Chicago, Illinois, as well as at the Hall of Fame (FLSP Box 9 and HP Boxes 104 and 105). The transcript from the January 1915 hearing in Chicago is on file at the Hall of Fame (HP Box 105), while the transcript from the February 1916 dismissal of the case can also be found at the Hall of Fame (FLSP Box 1, Folder 2).

Documents related to the *Camnitz* litigation can be found on file at the Hall of Fame (HP Box 108, Folders 21–23). Documents relating to the *Killefer* litigation (Case No. 1789) are available at the National Archives in Chicago, Illinois, as well as at the Hall of Fame (HP Box 109, Folder 10). Documents relating to the *Boston v. Hanlon, et al.* lawsuit (Case No. 120) can be found at the National Archives in Philadelphia, Pennsylvania. Documents related to the *Philadelphia v. Weeghman, et al.* litigation (Case Nos. 220 and 31,683) are housed at the National Archives in Chicago, Illinois, as well as at the Hall of Fame (HP Box 110, Folders 7, 8, and 11). Documents from the *Blanding* cases can be found at the Circuit Court of St. Louis Records Department (Case No. 295) and the Archives for the Circuit Court of Cook County, Illinois (Case No. 308988). Documents from the *Hamilton* litigation (Case Nos. 82557 and 4262) are available at the National Archives in Kansas City, Missouri. Documents relating to the *Chief Johnson* and *Madison* lawsuits (Case Nos. B2356, 308198, B2357, and 308197) are available at the Archives for the Circuit Court of Cook County, Illinois, as well as at the Hall of Fame (HP Box 109, Folders 1–8 and FLSP Box 5, Folder 6). Documents relating to the *Marsans* litigation (Case Nos. 4314 and 4562) can be found at the National Archives in Kansas City, Missouri, as well as at the Hall of Fame (HP Box 109, Folders 13–19). Documents from the *Schulz* case (Case No. 309300) can be found at the Archives for the Circuit Court of Cook County, Illinois. Documents relating to the *Chase* lawsuit are located at the Hall of Fame (HP Box 108, Folder 24 and FLSP Box 5, Folder 6).

Finally, the original correspondence between organized baseball's officials and attorneys can be found on file with the Hall of Fame (in both the HP and the FLSP). Chief Justice Taft's correspondence is from the William Howard Taft Papers, Manuscript Division, Library of Congress, Washington, D.C. (Microfilm Series 3, Reels 239–42). Justice Holmes's correspondence can be found in the Papers of Oliver Wendell Holmes Jr., Harvard Law School Library, Cambridge, Massachusetts (Microfilm Reel 71).

In addition to the original source materials listed above, the following sources were referenced in preparing this book:

Books

Abrams, Roger I. *Legal Bases: Baseball and the Law*. Philadelphia: Temple University Press, 1998.

Alexander, Charles C. *Our Game: An American Baseball History*. New York: MJF Books, 1991.

———. *Ty Cobb*. New York: Oxford University Press, 1985.

Ashmead, Henry Graham. *History of the Delaware County National Bank: With Biographical Notes of Its Officers*. Chester, Pa.: Press of the Chester Times, 1914.

Asinof, Eliot. *Eight Men Out: The Black Sox and the 1919 World Series*. New York: Holt, Rinehart and Winston, 1963.

Berk, Gerald. *Louis D. Brandeis and the Making of Regulated Competition, 1900–1932*. New York: Cambridge University Press, 2009.

Burton, David H. *Taft, Holmes, and the 1920s Court: An Appraisal*. Madison, N.J.: Fairleigh Dickinson University Press, 1998.

Cook, William A. *August "Garry" Herrmann: A Baseball Biography*. Jefferson, N.C.: McFarland, 2008.

Cordell, Eugene Fauntleroy. *University of Maryland, 1807–1907*. New York: Lewis Publishing, 1907.

Duquette, Jerold J. *Regulating the National Pastime: Baseball and Antitrust*. Westport, Conn.: Praeger, 1999.

Kohout, Martin Donell. *Hal Chase: The Defiant Life and Turbulent Times of Baseball's Biggest Crook*. Jefferson, N.C.: McFarland, 2001.

Levitt, Daniel R. *The Battle that Forged Modern Baseball: The Federal League Challenge and Its Legacy*. Lanham, Md.: Ivan R. Dee, 2012.

Lowenfish, Lee. *The Imperfect Diamond: A History of Baseball's Labor Wars*. Lincoln: University of Nebraska Press, 1980, 2010.

Marbury, William L. *In the Catbird Seat*. Baltimore: Maryland Historical Society, 1988.

Mason, Alpheus Thomas. *The Supreme Court From Taft to Warren*. Baton Rouge: Louisiana State University Press, 1958, 1968.

———. *William Howard Taft: Chief Justice*. New York: Simon and Schuster, 1964, 1965.

Monks, Leander J., ed. *Courts and Lawyers of Indiana*. Indianapolis: Federal Publishing, 1916.

Morris, Jeffrey Brandon. *Calmly to Poise the Scales of Justice: A History of the Courts of the District of Columbia Circuit*. Durham, N.C.: Carolina Academic Press, 2001.

Murdock, Eugene C. *Ban Johnson: Czar of Baseball*. Westport, Conn.: Greenwood Press, 1982.

Murphy, Paul L. *The Constitution in Crisis Times: 1918–1969*. New York: Harper & Row, 1972.

Nathanson, Mitchell. *A People's History of Baseball*. Urbana: University of Illinois Press, 2012.

Okkonen, Marc. *The Federal League of 1914–1915: Baseball's Third Major League*. Garrett Park, Md.: Society for American Baseball Research, 1989.

Pepper, George Wharton. *Philadelphia Lawyer: An Autobiography*. Philadelphia: J. B. Lippincott, 1944.

Pietrusza, David. *Judge and Jury: The Life and Times of Judge Kenesaw Mountain Landis*. South Bend, Ind.: Diamond Communications, 1998.

———. *Major Leagues: The Formation, Sometimes Absorption and Mostly Inevitable Demise of 18 Professional Baseball Organizations, 1871 to Present*. Jefferson, N.C.: McFarland, 1991.

Renstrom, Peter G. *The Taft Court: Justices, Rulings, and Legacy*. Santa Barbara, Calif.: ABC-CLIO, 2003.

Rosen, Evelyn Bodek. *The Philadelphia Fels, 1880–1920: A Social Portrait*. Madison, N.J.: Fairleigh Dickinson University Press, 2000.

Seymour, Harold. *Baseball: The Golden Age*. New York: Oxford University Press, 1971, 1989.

Snyder, Brad. *A Well-Paid Slave: Curt Flood's Fight for Free Agency in Professional Sports*. New York: Plume, 2007.

Spink, J. G. Taylor. *Judge Landis and Twenty-Five Years of Baseball*. Binghamton, N.Y.: Vail-Ballou Press, 1947.

Toot, Peter T. *Armando Marsans: A Cuban Pioneer in the Major Leagues*. Jefferson, N.C.: McFarland, 2004.

White, G. Edward. *Creating the National Pastime: Baseball Transforms Itself 1903–1953*. Princeton, N.J.: Princeton University Press, 1996.

Wiggins, Robert Peyton. *The Federal League of Base Ball Clubs: The History of an Outlaw Major League, 1914–1915*. Jefferson, N.C.: McFarland, 2009.

Articles and Chapters in Books

Abrams, Roger I. "Blackmun's List." *Virginia Sports and Entertainment Law Journal* 6 (2007): 181–207.

Alito, Samuel A., Jr. "The Origin of the Baseball Antitrust Exemption: Federal Baseball Club of Baltimore, Inc. v. National League of Professional Baseball Clubs." *Journal of Supreme Court History* 34 (2009): 183–95.

Anderson, Donald F. "The Anti-trust Act and the Supreme Court." In *The Collected Works of William Howard Taft*, edited by David Potash and Donald F. Anderson, 5:163–71. Athens: Ohio University Press, 2003.

"Baseball and Vaudeville as Interstate Commerce." *Central Law Journal* 96 (1923): 237–38.

"Baseball Law." *Law Notes* 25(1921): 24.

Belknap, Michal R. "Mr. Justice Pitney and Progressivism." *Seton Hall Law Review* 16 (1986): 381–423.

"Constitutional Law—Monopolies—Baseball Club Not Engaged in 'Trade' or 'Commerce.' " *Michigan Law Review* 19 (1921): 867–69.

Davies, Ross E. "A Crank on the Court: The Passion of Justice William R. Day." *Baseball Research Journal* 38 (2009): 94–107.

Devine, James R. "The Racial Re-Integration of Major League Baseball: A Business Rather Than Moral Decision; Why Motive Matters." *Seton Hall Journal of Sport Law* 11 (2001): 1–72.

Edmonds, Ed. "Over Forty Years in the On-deck Circle: Congress and the Baseball Antitrust Exemption." *Thurgood Marshall Law Review* 19 (1994): 627–61.

Finkleman, Paul. "Baseball and the Rule of Law." *Cleveland State Law Review* 46 (1998): 239–59.

Friedman, Jeff. "Antitrust Exemption Vital for Minor League Survival: MLB & Parent Clubs Must Put Money Behind 1991 Stadium Standards." *DePaul Journal of Sports Law & Contemporary Problems* 1 (2003): 118–22.

Gallagher, Robert C. "John Tener's Brilliant Career." *Baseball Research Journal* 20 (1990): 36–38.

Galloway, Russell W., Jr. "The Taft Court (1921–1929)." *Santa Clara Law Review* 25 (1985): 1–64.

Gillerman, Jonathan D. "Calling Their Shots: Miffed Minor Leaguers, the Steroid Scandal, and Examining the Use of Section 1 of the Sherman Act to Hold MLB Accountable." *Albany Law Review* 73 (2010): 541–73.

Grow, Nathaniel. "Defining the 'Business of Baseball': A Proposed Framework for Determining the Scope of Professional Baseball's Antitrust Exemption." *University of California at Davis Law Review* 44 (2010): 557–623.

———. "In Defense of Baseball's Antitrust Exemption." *American Business Law Journal* 49 (2012): 211–73.

Hailey, Gary. "Anatomy of a Murder: The Federal League and the Courts." *National Pastime* (Spring 1985): 62–73.

Ham, Eldon L. "Aside the Aside: The True Precedent of Baseball in Law." *Marquette Sports Law Review* 13 (2003): 213–21.

———. "The Immaculate Deception: How the Holy Grail of Protectionism Led to the Great Steroid Era." *Marquette Sports Law Review* 19 (2008): 209–30.

Holmes, Oliver Wendell, Jr. "The Path of the Law." *Harvard Law Review* 10 (1897): 457–78.

Hylton, Gordon. "Why Baseball's Antitrust Exemption Still Survives." *Marquette Sports Law Journal* 9 (1999): 391–402.

Jarvis, Robert M., and Phyllis Coleman. "Early Baseball Law." *American Journal of Legal History* 45 (2001): 117–31.

Johnson, Bruce. "Why Baseball's Antitrust Exemption Must Go." In *Stee-Rike Four!: What's Wrong with the Business of Baseball?*, edited by Daniel R. Marburger, 135–42. Westport, Conn.: Praeger, 1997.

McDonald, Kevin. "Antitrust and Baseball: Stealing Holmes." *Journal of Supreme Court History* (1998): 89–128.

Nathanson, Mitchell. "The Irrelevance of Baseball's Antitrust Exemption: A Historical Review." *Rutgers Law Review* 58 (2005): 1–43.

———. "Who Exempted Baseball Anyway? The Curious Development of the Antitrust Exemption That Never Was." *Harvard Journal of Sports & Entertainment Law* 4 (2013): 1–50.

Neely, Alfred S. " 'A Humbug Based on Economic Ignorance and Incompetence'—Antitrust in the Eyes of Justice Holmes." *Utah Law Review* (1993): 1–66.

Orbach, Barak, and Grace Campbell Reblin. "The Antitrust Curse of Bigness." *Southern California Law Review* 85 (2012): 605–55.

Pollack, Jason M. "Take My Arbitrator, Please: Commissioner 'Best Interests' Disciplinary Authority in Professional Sports." *Fordham Law Review* 67 (1999): 1645–1712.

Post, Robert. "Federalism in the Taft Court Era: Can It Be 'Revived'?" *Duke Law Journal* 51 (2002): 1513–1639.

———. "The Supreme Court Opinion as Institutional Practice: Dissent, Legal Scholarship, and Decisionmaking in the Taft Court." *Minnesota Law Review* 85 (2001): 1267–1384.

Powe, L. A., Jr. "What Does Bo Know?" *Virginia Law Review* 82 (1996): 1369–97.

Reynolds, William L. "Maryland and the Constitution of the United States: An Introductory Essay." *Maryland Law Review* 66 (2007): 923–53.

Roberts, Gary R. "The Case for Baseball's Special Antitrust Immunity." *Journal of Sports Economics* 4 (2003): 302–17.

Sigman, Shayna M. "The Jurisprudence of Judge Kenesaw Mountain Landis." *Marquette Sports Law Journal* 15 (2005): 277–330.

Waller, Spencer Weber. "The Antitrust Philosophy of Justice Holmes." *Southern Illinois University Law Journal* 18 (1994): 283–327.

Zimbalist, Andrew. "Baseball Economics and Antitrust Immunity." *Seton Hall Journal of Sport Law* 4 (1994): 287–320.

Web Site Sources

Federal Judicial Center, "Biographical Directory of Federal Judges, Oliver Booth Dickinson." Available at: http://www.fjc.gov/servlet/nGetInfo?jid=616&cid=999&ctype=na&instate=na.

Federal Judicial Center, "Biographical Directory of Federal Judges, Wendell Phillips Stafford." Available at: http://www.fjc.gov/servlet/nGetInfo?jid=2263&cid=999&ctype=na&instate=na.

Mears, Patrick E. "The Catcher, 'The Quick Lunch King' and Baseball's Reserve Clause: Major League Litigation in Grand Rapids." *Stereoscope*, Winter 2003. Available at: http://www.michbar.org/programs/milestone/PDF/Stereoscope%20w03_2.pdf.

Newspapers and Magazines

Atlanta Constitution
Baltimore American
Baltimore Sun
Baseball Magazine
Chicago Tribune
Christian Science Monitor
Cincinnati Enquirer
Milwaukee Sentinel
New York Evening Telegram
New York Herald
New York Times

New York Tribune
North American
Philadelphia Inquirer
Pittsburgh Gazette
Sporting Life
Sporting News
Washington Herald
Washington Post

INDEX

Nathaniel Grow is an assistant professor of legal studies at the University of Georgia's Terry College of Business.

The University of Illinois Press
is a founding member of the
Association of American University Presses.

Composed in 10/13 Sabon
by Lisa Connery
at the University of Illinois Press
Manufactured by Cushing-Malloy, Inc.

University of Illinois Press
1325 South Oak Street
Champaign, IL 61820-6903
www.press.uillinois.edu